Travel and Tourism Marketing Techniques

by

Robert T. Reilly

Merton House Travel and Tourism Publishers, Inc.

ISBN: 0-916032-08-6
Library of Congress Catalog Card Number: 79-92385

Copyright © 1980 by Robert T. Reilly

All rights reserved. No part of this publication may be reproduced, stored in a retrieval system, or transmitted in any way or by any means, electrical, mechanical, photocopying, recording or otherwise, without written permission of the publisher, except for quotations made for the purposes of a review. All inquiries should be addressed to the publisher.

Merton House Travel and Tourism Publishers, Inc.
2100 Manchester Road
Wheaton, Illinois 60187

Manufactured in the United States of America

Other books in The Travel Management Library series

BUDGETING FOR PROFIT AND MANAGING BY GOALS
COMPLETE GUIDE TO TRAVEL AGENCY AUTOMATION
THE DICTIONARY OF TOURISM
GUIDE TO STARTING AND OPERATING A SUCCESSFUL TRAVEL AGENCY
GUIDE TO TRAVEL AGENCY SECURITY
HANDBOOK OF PROFESSIONAL TOUR MANAGEMENT
LEGAL ASPECTS OF TRAVEL AGENCY OPERATION
THE TRAVEL AGENCY PERSONNEL MANUAL

TABLE OF CONTENTS

ACKNOWLEDGEMENTS vii

ABOUT THE AUTHOR ix

INTRODUCTION 1

CHAPTER ONE
MARKETING ASPECTS OF TRAVEL 2
Elements of the marketing mix, 2-6; product versus service, 6-7; special problems of the travel field, 7-9; questions and exercises, 10

CHAPTER TWO
THE TRAVEL AGENCY AND MARKETING 11
Locating and researching prospects, 11-14; research, 14-15; travel trends, 15-16; market segments, 16-20; commercial accounts, 20-21; planning, 21-22; questions and exercises, 23

CHAPTER THREE
THE ROLE OF ADVERTISING IN MARKETING 24
Role of advertising, 24-25; human behavior in advertising, 25-28; psychological appeals in advertising, 28-29; types of advertising, 30-33; cooperative advertising, 31-33; ethical and legal considerations, 33-36; questions and exercises, 37

CHAPTER FOUR
THE ADVERTISING AGENCY 38
Agency size, 38-39; agency activities, 39-40; costs and commissions, 40-42; relationships and structure, 42-45; in-house agency, 45; questions and exercises, 46

CHAPTER FIVE
UNDERSTANDING MEDIA 47
Newspapers, 47-49; direct mail, 49-51; television, 51-53; radio, 53-54; magazines, 54-56; out-of-home media, 56-57; other media, 58-59; media mix, placement, and charges, 59-66; questions and exercises, 66

CHAPTER SIX
CONSTRUCTING THE ADVERTISING MESSAGE 67
Creativity and research, 67-68; copy writing, 69-72; print ads, 72; headlines, 72-74; body copy, 75-78; styles and formats, 78-83; coupons, 82; questions and exercises, 83

CHAPTER SEVEN
THE DESIGN OF PRINT ADVERTISING 84
Principles of design, 84-91; layout and formats, 92-104; small space ads, 105-106; typography, 106-109; illustrations, 109-111; logo, 112; color, 112-113; paper, 113-114; travel page or section, 114; miscellaneous design problems, 114-115; questions and exercises, 115

CHAPTER EIGHT
THE MECHANICS OF PRINT PRODUCTION 116
Constructing the ad, 116-118; mechanics of type, 119-122; printing, 122; mechanics of photo production, 122-126; brochures, 126-129; color reproduction, 129-132; production tips, 133; questions and exercises, 133

CHAPTER NINE
PRODUCING RADIO AND TV SPOTS 134
Radio formats and writing, 134-141; television formats and writing, 141-148; travel shows, 148, 150; questions and exercises, 151

CHAPTER TEN
THOSE OTHER ADVERTISING MEDIA 152
Out-of-home media, 152-154; novelties, 154; directories, 155; direct mail, 155-160; questions and exercises, 161

CHAPTER ELEVEN
THE ADVERTISING CAMPAIGN 162
Planning, 162-164; sample campaign, 164-165; questions and exercises, 166

CHAPTER TWELVE
PUBLICITY AND PROMOTIONAL TECHNIQUES 167
Public, human, and community relations, 167-169; publicity, 169-174; travel article, 174-176; newsletter, 176-177; special events, 177-182; sample events, 182-184; questions and exercises, 185

GLOSSARY OF TERMS 187

INDEX 197

Acknowledgements

We wish to thank the following for permission to reprint materials: The Four Seasons Motor Inn, Colorado Springs; The Gramercy Travel System, Inc.; Qantas Airways; Range Tours of Colorado; H & M Landing; Copper Beech Inn, Ivoryton, Conn.; Samuel B. Crispin & Associates and the Negril Beach Village; TravLtips; International Travel & Resorts, Inc. and Gentle Winds, St. Croix; Cartan Travel Bureau; Caravan Tours; Ameropa Travel, Inc.; Travel & Transport, Inc.; Sans Souci Hotel, Jamaica; Japan Air Lines; The Delta Queen Steamboat Co.; Four Seasons Hotel, Toronto; Ramada Inn, Casper, Wyoming; South Carolina Division of Tourism; Granada Royale Hometels; The Pointe Resort, Phoenix; Xanadu Beach Hotel, Grand Bahama Island; Frantel Hotels; Sunny Land Tours, Inc.; Penn Center Inn, Philadelphia; East Wind Inn, St. Lucia; Doral Hotel, Miami Beach; Windward Passage Hotel, St. Thomas; El Convento Hotel, San Juan; Bermuda Department of Tourism; Canadian Pacific Hotels; Travelink Tours International, Inc.; Glenwood Manor, Kansas City; Sans Souci • Versailles Hotels, Miami Beach/Primak Associates; Travel International; President Hotel, Taipei; Pavilions and Pools Hotel, St. Thomas; Caribbean Club, Grand Cayman; Half Moon Hotel, Jamaica; Hampshire House Hotel, Denver; Colony Club, Barbados; Montego Bay Club Resort, Jamaica; Tours Specialists, Inc.; Far Horizons Beach Resort, Sarasota; Traveluxe; Simson Bay Beach Hotel, St. Maarten; Estes Park Area Chamber of Commerce; Vail Reservations, Inc.; Sitzmark Ski Lodge, Winter Park, Colorado; Black Mountain Ranch, Vail, Colorado; Mexican National Tourist Council; Paquet Cruises, Inc. (Warren Pfaff Inc., agency); Swissair; Air Canada; Trans World Airlines, Inc.; Vacation America, Inc.; Ogilvy & Mather, Inc.

About the Author

While this is Bob Reilly's first venture into the field of travel texts, it's his tenth book. The others, fiction and nonfiction, cover a wide range of topics, from the Indian Wars to a textbook in public relations. Many of his books have Irish themes, including *Come Along to Ireland,* which combines a tour through Ireland with glimpses of the country's history and culture, and *Red Hugh, Prince of Donegal,* which was made into a Walt Disney film in 1966. Reilly has also published over 400 articles in a variety of national magazines, writes poetry, scripts films and TV shows, and has produced material for Mike Douglas, Fred Waring, and Capitol Records.

A native of Lowell, Massachusetts, Reilly now lives in Omaha, Nebraska, where he's a professor of journalism at the University of Nebraska at Omaha, teaching courses in advertising, public relations, and advanced writing.

The author spent 30 years in the advertising-public relations field before returning to teaching in 1972. During these years he worked on travel accounts in Boston and Omaha, served as public relations director for Creighton University, and was a partner in Holland Dreves Reilly Inc., the state's largest home-based advertising-public relations firm.

Reilly has travelled widely, leading tours to Ireland and the British Isles, touring the South Pacific on various film assignments, and serving with the infantry in Europe during World War II. He has visited virtually all of the United States as a public speaker.

Reilly has a masters degree from Boston University, where he also spent two years toward his doctorate in English.

He's been a consultant to the Ford Foundation, provided counsel to numerous commercial and nonprofit agencies, and once lost a close race for Congress.

His honors include a number of foundation grants; the Fonda-McGuire Best Actor Award at the Omaha Playhouse (1954); Hall of Fame Award from the American College Public Relations Association (1965); Boss of the Year Award in Nebraska (1969); Midlands Journalist of the Year (1977); and the Kayser Chair at the University of Nebraska at Omaha in 1979.

Reilly is listed in *Who's Who in Advertising; Who's Who in Public Relations; Who's Who in the Midwest; Contemporary Authors; The Dictionary of British and American Writers; Dictionary of International Biography; The International Writers and Authors Who's Who,* and *Writers and Photographers Guide.*

Introduction

All facets of the travel agency business are important—the staffing, the selling, the budgeting—*and* the advertising.

Ideally, the travel manager would be able to employ the services of a professional advertising agency; practically speaking, however, this is seldom possible. Most managers must settle for what they can create themselves, or for what they can obtain from the media. That's why a book on advertising for travel agencies seemed imperative. If managers are to be responsible for this facet of the business, they should know as much as they can about the subject.

This text, however, is merely a beginning. The wise manager—and student—keeps abreast of advertising as a live form, noting the routine and exceptional advertising in the travel field, and saving samples which merit imitation.

Because of the growing number of colleges and universities which offer courses or degrees in travel management, the publishers opted for a textbook which would have equal value for the professional travel employee as well as for the student. While the questions and exercises may seem more appropriate to a campus atmosphere, they also serve as a checkpoint for those in the travel business who want to improve their skills.

Advertising, then, is a *practical* endeavor. It needs to be implemented in order to be learned. This text opens the door—but it doesn't furnish the room. The development of successful advertising techniques remains up to the individual.

Robert T. Reilly
University of Nebraska at Omaha

CHAPTER ONE

Marketing Aspects of Travel

If you do build that better mousetrap, will the world really beat a path to your door?

Not if they don't know about it.

You can't rely on luck, good will, or the law of averages to provide customers for travel services. Even when you have an exceptional tour to sell, this tour must be promoted. That's doubly true of regular travel services, which tend to be similar in nature and price.

Because of competition for attention, the wise travel manager must become familiar with all aspects of marketing, including advertising. Researchers tell us that the average consumer is assaulted by more than five hundred advertising messages daily—radio, television, newspapers, billboards, bulletin boards, magazines, shop windows, and so on. Of these five hundred messages, the average person sees fewer than ten percent. To half of these, he or she reacts negatively.

That means that, out of five hundred chances to capture favorable attention, you have a five percent chance. Probably less. That's why the more you know about the whole process of marketing, the better you'll run your travel business.

Marketing simply means all of the activities necessary to bring a product or service from a manufacturer or creator to the ultimate user. These activities include:

- The product or service itself
- Method of distribution
- Method of pricing
- Means of promotion
- Personal selling
- Advertising

The Product or Service

First, you must have a good product or service, one that fills a need or creates a demand. If the product or service is no good, or if it fails to provide satisfaction, no amount of promotion or advertising can sustain it for long.

When Metrecal came on the market as a diet drink, nearly one hundred dietary formulas also appeared. Only Metrecal survived. Thousands of products or services arrive and depart annually, costing their sponsors millions of dollars. Even giants like Campbell Soups and General Motors have guessed wrong and have been forced to call back their new offerings.

Travel agency managers should stand back and study their agencies. Does it meet a real need? Does it offer a superior product? Is there something wrong with what it's trying to merchandise? Inadequate and inexperienced staffing could be one problem. Lack of efficiency could be another. Poor management, lack of adequate financing, poor location, and faulty planning could be other product errors. These should be corrected before launching any public phase of marketing.

It's a truism that good advertising only calls attention to a bad product. If a restaurant, for example, hasn't worked out the kinks in its operation and hasn't yet developed an acceptable cuisine, this is no time to buy space and time in print and broadcast media. An influx of customers will only result in a devastating word-of-mouth campaign against the restaurant. It will take months, perhaps years, to recover.

Travel agencies, too, should not put out the word to potential clients until they're ready to handle them.

Distribution

This aspect of marketing may be more of a problem for a manufacturer who makes a complicated piece of machinery which must be transported great distances, or bakes a product with short shelf life, or produces an item with nationwide demand. The marketing manager must work on ways to transport the product to the consumer. This may include a decision on trucks versus trains versus airplanes; or it may encompass the question of selling via mail versus direct selling versus the use of dealers or distributors.

Travel agencies also have certain distribution problems.

The travel manager must consider means of reaching potential customers within a geographical range where the delivery of services is both possible and practical. It's unlikely, for example, that your agency can count heavily on drawing clients away from Agency B if Agency B is more convenient to these clients and is doing a good job. Besides, even if you manage to secure some of this clientele, can you handle them profitably?

Let's assume you have an opportunity to take one, two, or three large commercial accounts. Do you have the personnel to provide the sort of service they will require and, if so, can you make money on the transaction? If you haven't the people, can you recruit them? If not, it's best not to overextend yourself and risk losing all the accounts. Settle on one or two.

Another distribution problem centers on the number of tours you may want to actively handle at one time. They become like inventory in a product-oriented business. No manufacturing firm wants to keep too large an inventory. They want to keep it moving. Similarly, the travel agency should be reasonable in the number of items it decides to concentrate on.

Pricing

Much of the pricing in travel agencies has been traditionally dictated by supplier costs. Airline tickets, hotel rooms, package tours—these arrive with basic price tags. Even when an agency builds its own tour, much of the price represents standard supplier charges. There are variations. Anticipated volume can lower costs, as can the ability of the travel manager to promote a better basic arrangement. The desire to make more money can, of course, increase costs.

Like advertising agencies, travel agencies in the past have wrestled with the low margin of profit. Because of this factor, and because of changes contemplated by governing bodies like the Civil Aeronautics Board, new methods of securing revenue may be added. The "net fare" concept, for example, will allow agencies some freedom in establishing their own consumer ticket prices. Smaller agencies are fearful that this trend could drive them out of business, since larger agencies, perhaps with a number of branches, may contract for an entire plane, and thus be able to compete unfairly with the smaller agencies on a volume basis.

There may well be other innovations—a different commission schedule, add-on charges for certain services, and the like.

Travel, however, will always be competitive. Not only will people gravitate toward the more economical offering (other things being equal), they will also resent an agency that seemed to over-price a trip. That's why pricing should receive high priority in a travel agency, with both profit margins and competition receiving consideration. Even clever and continuous advertising can't save an overpriced tour.

Another pricing factor is the problem with consumers understanding what travel agencies do and what their services cost. A significant majority of Americans still think they will be facing a number of extra charges when they use a travel agency. While this practice may change in the face of inflationary costs, extra charges are currently a rarity. Most services are free. Customers need to know how agencies are compensated, what services they can perform, and what these services mean to the client in terms of convenience and economy. A number of travel agencies have mounted promotional campaigns addressing this point, but the misconceptions persist.

As changes in the service and revenue phases of travel agencies take place, such information must be speedily and continually disseminated.

Promotion

Ways to promote travel will be covered in detail in chapter twelve. All that needs to be mentioned here is that there are many methods of selling merchandise or services. Advertising and salesmanship are merely two routes.

Wall-to-wall carpeting, two cars for a family, dieting for health—these and hundreds of other concepts have been sold as the result of publicity and promotion. Look at all the newspaper and magazine columns which promote—often by brand name—certain foods, flowers, movies, plays, books, sports events, medicines. And travel.

Demand for travel space to places like China and Russia stems more from external information tourists absorb than from any advertising list of scenic pleasures. Conversely, the bad publicity about a place like Northern Ireland seriously cut into travel to the Irish Republic, where no fighting was taking place.

A movie like *Close Encounters of the Third Kind* produced a boom in travel to South Dakota's Devil's Tower, where the film ends. A successful television series like *The Love Boat* gets more people thinking about cruises.

Sometimes a locale or a tour or a mode of transportation gets an inadvertent boost from some promotional venture. More often, though, the promotional effort is calculated and orchestrated.

Personal Selling

This could take several forms, the most common of which are over-the-counter selling and the practice of calling on prospective commercial clients. To these might be added phone solicitation and the use of social occasions to subtly introduce the subject of travel services.

Individual salesmanship is important. Advertising and promotion alone rarely sell travel. They are more likely to provoke interest, to stimulate inquiries. At that point, the expert salesperson takes over and closes the sale. That's why intelligence, experience, perseverance, and a grasp of human psychology are indispensable for travel counsellors. The able salesperson can turn mild curiosity into a solid booking; can make a customer out of a walk-in spectator; can extend a trip or services on that trip; and can save a wavering prospect.

The person who makes calls on large institutions, like corporations, universities, hospitals, and other major employers, must know his or her business thoroughly, must be able to deal with all types of people, and must be committed to an extra dimension of service at all hours of the day and night.

Weak salespeople are a drag on any agency. Clients who come to the agency as a result of advertising, promotion, or word-of-mouth appeals, can be quickly turned away by lack of enthusiasm, inattention, rudeness, ignorance of travel needs, inefficiency, or failure to provide real service.

Advertising

Since this is the principal subject to be covered by this book, this topic need only be defined here. Advertising includes all of the messages in print or broadcast media that are purchased by the travel agency and whose content is controlled by the travel agency. This involves everything from a small two-inch advertisement in the Sunday travel section to the printed brochure mailed to prospects.

The inexperienced manager may think that advertising can do it all. Not true. The reason for listing all of the aspects of marketing is to emphasize that each of them has a role in the successful conclusion of any travel transaction.

In short, you must have something the client wants; you must be able to deliver it; it must bear an affordable and reasonable price tag; it must be communicated to the public in an interesting and appealing manner; and it must be clinched by some personal selling or service.

The Marketing Mix

Since most travel agencies are relatively small enterprises, there is no need for an elaborate marketing plan, such as major corporations would compose. Still, if a shrewd manager wants to get the most for the dollar, it makes sense to budget wisely within the marketing framework. Specific amounts should be assigned to areas like newspaper advertising, direct mail advertising, promotional activities and other budget items. This is called a *marketing mix,* and the goal is to achieve the best blend of expense to produce maximum sales at minimum cost.

Let's say a medium-sized agency decided to allot $6,000 annually for all of its marketing activities. This amount might be spent in this fashion:

- Newspaper advertising—Sunday travel section—
  200 column inches at $15 per column inch....................$3,000.00
- Quarterly newsletter to clients (printing and postage) $1,400.00
- Other direct mail ....$ 300.00
- 30 radio spots at $30 per spot (Two short campaigns) ....$ 900.00
- Special events, production, miscellaneous ....$ 400.00

$6,000.00

This, of course, is only one way to allocate funds. Some managers may decide to go heavier on direct mail, or eliminate radio. Others may want to add television—but this calls for a larger budget.

The point is, you should use a variety of approaches, putting them together in a proportion that works for you.

Product Versus Service

Selling a tangible item is different than selling a less tangible service. Marketing and advertising specialists are generally better at moving merchandise than they are at promoting services. For one thing, they've had more experience and have been able to gather more data. Learning how to properly market services is still a relatively new science.

For another thing, there are more variables in services. When you manufacture a product, you can exercise a considerable amount of control over it, virtually all the way to the consumer. With services, you rely more on the individual abilities and personalities of people. Many times, particularly with similar services—like banks and restaurants and hotels and travel agencies—you are really selling people. People are harder to control than products. They have their good and bad days; they can be superbly efficient or miserably inept. Therefore, when you make advertising and promotional claims about your service, you feel less secure than you do when making them about a tangible product.

Your ads tell readers how easy it is to get a loan at a certain bank, but, when they go there, they find it nearly impossible to qualify. Your travel ads refer to fast, congenial, knowledgeable people, but the customer finds long lines, delays, brusqueness, and insufficient information.

Another difference between products and services is that, while both are sometimes bought for emotional reasons, services are more frequently purchased that way. As we'll see in chapter three, emotion figures heavily in advertising. Items like cosmetics (male and female), clothes—even large items like houses and cars—are bought, at times, for emotional reasons. With travel, except for business and other necessary travel, the reasons are virtually always emotional.

In an *Ad Age* interview (May 14, 1979), Robert Catlin, senior vice-president of N. W. Ayer ABH International, commented that "people tend to use products because they believe they work. People tend to use services because they believe they like them."

This phenomenon explains the competition among airlines in decor, dress of stewardesses, exotic menus, and other externals. Where airlines were competitive in scheduling, they sought to accentuate some aspect of their service that set them apart—even in a minor way.

What this means for the travel business is that those selling services need a great deal of research into what people like and dislike about specific services; why they choose one over the other; why they change from one to another; what they perceive to be the difference.

You can sometimes recover fairly rapidly from a bad product by removing it from the marketplace, by redesigning or repackaging it, by repricing it, by moving it aside with an acceptable substitute. With services, this is much more difficult to do. A bad experience with a service leaves an impression that's hard to turn around, especially if the consumer has an alternative.

Travel agency managers know that a client whose travel plans have been messed up, perhaps without any fault being laid at the agency door, will start looking around for another agency. The bank customer who fails to get that loan and succeeds elsewhere will probably boycott the first bank forever, regardless of advertising.

That's why it's important to have good people (who are, after all, your product), to train them well, to monitor their performance, and to reward excellence.

Market Problems of the Travel Business

While this topic will be discussed more fully in the next chapter, it's well to reflect here that, even among services, the travel business is a little different.

Perhaps, as with so many things, money is the bottom line. So many services travel agencies perform are unprofitable. There are the people who drop by to chat, or to pick up brochures; there are those who make dozens of costly itinerary changes and then scrap the idea of the tour; and there are a number of client services whose profit margin is too low for any real agency benefit.

When you consider that many of the nation's advertising agencies argue that they can no longer make a living on the basis of fifteen percent commissions, you realize how narrow the gap is between financial success and failure in the travel business.

Money also has something to do with the number and kind of people you employ to give service, and the length of time you can expect to have them with you. Money affects the office surroundings, even the kind of image you are able to project through your advertising and direct mail.

External Problems

Travel agencies also differ from many other service firms in that, even when they manage situations properly, they remain at the mercy of other individuals and circumstances.

If a bank handles a new account correctly, chances are no external event will erode customer satisfaction. If the postal clerk is courteous and helpful, the patron feels good about this contact. A clean, attractive hotel, with genial and efficient staff members, can control a majority of the factors included in a traveler's stay. Oh, the mail may take longer than you anticipated, and there could be a noisy party next to you in the hotel, but those risks are minimized.

With a travel agency, events are less certain. Because travel agencies broker for other services, the dangers multiply. A beautifully conceived tour, economically priced and well led, can still experience surly waiters, governmental red tape, airline delays, and distasteful companions. There may be transportation strikes, inconvenient bank holidays, student riots, and miserable weather.

People and Money

Ultimately, staffing and financing affect agency performance. Travel agency personnel have to know what customer service is, what customer needs are, and how to relate to customers one-on-one.

Thomas Engel, product group manager for Lever Brothers, told an *Ad Age* interviewer (February 19, 1979) that the reason people with package goods experience are sometimes driven out of the service industry is because they feel less loved and less needed.

"You've got to have a zealous missionary spirit," he adds. "You also have to have resiliency."

Travel agencies almost always have less personnel than the volume of business requires, meaning that they work long and full hours. This places an extra burden on all of the personality traits which must be part of decent customer relations.

Unlike banks, which have both more personnel and more money for advertising, travel agencies rarely venture into image ads, which don't sell anything directly but which attempt to create a favorable opinion of the agency. They are also short of funds to underwrite research, to attract advertising agency attention, or to take advantage of advertising opportunities.

Timing

Perhaps one final difference between service and product advertising is that product ad philosophy advises pouring additional dollars into promotion when the product is selling well. The "strike while the iron is hot" syndrome is at work here. With service industries, this may not be true—particularly in areas like travel. If a motel chain has no rooms to sell, it is unlikely to beef up its advertising campaign. If the travel agency (happy thought!) has filled all tours to capacity, it is not likely to increase advertising expenses.

Do the Best You Can

Most astute agency managers can't really afford to do the best they *know how*; they merely do the best they *can*. They adapt the research that is available to their own situation, using common sense in applying it to their market. They use all the services supplied by carriers, hotel and motel chains, tour operators, and others. They read their professional travel publications and keep up on trends. They review advertising by competitors and by similar agencies in other areas and imitate what they can afford to imitate.

In short, they husband the dollars that go into advertising and promotion, carefully allocating each hard-earned dime.

Questions and Exercises

1. Is there a communication overload in travel advertising?
2. Check several Sunday newspaper travel sections at your library and compare prices of similar tours. What differences do you find?
3. What do we mean by a *marketing mix*?
4. What are some of the differences between selling product and selling a service? Can you add any differences not covered in the text?
5. If personnel form the most critical aspect of any service industry, what things would you do as manager of a travel agency to increase the chances of good customer service?

Case Problem

You are the manager of a new travel agency which is scheduled to open October 1st. You've sent out 20,000 pieces of direct mail announcing the opening, have ordered punch and cookies, have begun a series of radio and newspaper ads announcing the date. With a week to go, however, you realize that two things are wrong. The contractor will not have your office in final shape by October 1, and you are beginning to feel shaky about the number of employees you'll have available by that date and about the lack of experience of some of them.

Would you postpone the opening? Would you change the nature of the event? Would you alter the advertising campaign? What would you do?

List the steps you'd take, explaining the reasons for each, and putting them in their proper sequence.

CHAPTER TWO

The Travel Agency and Marketing

Many of the marketing skills which work in other businesses will also work in the travel business. Research, testing, good salesmanship, innovative advertising, superior products—these work anywhere. Many agencies, however, don't have the wherewithal to perform these functions in a sophisticated and dependable manner. Consequently, they have to rely more on common sense and on practices found successful by other agencies.

Sig S. Front, director of marketing for the Sheraton Corporation, contends that too many travel agency managers spend their time on bookkeeping when they should be devoting this time and energy to the people side of their business. Writing in *Travel Weekly* (February 12, 1979), Front says:

> The businessman who is willing to spend 30% to 40% of his time getting business is going to be successful. Those who spend 80% to 90% of their time controlling the business may eventually have to take a back seat to someone else.

Any business has to be managed, of course, but the travel business also requires more time spent listening to clients, talking with staff members, reading professional materials, making personal calls. This sort of people-consciousness can atone for much of the shortfall dictated by the budget.

Who Are the Prospects?

The first thing you have to realize in marketing any product or service is that not everyone is a real prospect. What you try to do is locate those individuals who constitute the more likely prospects. What you aim for is a *market segment*.

Three things characterize a market segment:

Ability to pay. In travel as in other areas, the ability to pay is not related solely to income size. Studies show that people who are making identical incomes make purchases based on the way they view that income. Some feel the present salary is their peak and that it will decline in the future. These people make poor travel prospects. A second group feels this salary will remain about the same. They are only fair prospects. The third group sees themselves as moving up from here and, even though they are holding identical paychecks at the moment, they make the best prospects.

It's obvious, however, that a person making $10,000 a year, regardless of how he or she feels about that income, is not a prime prospect for an $8,000 luxury cruise.

Ability to make a buying decision. You want to reach the person who has the largest say in selecting a product or service. Men usually exert a larger influence in buying insurance, for example, while women are most likely to have the deciding vote in home furnishings. Perhaps both carry equal weight in purchasing a car or home. College-age students affect the choice of university, even when parents are footing the bills, and children have a lot to say about things like breakfast cereals, fast food restaurants, and toys. In this chapter we'll examine the buying decisions involved in travel.

Ability to derive satisfaction from the product or service. The best prospects have to be able to enjoy what they have purchased, either directly or indirectly. A housewife may enjoy a beef roast herself or may get vicarious pleasure out of serving it to her family or guests. A father may detest rock music but may feel good about selecting a record album his teenage son admires. With travel, the purchaser usually anticipates personal happiness, but the individual could also be travelling to please a spouse or could be underwriting a trip for a son or daughter.

Those three elements are present in the prime prospects. The problem is to locate these individuals, and that's where research is valuable.

Researching the Prospects

If travel agency managers could merely refer to a directory to discover the most likely clients for specific tours or services, the job would be simple. Unfortunately, there are no such directories. The agency may build a client list and know certain things about the preferences of its regular customers, but this is a small sample and not always reliable.

Some travel agencies do periodic surveys to take some of the guesswork out of their marketing plans. One large Midwestern agency conducts such a survey every three years. In a recent survey, here are some of the things it concluded:

1. Why Do People Travel?
Adventure led the list of reasons; followed by business, a change of climate, visits to relatives, education, a search for roots, a chance to shop, an opportunity to meet people of the opposite sex, boredom at home, the availability of exotic cuisine, and several other minor reasons.

The agency feels that it's relatively easy to sell to the adventurous souls; difficult to convince the homebodies. They also find women more adventurous than men as the two sexes get older. Not infrequently, it's a woman who brings her reluctant husband to the travel agent.

In 1954, Abraham Maslow cited five motives for behavior, beginning with survival, then moving up to security or safety, then on to the need to belong or to be accepted. The top two motives in his hierarchy of values are the desire for status or recognition, and self actualization—the desire to know and understand. These last two motives make the best travel prospects.

2. What Things Are People Concerned About When They Travel?
They ask about safety items: food, water, language barriers, money exchange, the political situation.

They are concerned about clothes to wear, and extra money they may need, and about things they may buy.

They ask about climate, and the pace of the trip, and the living conditions.

They want to know what sort of people they will be with (if on a tour), and whether they'll really have fun.

Many travellers really want to take their home conditions along with them. This means the travel agent has to *sell up* their travel, providing them with better facilities at a slightly higher cost. Even tourists who declare they can make do anywhere may get pretty upset after a week in accommodations that are Class C or lower.

3. What Sort of People Are the Best Prospects?
This Midwestern survey unearthed the following statistics:

For nonbusiness travel, the prime market segment is:

- *51-60 years of age.* This represents just under a fourth of the tourists. Next come the 66 and over group (20%) and the 41-50 group (18%).

- *Married people* account for 68% of the travellers, with single persons making up 17%, and divorced or widowed individuals making up the remaining 15%.

- The highest categories in terms of employment were, retired (20%), business and clerical (14%), and professional (12%).

- Approximately 40% of those responding to this survey indicated their incomes exceeded $25,000 annually. This was combined family income. In the single income category, the income levels were widely scattered, with an income of between $10,000-$15,000 the most common, but still only 17% of the total.

- Better than half of those surveyed (55%) reported that the travel decision was a joint one. Another 30% said that the female made the decision, with the remaining 15% being credited to male influence.

- Favorite months to take vacations were August (16%), followed by September (15%), and then June and July tied at 12%. It should be noted here, however, that these figures would be down from a decade or two ago because of the increase in the number of winter vacations.

- In this particular Midwestern area, the most popular areas to visit were:

    a. The United States (57%), with Las Vegas, Southern California, Arizona, New York, and Florida leading the list of continental American vacation spots.
    b. Hawaii (10%)
    c. Central Europe (8%)
    d. England-Ireland (4.5%)

e. Caribbean (4%)
f. All other areas (16.5%)

These decisions will vary considerably depending on where the travelers live. West Coast residents would be more interested in Far East travel, whereas East Coast residents might be better bets for the Bahamas, New England, and Europe.

• This particular survey also attempted to determine how much money each traveler spent, on the average. This figure, of course, will be increasing rapidly as inflation hits virtually all of the tourist havens. Just over a third of the travelers stated that they spent between $500-$1,000 each. A fourth of them spent between $1,000-$1,500 on their trip and 22% of those surveyed reported additional expenses of up to $500. The remaining 20% of the spenders were equally divided among those who spend $1,500-$2,500, and those who spent over $2,500.

To learn more about its clients, this Midwestern agency also surveyed them regarding the travel agency itself and came up with these conclusions:

• Considerable confusion still exists as to the nature of travel agency services (some people feel they handle only tours or major excursions), about presumed charges for service, and about the relative convenience of using an agency as against, say, going directly to an airport ticket desk.

• Planning the trip, making air and hotel reservations, and imparting travel knowledge were given as the most satisfactory service performed. Criticisms of the agency ranged from insufficient information to the difficulty of reaching counselors via telephone.

These findings pertain to that particular chain of agencies, in that particular area, at the particular time. Any agency, however, could conduct a similar survey to get a better grasp of how its own clientele feels.

Once you appreciate who the best prospects are, you are better able to design a marketing campaign to reach them.

Research Is Always Helpful

It's dangerous to base assumptions about travel—or about any product or service—on hunches and instinct. You may often be right, especially when you've logged a lot of hours in the business. Those times when you are wrong could be disasters. You miscalculate interest in a particular travel area, or misdirect your advertising appeals to the wrong clientele, or fail to take into consideration some of the changing elements of this fast-paced world.

If you reviewed airline advertising, for example, you might conclude that passenger interest was centered on friendly stewardesses, short waits for the rest rooms, low fares, latest equipment, good meals and beverages, passenger agent help in planning the trip, and in-flight movies. A Harris poll conducted in 1977 did indicate that these items were considered important by travelers.

What they considered even *more important,* however, were:
- Capable pilots
- Good safety and maintenance records
- Fast baggage claim, check-in, and reservation services
- Sufficient leg room
- Friendly and courteous ground services

True, some of these items may not make the best advertising themes, but the marketing person should always be aware that these are the *prime* concerns, and not cuisine or an extra drink.

Research, properly handled, is a skilled science. The population segment to be sampled must be chosen correctly, so that it represents the cross section you wish to examine; the questions must be appropriately worded so that they neither lead nor confuse; the timing must be right so that responses will be accurate; and the evaluation of the results must be carefully done so that the correct interpretations are placed on the data.

If you survey only your own clients, for example, as did the Midwestern agency cited earlier, you've already restricted your sample. You are not getting a true picture of the public at large. After all, these people are already travelers. If you sought to get similar statistics from the so-called average citizen, you would have to go through the technical exercise of randomizing a sample segment of the population in order to interview those whose responses would approximate the findings you'd achieve if you could contact *everyone* in your target area.

In wording the questionnaire, the aim is to elicit genuine and accurate replies. You must avoid including terms which have *different meanings* to different people. If you ask whether respondents eat out "often," that word *often* can be viewed as twice a week or twice a month or ten times a year.

Another thing to avoid is the use of words which may be *unfamiliar* to many people receiving the survey. "Would you approve of arbitrary surcharges for FIT travel?" would be a bad question.

General questions can also be dangerous. If you asked individuals if they would be willing to pay more for travel services, they'd want to know how much more. A better way to phrase that would be to give them choices of charges, from zero to some higher amount.

Those framing questions should not *anticipate the response* in the query, as politicians sometimes do when surveying constituents. If you ask people if they "get unhappy with the long, slow-moving lines at airport ticket counters," naturally the majority will answer in the affirmative. A better way to phrase that would be to inquire what aspects of reservation or check-in services they liked and disliked.

Observing Trends

In addition to gathering research data, either your own or that of others who share similar goals, you, as agency manager, must also become aware of trends that affect travel and the advertising of travel.

Inflation is one major trend affecting all business. Consumers are more conscious of price and are shopping harder for bargains. This is true in travel as well. Comparison shopping for trips and tours is more prevalent than ever. Inflation also influences the way people feel about travel. Some individuals figure things are going to continue to skyrocket, so they decide to travel *now*. Others feel the economic pinch so much they decide to defer their travel plans until later.

The energy shortage has had a marked effect on travel by automobile. Some national parks report tourism off as much as forty percent and many travelers simply declare they'll vacation closer to home. Airline and bus travel will rise in the wake of such conditions.

There is a move toward less structured tours, brought on by the freedom of the sixties, perhaps, or the media image of regimented travel. And the revived interest in one's ancestry has provided an entirely new reason to travel.

The removal of many sexual taboos has made an impact on travel advertising. Illustrations are more daring; headlines proclaim "ecstacism" or "hedonism" or provocatively invite the traveler to "come and get it." The titillation of physical gratification has moved from the honeymoon ads to the general travel sections. Even the hometown hotels have "run-away-with-your-wife-for-the-weekend" specials.

Another trend is the growing power of the feminist movement. Finnair ran a print advertisement featuring cartoons and a headline that read:

HOW VILHO VATENEN, THE FINN, CREATED THE WORLD'S FIRST SAUNA WHEN HE LOCKED HIS WIFE IN THE SMOKEHOUSE, SET IT ON FIRE, BEAT HER SOUNDLY WITH BIRCH LEAVES, AND DISCOVERED SHE LOVED IT.

The creators of this message thought they had something amusing; women found it degrading. Many of them took the trouble to write to Finnair, explaining that wife abuse was no laughing matter.

Other trends—all of which are of importance to travel—are the increase in the amount of leisure time, the move toward a more casual life style, changing concepts of what is masculine and what is feminine, the desire to be considered modern rather than old-fashioned. Even the current emphasis on dieting and fitness influences travel decisions.

All of these trends dictate what is to be carried in the advertising message. Because of both inflation and consumerism, for example, ads must work harder. Readers are more sophisticated and they will regard exaggerated claims and promises with suspicion. They want more facts, less showmanship. That doesn't mean that advertisements must read or sound like catalog copy, but it does warn the writer that he or she must stay within the bounds of credibility.

Isolating Market Segments

The more personal you can make an advertising message, the more successful you will be. If you could gather all of the best prospects for a

THE TRAVEL AGENCY AND MARKETING 17

Figure 2-1 Pop art forms the basis of this ad. Advertising has popularized many art trends.

particular kind of travel in one room and expose them to a message aimed directly at them, this would be a much more efficient way of approaching sales than placing an ad before an audience of half a million readers, most of whom won't even see it.

Unfortunately, you can't do this. Advertising remains largely a mass media game. However, you can target in on audiences more through direct mail. And even in mass media advertising, you can present information in a way that seeks out the best prospects.

Let's look at a few special groups:

1. *Working Women.* Nearly two out of every three women are employed outside the home, and they constitute approximately half of the total labor

force. Working women, on the average, are better educated than nonworking women, are younger than their nonworking counterparts, watch less television, but read more magazines. These facts would affect the media decisions of an advertiser desiring to reach the working woman. Nearly 10% more working women take vacations than do housewives, and they are more likely to travel by air. The households in which they live also have higher median incomes.

Advertising must be attuned to this profile, considering in its approach the fact that portraying women in home or play situations is no longer realistic—or relevant.

2. Youth Market. Just four decades ago, it was the rare young person who could contemplate a trip to Europe. That pleasure was reserved for the rich. Today, because of increased mobility, more available resources, and because of the desire for travel, young people form a special audience for travel. Their needs differ from those of their parents. They are likely to stress economy and will put up with more discomfort. They are also likely to opt for travel on their own, seek out places where they will encounter other young people, and look for entertainment which is compatible with their age.

Some travel agencies specialize in youth travel, and there are any number of brochures directed to the younger set.

3. Senior Citizens. With the increase in the number of individuals over 65, and in improved health care, older Americans have become an even more important travel segment. The tour member heading for Europe has been categorized as a widow in her sixties and, indeed, there seem to be an abnormal number of package tour members who fit that description. Women do live longer than men and, in the over-65 group, this imbalance shows only 70 men for every 100 women.

The basic pattern for older people is one of geographic stability, more concerns about travel, desire for warmer climates, and, for a majority of them, the necessity to practice economy.

4. Minority Citizens. Some advertising executives claim that audiences like the black consumer market are virtually untapped. Blacks make up 11% of this nation's population, have approximately $80 billion in spendable income, and are showing a greater financial growth rate than the economy as a whole. These facts don't obscure the high unemployment rate among black Americans and other minorities but they do indicate that there is a potential here which has scarcely been reached. Like many minorities, blacks have their own media, which often give advertisers an effective entry into this market.

Jewish Americans are generally better educated than the average prospect, read more extensively, have higher disposable incomes, and travel more. A number of advertisers have been able to target in on this group. American Airlines, for example, produced a pocket-sized paperback entitled *Tourist's Guide to Jewish History in the Caribbean.*

Spanish-speaking citizens also form a significant proportion of our

Figure 2-2 These tours focus on youth and singles as market segments.

population and advertising programs are being designed to meet the needs and aspirations of various groups within this category, realizing that even the shared language has different shades of meaning for Mexicans and Puerto Ricans, for example. Orientals have occasionally appeared in ads; the American Indian rarely. When a particular minority can't identify with the advertising campaign, it's at least a partial failure for them.

Figure 2-3 Ads often seek out special audiences.

5. *Foreign Visitors.* It took a number of years for travel promoters to realize that foreign visitors had some different scenic interests from Americans. They have beaches in Europe, and mountains, and lakes. What they wanted to see were signs of the Wild West, or the skyscrapers of New York, or the wonders of Disneyland.

America has also been slower to accommodate visitors in terms of the language barrier but this is being handled more expertly now, with linguists available as greeters at many of the international airports and seaports.

Other Groups. Look through travel pages and travel magazines, or through the brochure racks at the travel agency. You'll see travel designed for single people ("Meet other singles. Attend special get-together parties. Trained escorts. Guaranteed share rates."), for photographers, for business people, and for a variety of other potential travelers.

Commercial Accounts

Not much media advertising is directed at commercial accounts. Most of this business comes as a result of personal selling, direct mail, phone calls, or referrals. These accounts sometimes make up as much as two-thirds of the business in agencies located in metropolitan areas. While they can be lucrative, they also come equipped with their own set of problems. For one thing, commercial accounts expect a lot of service. A number of large companies began with an in-house person handling travel, then switched to using an agency when they found this more efficient and economical. Some firms prefer the in-house service and make all of their own travel arrangements. And still others combine both in-house and travel agency service.

What companies find attractive about the agencies is their ability to simplify most transactions, their delivery of tickets, single billing, convenience, saving of executive time, and, in some cases, the broader experience represented by the counselors.

Among the complaints about commercial accounts are computer malfunctions; errors in charges; less interest than an in-house person, which results in failure to go the extra distance to get reservations or make changes; difficulty in reaching the agent by phone; and failure to follow up on travel requests.

Travel agencies of any size find it profitable to assign one or more individuals to these commercial accounts, rather than to leave such service to whoever happens to be staffing the desk or answering the phone. Mailings to these accounts are also designed differently. They focus less on romance and color, and more on facts and figures.

Developing a Futuristic Outlook

In addition to research, the study of personal and international trends, and the categorizing of audiences, the travel agency manager must also analyze the projections of the various suppliers with whom he or she deals. These suppliers also look at the trends and mix in other concepts which they feel will produce changes in the way they do business.

Later marriages and fewer children, for example, mean more travel possibilities among young married couples. So does the larger combined income. The working woman means more female business travel.

These prognosticators see more travel from Europe to the United States; little impact of the fuel shortage on airlines, except in terms of cost; a danger of overselling some tourist areas; more federal regulation; innovations in travel safety, comfort, and efficiency. They also see greater competition among carriers and, perhaps, among travel agencies.

Many agency managers are so busy wondering how they'll meet the demands of the current week, they feel they haven't time to look to the future—but they must.

Developing a Marketing Strategy

All planning shares some fundamental characteristics. There must be goals and objectives, short-range and long-range strategies, a means of implementing the plans, and a method of evaluating results.

A travel agency, for example, might have a five- and a ten-year plan, based on anticipated growth and the changing nature of travel services.

These long-range plans would incorporate income and expense projections, space and personnel needs, and volume needed to realize these objectives.

Short-range plans would be for a period of a year, perhaps less. The goals set for this time frame must be in accord with the longer view. They would also be more specific, since it's easier to anticipate what will happen in the short run than it is over a longer time span.

Good planning is essential in marketing because it establishes an orderly procedure for doing business, makes it easier to budget, helps set standards for employees, aids in coordinating all agency programs, prepares the agency for sudden changes in external conditions, forces all those involved to think more clearly, and gives the planners some basis for later evaluation. If your agency is part of a larger company, good planning also makes budget requests sounder and more likely to be funded.

How to Plan

When you develop a marketing plan, you feed in everything you know or can anticipate about your firm, everything you know or can anticipate about the travel industry, and everything you know or can anticipate about those you serve or would like to serve.

Then you'd set some realistic sales goals, based on a year-end sales forecast. This is where you think you could and should be a year hence.

This forecast is broken into individuals goals. You try to determine how much commercial travel needs to be sold, how many tour spaces have to be booked, what over-the-counter sales need to be made, and so on.

When this has been done, you implement the plan, monitoring regularly to be certain the work is on target and on schedule.

The more detailed you can make the plan, the easier it is to implement and monitor it. Each element of the plan should be written out, should indicate whose responsibility this portion is, and what it will cost, and when it's to be completed. All of the elements must work together to produce the overall objective.

If the agency manager sees that some facet of the plan is not working, he or she should review the situation, decide where the problem lies, and revise things to bring the program back in line.

As the plan is being implemented, various tools are used—tools that will be discussed in succeeding chapters—tools like publicity, personal selling, and advertising.

When the year ends, and before the next year's planning is complete, all those involved should go over the twelve months' activity, seeing where they exceeded goals or fell short, trying to determine why things worked well or didn't work at all.

If you don't know where you're going, you'll never know when you get there; and if you don't know *how* you got there, you'll never get there again; and if you don't know why you *didn't* get there, you are doomed to repeat the discovery process.

Questions and Exercises

1. Besides those trends mentioned in this chapter, list five other trends you feel will have an impact on future travel and tell why.
2. What three factors characterize a market segment?
3. From your experience with your own peer group, what factors do you feel influence them most in their travel choices? Can you explain why these influences are at work?
4. Conduct a brief survey among ten relatives or friends who travel and try to find out what they look for in hotel or motel accommodations. You draw up the list—comfort, convenience, decor, friendly people, price, swimming pool, or whatever other factors you consider likely. Tabulate the results. The class might do this as a whole and total the results.
5. What are some things to avoid when wording questions in a survey?
6. Bring in half a dozen travel ads that you feel demonstrate an awareness of today's travel climate; bring in three which you feel miss the mark. Explain your reasons for each selection.
7. What are the steps in planning?

Case Problem

You want to market tours to the Fiji Islands but discover that one of the major problems is that Hawaii is closer and cheaper, and prospective tourists view these two resort areas as about the same. What would your marketing strategy be? How would you try to sell Fiji against Hawaii? Who do you think would be your best prospects, and why?

CHAPTER THREE

The Role of Advertising in Marketing

There are many definitions of advertising, some of them humorous, some cynical, some only partially accurate. Perhaps any definition will limp a bit, but here's a working description:

> Advertising is a method for presenting goods and services to the public, using the mass media rather than personal selling, and carrying the signature of an identifiable sponsor.

Perhaps we should add that this is a *paid* form of presentation, to distinguish it from publicity, which is an unpaid form of presenting products, services, and ideas.

Keep in mind that, while the ad replaces the salesman for the more distant audience, it still relies on many of the selling points and techniques employed by salespeople. It tries to put into a limited space or time block what a good salesperson might say to a prospect.

It's important, too, to recall that the sponsor is identified. This is not really a *news* item, nor is advertising normally bipartisan. It strives to deliver a message—the message of the sponsor who paid for it.

Of course, advertising *can* be news. That's one of the ways in which it works. A travel ad can communicate a new fare or new schedule or new tour offering.

Besides presenting *news*, advertising can also:

- *Remind you* of a product or service. This works well in travel, where repetition about a trip may eventually sink in. Or where an individual advertisement may trigger thinking about some place a reader intended to visit.
- *Convey information* that will make the product or service better known. This may not be news, but it is of interest. The more people know about a subject like travel and travel agencies, the more likely they are to use an agency.
- *Enhance the image* of the service or product. Good writing and strong illustrations can make travel even more appealing. Copywriters who can come up with prose that "sings" are invaluable.

- *Close the sale.* Well, perhaps advertising doesn't really close many travel sales but it can make it easier for the salesperson to get a chance for the clincher. Good ads can stimulate readers to action, get them to mail a coupon, or write for a brochure, or visit the travel office.

Many businesspeople don't understand advertising. They consider it a necessity but, if they could do well without it, they'd probably scrap it. They fail to realize both the long- and short-range effects of advertising. Advertising, in fact, does many things that the consumer doesn't grasp or appreciate.

Ads don't merely sell products or services, they accomplish a variety of tasks. They get people to switch brands, or they solidify brand loyalty. They try to correct confusion about a brand, as Goodrich's "other guys" campaign tries to do in connection with Goodyear. They may seek to get you to use a familiar product in a new way, or to buy more of it at one time ("When You're Out of Schlitz . . . "), or to extend the buying season—as tour operators have managed to do. They turn a minus into a plus ("We Try Harder") or explain a problem or enhance the image of an entire industry, as the million dollar ASTA campaign focusing on travel agents was designed to do.

Keep in mind that you are directing ads to certain groups of people for certain reasons. It makes no difference if men (and some women) snicker at television spots for household products; these men don't buy the products; their wives do. Casual readers who don't understand a sophisticated ad in *The New Yorker* don't worry the people who created that ad; they are after sophisticated readers and buyers. People who never intend to go to Mexico can complain all they want about your ad for a Mexican vacation; you're not writing for them.

This fact also tells us something fundamental about human behavior.

Understanding Human Behavior

Every good travel counselor knows there is a certain amount of psychology in selling. Advertisers understand this, too. Not only must you know who the prospects are and where they are, you should also know how they tick.

For example, needs and wants differ among individuals. This may be the result of age, taste, income, family size, background, station in life, and other factors.

Not too many years ago a winter vacation was something only very wealthy people could afford. Or so the others thought. Today winter vacations are commonplace, and some people state that they positively need them because of the pressures of their work.

Air conditioning has become a virtual necessity in most states, and two-car families are the norm. Even the agreed-upon necessities, like food, shelter, and clothing are subject to the whims of the purchaser.

There are diet foods, health foods, people who think steak is the ultimate, others who lavish money on gourmet meals. There are those who fancy jeans, those who prefer three-piece suits, and those who will pay anything for a fashion first. The choice of a home has something to do with income, family size, proximity to work, personal taste, even the image you want to convey.

Travel is affected by all of these variations, based on individual preferences. Time of year, locale, group or singly, city lights or solitude, luxury or economy—all of these factors will strike people differently.

Motivation, Perception, and Learning

Psychologists tell us that the three things fundamental to an understanding of human behavior are motivation, perception, and learning.

Motivation deals with our inner drives and urges, the reasons we behave as we do, the things that move us toward goals.

There are *primary* motives (like pain avoidance, self preservation, satisfying of hunger and thirst) and *secondary* motives, like the desire for security or success. Obviously, travel agents are concerned only with the secondary motives.

Think of the reasons people travel, their motivation for spending the money on a trip. They could be after pleasure, amusement, a chance to talk about the trip later, an opportunity to satisfy their curiosity, or after an improvement in health, a degree of comfort, or an educational experience. Each trip, in fact, probably stems from a combination of motives. Good salespeople try to ferret these out, to learn *why* a person wants to go to a certain place and travel in a certain way.

Primary motives may assert themselves on occasion—if, for example, the prospective traveler saw some physical danger in an otherwise attractive journey—but the secondary motives, largely emotional but sometimes rational, dominate in selling.

Perception refers to the way we see things. Everyone is familiar with the conflicting stories that come from witnesses to an accident or a holdup. We may be subject to the same external stimuli as those with us, but the way we translate these objective facts can differ. Perception has a great deal to do with our taste in certain things, including travel.

If all we can think about when we hear "Mexico" is the possibility of dysentery, we are not much impressed with the promise of lovely senoritas and classical flamenco. On the other hand, people with an intense curiosity about Aztec ruins are not going to let a little water stop them.

When we read an advertising message, we color it based on what we believe. One of the old tricks used to demonstrate this was to hold up two signs reading "Fresh Eggs," one written in a formal style, the other rather clumsily handwritten. Which one had the most credibility? The second one. Why? Because readers thought of farmers as simple, honest folks, who would just scratch out a sign.

Another aspect of perception is that we see what we are looking for. There are towns you never heard of until you meet someone from that place, and then the papers seem full of stories from that locale. If you've just bought a new Buick—or if you are planning to buy one—you really see the Buick ads.

That's why consistency and repetition are important in travel advertising. Last month your prospect wasn't even thinking about a vacation, let alone Europe. This month he begins looking ahead and decides he wants to go to Paris. Your ad for a French tour has been running for six weeks, but he doesn't see it until this week—because now he's looking.

Our experience teaches us to adopt certain behavior in certain situations. We call this *learning*. It is a relatively permanent behavioral change. If we have a reaction to specific foods, we stop eating them. We learn how to turn the key in a pesky lock, or how to nurse a balky automobile. Once we've dropped a tray of slides, we remember to check to see the ring is tight.

Travelers also store up experiences, good or bad, and they learn by them. They may avoid various countries or cities, or select favorite restaurants, or choose new modes of transportation, or pick a different time of year.

Travel agents do likewise. Everything they experience, either directly or via reports and reading, should be stored away. It should modify their behavior and influence their counselling.

Emotion Versus Intellect

People like to consider themselves rational human beings—but all of us act emotionally a good share of the time. That's why one of the advertising adages tells us to "sell the sizzle and not the steak," meaning that purchasers buy the *image* of the product or service. Few people arrive at their travel destination thinking, "I hope that I shall return a much more educated individual, healthier in mind and body." Most travelers are after fun and excitement—after emotional rewards. That's why travel copy talks about sun-drenched beaches and lush vegetation and warm hospitality and intimate lounges.

Some elements of travel advertising have a rational side—price, for example, and details on items covered and not covered in tours. But the appeal is more to the senses than to the intellect.

Travel agencies also have their images. They are looked upon as pleasant and efficient, or as cluttered and irresponsible. The image comes, not only from personal contact, but also from the advertising and print materials issued by the agency.

Persuasion and Reinforcement

Advertising is criticized for many reasons. Television viewers dislike the interruptions; motorists complain about highway signs; economists state that advertising interferes with the normal course of supply and demand; readers, listeners, and viewers protest that advertising is degrading, immoral, or just plain dumb.

Above all, advertising is feared because it *persuades*.

This is foolishness. Persuasion is the civilized way to accomplish things. The alternatives are force and payment. Persuasion is the art of bringing the other person to your point of view. We do it all the time, from our childhood years through senility. As we mature, our arguments on our own behalf become more sophisticated, combining what we know about our audience with what we know about the subject.

That's also what advertising tries to do.

In advertising, however, we are trying to persuade a mass audience, so we aim for some general psychological motives. We assume that viewers would rather look at an attractive man or woman opening a new car door, than to see some disheveled bum performing the same chore (although this might have shock value). We also assume that readers will be attracted by a bargain, by a familiar name, by the image created by some imaginative prose or a compelling illustration.

Advertising *is* trying to convert people to your view. You are convinced they will love this raft trip down the Grand Canyon. You must, therefore, convey to them the same sort of excitement and enthusiasm you have for the journey. That sells!

You cannot successfully persuade people to do things they don't want to do. If you could, we'd still be driving Edsels, riding trains, wearing flat shoes, and eating only natural foods.

The *reinforcement* merits of advertising come about in several ways. Repetition is one way. Reaching the prospect with exactly the right message is another. What happens here is that a person, inspired by an ad, tries the product or service advertised. That person is satisfied with the experience, and so is likely to repeat it—and likely to see the advertisements that offer something similar from the same supplier. That's why readers return to favorite authors, gourmets to favorite restaurants, and travelers to agencies which have met or exceeded their needs and desires.

Psychological Appeals of Advertising

Built into most advertising are appeals which focus on some psychological trait, appealing to the motives mentioned earlier, and drawing upon what the advertiser knows are basic behavioral patterns. Figure 3-1 shows some of them that you might recognize in all types of advertising, including travel ads.

• Advertising that emphasizes *peer identification* or *snob appeal.* Clothing comes to mind here, or cars, or brands of liquor. Both motivations could also be at work in booking travel—young people wanting to go "where it's at" or older adults looking for locales that will impress their friends.

• Advertising designed with a *cultural trend* in mind. You notice this in the type of art used, or in headlines that take off on current slang, or the use of celebrities who are hot, or the featuring of themes that are popular: tours to Dracula country, or an appeal to a search for roots, or headlines like "Welcome to *our* fantasy island."

• Advertising that stresses *saving money or time,* that promises *entertainment,* or a chance to *meet the opposite sex.*

• Advertising that appeals to *health, physical* or *mental comfort, good food* or *drink, concern for your family.*

Think of the travel ads which rotate around these themes—the get-away-

THE ROLE OF ADVERTISING IN MARKETING   29

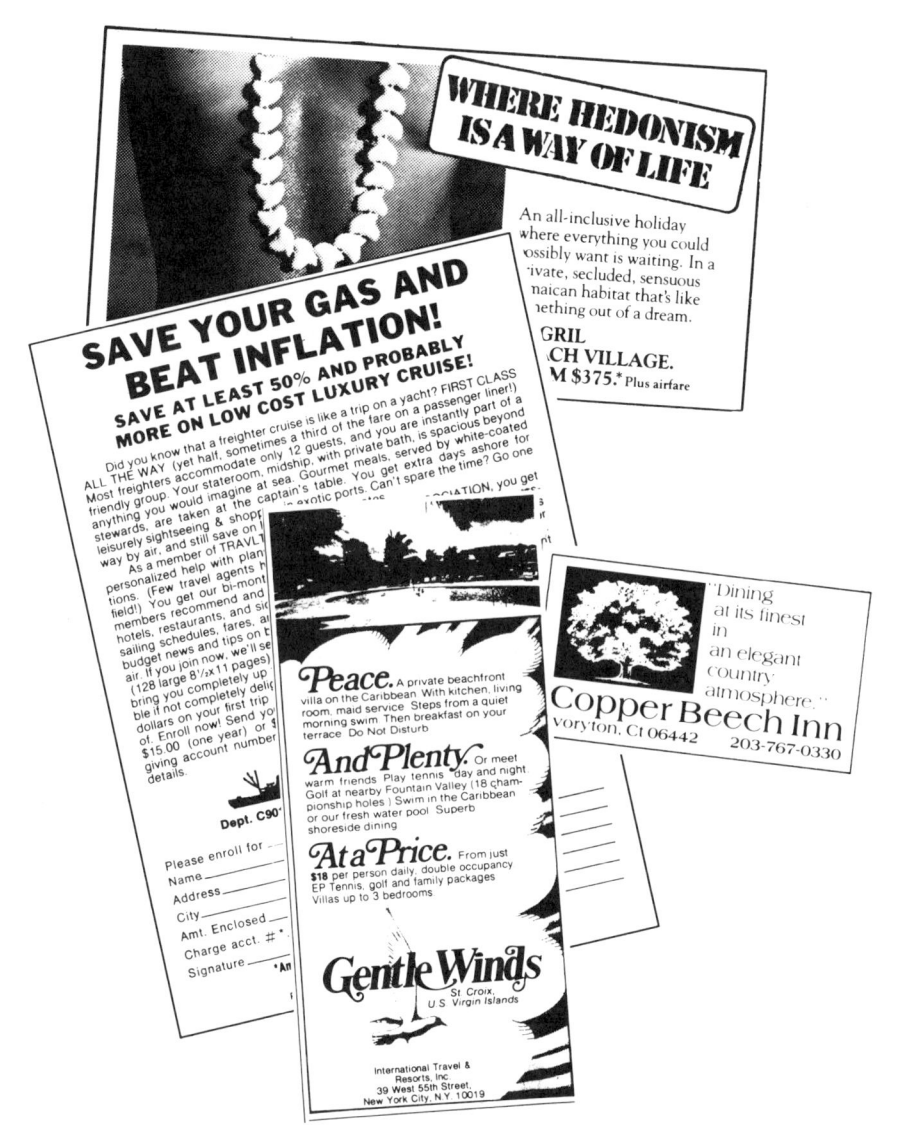

Figure 3-1 Psychological appeals characterize much of advertising.

from-it-all sun havens, the tours that take the worry out of traveling, the cuisine offered by airlines, the series of television commercials that urged the businessman to take his family on his business trips for just a little more.

Sometimes these categories naturally fit the travel being advertised; sometimes you dig out these ideas as additional reasons for travelling.

Advertising by Type

There's another major way to classify advertising—by noting what it sets out to do and where it appears. There are a dozen generally accepted classifications of advertising. We'll mention them all, but only a few really pertain to most travel agencies.

Institutional Advertising

These ads sell *ideas*. They are the image-making ads which companies are using in greater numbers, partly because of consumer movements, and partly because, with the clutter of advertising, it's important to make known the company behind the product. These ads may tell the public what the firm is doing to help society (note the environmental ads) or they may merely use the firm's name as sponsor of an ad about some national problem (drugs, voting, drunken drivers).

Commercial Advertising

This is advertising directed to middlemen, to the business people who will eventually sell to the consumer. You see ads for products or services (like desks, copy machines, and tax preparation) for use by businesses; or the merchandising of products or services to those who will sell them to others (everything from precooked fried chicken to Christmas cards), and professional ads directed at professional people (like physicians and dentists and lawyers) asking them to recommend products and services to clients.

All three of these categories affect travel agencies, although the second one is rare. Agencies do use both routine office furniture and some specialty items, like brochure racks; and trade magazines like *Travel Weekly* and *The Travel Agent* contain ads which appeal to agents, as professionals, to recommend certain tours, locales, resort hotels, carriers, and other competitive services to their clients.

Consumer Advertising

This category is, of course, the most common, the one we generally associate with advertising. It has three main divisions, all of which embrace travel advertising. These are: mail order, national, and local or retail advertising.

Mail order advertising is not the same as direct mail. Mail order advertising *sells* things through the mails, *directly*. You see these ads in hundreds of different magazines, where you are directed to fill out a coupon and enclose two dollars and you'll receive a monogrammed T-shirt. Or you may be given an address to which you post your check for assorted cheeses.

Travel isn't sold this way—although travel accessories may be, and travel books. Returning a coupon to receive a brochure is not the same thing, because the brochure is not an item of sale, it's an introduction to a personal sale.

Tour operators, airlines, hotel chains, and resort areas use *national advertising* in their campaigns. As normally defined, national advertising doesn't mean simply that the ads are seen nationwide; it means that you are pushing a brand name or a general service, and you are not particular where the customer purchases it. Advertising for beer and cigarettes and cosmetics falls into this area. So do ads for Holiday Inns, American Airlines, Maupintours, and those which promote trips to specific states or countries—like "Mexico—The Amigo Country."

National advertising affects travel agencies in a number of ways. These ads provide referrals, inspire curiosity, and may even direct the reader to see the local travel agency. Local agencies may also tie into such ads by putting their names at the bottom as the local contacts.

National advertisers buy schedules in the various media (principally newspaper, magazine, and television) to call attention to travel offerings. They may use the network on television, for example, or they may select fifty cities in which they want the spot to run. They may also specify billboard locations across the country, aiming for areas where the best prospects live, or they may pick radio stations that cover target markets.

Local or *retail advertising* is what virtually every travel agency uses, even when it is part of a larger geographical chain. This form of advertising specifies the supplier, asking that the consumer shop at a certain place of business. It isn't a matter of asking the reader or viewer to buy herbal shampoo; this form of ad asks him or her to buy herbal shampoo at Walgreen's Drug Store, at 16th and Douglas Streets.

Similarly, tours by major tour operators share space in local ads with trips organized by the local agency. Both of these may be joined with information on popular resort areas, like Hawaii or Las Vegas. The clincher is an appeal to visit this agency, or to call for information, or to return a coupon for further details.

As we'll note in the next chapter, local or retail *print* advertising is usually not commissionable, meaning that advertising agencies cannot earn fifteen percent from newspapers for placing local ads. That's why most retail newspaper ads are done by travel agency personnel.

Radio and television advertising, even on the local level, is generally commissionable, and may involve an advertising agency. Ditto for printed materials, like brochures and newsletters, which are not commissionable, but which the travel agency probably turns over to a specialist, paying this person or firm a fee for services.

Cooperative Advertising

Cooperative—or *co-op*—advertising is the name given to ads that are jointly sponsored by two mutually interested parties. Newspaper ads for new cars, for example, may be a collective venture in which the manufacturer and the local dealer share costs. Clothing stores also avail themselves of matching funds and other services from brand name suppliers.

Travel agencies, too, can look for help in a variety of ways.

• Carriers, resort hotels, tour companies, and other travel-oriented suppliers may make available newspaper mats or glossy proofs which can be incorporated into the agency's print ads, or which may be used as ads themselves, with the agency adding its name at the bottom.

• These same firms may also furnish items such as radio commercials on

Cartan Escorted

EUROPE WONDERLAND HOLIDAY

**FULLY ESCORTED
13 HOTEL NIGHTS
IN EUROPE**
Selected Saturday Departures.
Visits London 3 nights, Amsterdam 2 nights, Cologne 1 night, Mainz 1 night, Lucerne 2 nights, Besancon 1 night and Paris for 3 nights. 24 meals plus tax and waiters' tips. 11 Sightseeing Trips by Deluxe Air-conditioned Motorcoach. All airport transfers, handling and tips for 2 pieces of luggage. Total cost per person sharing twin including airfare $000.

**YOUR NAME
ADDRESS
PHONE NUMBER**

Cartan's MEXICO

**ESCORTED
ROMANTICA—MEXICO CITY, IXTAPAN, TAXCO AND ACAPULCO
FULLY ESCORTED**
9 Hotel Nights in Mexico
Selected Sunday Departures. Visits Mexico City for 3 nights at Fiesta Palace, 1 night at Spa Ixtapan, 1 night in Taxco at De la Borda and 4 nights in Acapluco at Condesa del Mar.
4 Sightseeing trips by Deluxe Air-conditioned Motorcoach, 7 meals including tax and waiters' tips. All transfers in Mexico, handling and tips for 2 pieces of luggage.
Total cost per person sharing twin including air fare $000.

**YOUR NAME
ADDRESS
PHONE NUMBER**

Caravan Africa 1978

Africa

Free! Beautiful New Brochure

Thrill to wild game viewing, tribal dancers, etc., on East Africa Safari or Cape to Kenya tour. 3 weeks, all expense, all meals, escorted, best hotels, $1875 to $1995 per person, double occupancy, plus air. Frequent departures.

For your free copy write or phone:

Figure 3-2   Tour operators and other suppliers provide materials for co-op advertising.

tape or cassettes, television spots on video tape, slides, scripts which may be worked into your own broadcast commercials, films for special showings or for television programs, posters for display, brochures, brochure shells into which you may insert copy for tours you originate, point-of-sale materials like counter stands and model airplanes, even giveaway items for clients and prospects.

• Suppliers of travel services may also agree to participate with you in a proposed advertising campaign, supplying part of the money to pay for the advertising. The amount they will commit depends on such considerations as the amount of space or time they get in the ad, the extent to which they feel they need the business, the way in which they view the travel agency, their own budget allocations, and other factors.

The travel agency manager should discuss these co-op opportunities with the airlines, hotel chains, tour operators, resort managers, and others who might share an interest. Find out what their policies are, what they can supply in the way of materials, and what their requirements are for allocating matching funds.

The Ethics of Advertising

This subject needs airing because of the many complaints about the advertising profession. As in all fields, there are those in advertising whose ethics may be marginal. These people generally don't last. Most practitioners are as ethical as those in any line of work.

Advertising gets blamed for the low moral tone of the nation and for persuading people to buy things they don't want with money they don't have. It is also attacked for debasing our cultural standards, increasing the cost of goods, dictating television programming, establishing public taste, and deliberately misleading the consumer with false product claims.

Let's look at these criticisms very briefly.

There may be some truth in the complaint that advertising has adversely affected our culture. Certainly, language has been altered, with superlatives losing much of their impact because of overuse. A number of television commercials, too, seem to take a low view of the intelligence of viewers. At the same time, advertising has also helped to popularize various art styles, to pioneer TV techniques, to promote thousands of good causes, and to raise awareness in a variety of social and cultural areas.

Advertising doesn't increase the cost of goods. True, the cost of advertising must be included in the price charged for any product or service but, without such advertising, how would the public know of the item's existence? Most selling is a volume business, and volume can only be achieved through advertising. Volume is one of the factors that can actually lower the cost of goods, rather than increase it. The travel agency that waited around for the public to discover its wares would be in for a long wait.

Television programs are retained or retired because of viewers, not advertisers. A program that attracts a large audience will also be supported by advertising, regardless of the sponsors' personal views about content (except where such content conflicts with their own goals and philosophy). If an inane and repetitive situation comedy stays on while your favorite symphonic program disappears, that's because the former, whatever its relative merits, simply has more people watching. The advertising dollars follow audiences.

Similarly, advertising follows taste in other things rather than establishing taste. Unfortunately, advertising was not in the vanguard of the fight for minority rights (although it has an exemplary record as an employer of minorities); it followed trends. Black people began appearing more often in commercials at about the same time white Americans were becoming more sensitive to the evils of discrimination. In general, ads react to trends, extending them perhaps, but rarely creating them.

Finally, *good* advertising doesn't make false claims. This practice doesn't work over a long period of time, is unethical and immoral—and also illegal. Sometimes advertisers do exaggerate, often because they think superlatives make for strong ads. They're wrong. Credibility is to be preferred over extravagance.

Legal Considerations

Some critics think advertising gets away with murder. Actually, advertising is a highly regulated business. Some ad execs have groused that major conglomerates withhold millions in taxes and get a slap on the wrist but, when an advertiser punches holes in a can of radiator stop-leak, the government jumps all over him. One of the reasons for such vigilance is that advertising is highly visible and any lapses are certain to be noticed. Another reason for the number of cases involving advertising is that there is a considerable body of law affecting the practice.

Most complaints against advertising stem from false and misleading claims.

A prohibition against such claims came into law in 1938 when the Wheeler-Lea Act substantially amended the earlier (1914) Federal Trade Commission Act which regulated unfair competition. "Unfair or deceptive acts or practices in commerce" were viewed as giving an edge to the violator, thus making them illegal.

This concept has been refined and expanded through the years in a series of laws and court cases which cover packaging, labeling, the distribution of obscene material through the mails, the use of false statements about competitive products and services, and other matters. Even the location of outdoor advertising is rigidly controlled, particularly along the interstate system.

Some areas of the law covering advertising are vague. In the past, advertising was excluded from the interpretation of First Amendment protection as freedom of speech. Courts looked upon it as commercial, rather than an expression of opinion or protest, or a means of communicating information. This view has softened somewhat. Advertising which expresses political opinions, for example, is considered protected and, if there is any trend, it is moving toward a liberalization of the coverage afforded all advertising.

Another grey area is the question of libel and slander. In the past two decades, judgments expanded the definition of who was a public figure, a person whose activities were inherently newsworthy. These individuals were —and are—entitled to less protection under the laws of libel than are private citizens. The principle is that these men and women—political leaders, entertainers, socially prominent citizens—are in the public eye and reporting about their foibles, even in a critical way, is acceptable. The reporter—or advertiser—had to be careful, however, about separating the public figure's public life from his private life.

How could travel agency advertising run afoul of these laws?

For one thing, if photos of any recognizable individuals (and this doesn't mean prominent, but merely identifiable) are used in ads, written permission must be obtained. The same thing pertains to the use of a person's name in any sort of endorsement copy.

Obviously, too, you cannot merely appropriate a photo or a piece of artwork without clearing with the owner. You must secure a written okay and pay whatever fee is agreed upon.

If you purchase a photo for use in an ad, that doesn't mean you can later use this photo in a brochure or newsletter, unless the permission you obtain covers all uses.

(In cases where photos are supplied by airlines or hotels, along with approval for use, you need no further okay.)

Travel advertising has to be as factual as any other advertising. The copy must fairly represent the actual tour and the price structure must not be misleading. You couldn't, for example, advertise an "All-Expense" tour and then indicate in the small print that this covers only transportation to and from the destination and some hotels. Nor would you be allowed to show photos of first-class hotels but put the tour members in third- or fourth-class hotels.

You can't use a "bait and switch" technique, advertising a terrific travel bargain, then, when the customers arrive, telling them this trip is sold out, and selling them on a more expensive vacation.

You can't subvert competitors by spreading false rumors about their methods or their lack of solvency or their treatment of other clients. This goes back to the original principle of unfair competition.

In terms of cooperative advertising, a supplier is supposed to make available to *all* agencies, large or small, the same sort of participation. Just because one agency does a large volume of business and the other a small volume, the supplier can't offer the first agency 80% of costs for an ad campaign and the second agency only 20%. All middlemen must be treated equally.

The media are generally aware of these legal problems and will often counsel an agency in the event of some questionable copy or practice. However, the agency shouldn't automatically count on this. It should police its own advertising, making certain it's in conformity with both legal and ethical standards.

In addition to federal laws governing advertising, there are also state laws. Not every state has such legislation (most of which is based on the Printers Ink Model Statute, drawn up in 1911, revised in 1945) and less than half the states have what we call effective legislation.

Besides the major legal concerns cited above, there are also some less likely, but also important, considerations:

• The use of obscenity (which may be broadly interpreted by each community) in copy or illustrations can get you into trouble.

• Infringing on another's copyright—by stealing a slogan or identifying logo or other copyrighted item—could lead to legal action.

• Participation in a lottery—such as the offering of a free trip—could be dangerous. To constitute a lottery, there must be three elements present: *prize, chance,* and *consideration.* If any of these three is missing, the contest is not a lottery and is, therefore, not illegal. Let's say you offered a trip for two to Hawaii, based on the drawing of numbers, and open to anyone, whether or not they ever did business with you, you'd be okay on the lottery score. If you limited the contestants to those who had travelled with you, or who purchased an airline ticket, or who performed some task (even a visit to your office, as interpreted in some states), you could be in violation of the lottery restriction. In addition to watching your own possible offerings in this area, be careful about tying in with any other companies who plan to use you as a supplier of the trip in return for advertising and promotion.

• Remember that the consumer and the competition have access to corrective and counter advertising, forcing a statement which amends an earlier ad, or securing equal space or time to express a point of view counter to the advertiser's.

If, for example, you aired a television commercial stating that using a travel agency saved you time and money, a private citizen *might* have the right to dispute this, forcing the TV station to grant him equal time to express an opposing viewpoint. This is less likely than in the case of controversial items, like cigarettes or utilities, but it could happen.

* * *

Some helpful books in this legal area are:
WILLIAM E. FRANCOIS, *Mass Media Law and Regulation,* Columbus, Grid, 1975.
EARL W. KINTNER, *A Primer on the Law of Deceptive Practices,* New York, The Macmillan Company, 1971
NATIONAL BETTER BUSINESS BUREAU'S *Do's and Don'ts in Advertising Copy,* New York, National Better Business Bureau, 1968
GEORGE ERIC ROSDEN and PETER ERIC ROSDEN, *The Law of Advertising,* New York, Matthew Bender, 1975

Questions and Exercises

1. Name five things that advertising can accomplish.
2. What three things are fundamental to an understanding of human behavior?
3. How would you argue against an individual who state that the riots in Watts were caused by television commercials which showed the poor blacks of that area that there were all sorts of consumer goods available but denied to them because of their low incomes?
4. Find twelve print ads that are directed toward *different* psychological appeals.
5. Find these three types of print ads in the *travel* area:
    a. An ad directed toward the travel agency itself.
    b. An ad by a national firm without a local reference.
    c. A local ad incorporating a national advertiser's copy.
6. Why should a public figure have fewer rights under the First Amendment than a private citizen? Discuss.

Case Problem

As a travel agency manager, you are bidding for a major tour to be underwritten by a large insurance company for its top producers. There will be at least 500 bookings and the tour package involves all costs of a 5-day vacation in Acapulco. This would not only be a nice piece of business but could also provide a foot in the door for the insurance firm's ongoing commercial travel. Consequently, you bid the tour as low as possible, barely covering expenses, and showing virtually no profit. You discover, however, that you have been substantially underbid by another agency whose reputation within the advertising fraternity is nil. This particular agency has lost its accreditation, has gone bankrupt twice, has been denied credit by several of the major airlines, and has been suspected for some time of using unethical practices to garner business. At the moment, it is operating through a national tour operator who does hold a legitimate accreditation.

What should you do? Forget about it and figure you were just outbid? Blow the whistle on the agency by reporting all to the client? Mobilize your fellow agents against this agency? What? (Remember the legal implications of any action you initiate.)

CHAPTER FOUR

The Advertising Agency

No profession's image has been as distorted by the mass media as has advertising's. The ad agency exec is depicted as a flashy, ulcer-prone, unscrupulous entrepreneur who fawns over clients, plots against his own colleagues, and espouses even the shoddiest ideas if they sell merchandise. He arrives late to work, takes three hours for martini lunches, and spends enormous amounts of time losing to client-golfers on the nation's courses.

Every stereotype has some exemplars, but most of those who work in advertising are not only creative; they are also intelligent and productive and diligent. They are used to pressure and committed to a life of deadlines. Unlike some other professionals, their efforts are publicly displayed and their results are obvious and measurable.

The advertising agency is largely a product of this century, although its roots go back to pre-Civil War days when *space brokers* would purchase several pages of a newspaper and then resell this space to advertisers at a profit. Just over a hundred years ago, N.W. Ayer & Son agency begin the practice of lining up clients who agreed to buy space through their agency. Ayer would then contract with the newspaper for this space.

A natural consequence of this arrangement was that clients began to request additional services from Ayer—things like copywriting and layout and artwork. From this model, today's agency was born.

Agency Size

There are some four thousand advertising agencies in the United States and they range from firms which employ thousands of people to those which have only a handful. Size, however, is determined, not by personnel, but by *billings*. Gross charges for all agency activities are totaled and that dollar figure is used to measure ranking among the nation's advertising firms.

When *world billings* are calculated, for example, J. Walter Thompson would lead American agencies with annual billings in excess of a billion and a half dollars. That would result in an income of approximately $225 million. Young and Rubicam listed income in 1978 as $118 million, which ranked at the top in terms of United States (only) income.

The ten largest American world agencies would all have annual incomes in excess of $100 million while the top ten agencies in the United States income would range from Young and Rubicam's $118 million to Ted Bates and Company's $55 million.

These are the big boys; they're the exceptions. They handle the airlines accounts and the steamship lines and the international tourism accounts. They people either coast and a few of the larger inland cities, like Chicago and Detroit. While one of their branches might work with a travel agency, such an arrangement is unlikely. You'll be doing business with a smaller agency.

Most ad agencies, in fact, are small businesses. A majority bill less than a million a year, making their income between a hundred and a hundred and fifty thousand dollars each annually. Many agencies bill substantially less than this—perhaps half a million or even a quarter of a million dollars. Some are "ma and pa" shops which operate out of an individual's home, cutting down on the overhead, and may feature a single employee, often an older executive who wants to taper off, or a younger one who wants to build his own clientele.

The fact is, many advertising agencies are modest operations, just like many travel agencies.

What Can an Ad Agency Do for Me?

Obviously, the larger the agency, the more services will be available on the premises. A *full service* agency is expected to provide media services, marketing advice, research, copywriting, art services, public relations, production capabilities, and other specialities. Smaller agencies may not have research and marketing experts and may also try to double up on public relations activities. Even smaller agencies may merely provide ideas, writing, and make media placements, contracting out the other specialties, such as artwork and production.

Let's assume you have a campaign in mind to sell winter tours to Midwestern farmers who will have more leisure time during the cold weather and, in good years, will also have sufficient funds to travel. You decide you need the help of a professional advertising firm. How do you find one?

Advertising agencies are listed in the Yellow Pages, of course, and are also catalogued in national directories. Chances are, however, you'll come up with a name as the result of the recommendation of a friend who advertises or via consultation with someone in the media.

You bring your problem to the agency. At this point, the agency has to decide whether or not it wants you as a client. It may already have a travel account and this usually means they will not take on a competing account. Or it may analyze your proposed budget as being too small to deal with profitably.

Let's say you do get an affirmative response and you like what you observe about the agency. You agree to go ahead. This could call for a contract, but most agencies have only short range agreements which can be cancelled by either party after sufficient notice or, often, only verbal agreements. With larger agencies and larger accounts, this is different.

The agency would assign someone to work on your account—an account executive. That person listens to what you have in mind and then, working with a creative team within the agency, tries to come up with a campaign that will meet your needs and goals.

The Campaign

This campaign would focus on a theme, involve some print and broadcast ads, perhaps, and direct mail and other media. The agency would show you some sample ads or scripts and also present you with a recommended budget that would spell out its choices of media, programs, broadcast dates and times, and other items. You always have the right to turn down the campaign, suggest alterations, or trim the budget. It's your money that's being spent!

When you've agreed upon the creative work, expenditures, and general use of media, the agency goes ahead and completes the production of the print ads or the radio and television ads, contacts the media to reserve space, keeps track of the costs, and submits a bill to you. In a sense, it also serves as a bank, since the media know and trust the agency and see it as a guarantee of payment. They may not be as familiar with your credit record.

What Will This Cost Me?

It could cost you nothing—depending on a number of things. Advertising agencies are something like travel agencies; the majority of their income comes from commissions from the media they use. *If* the medium chosen allows the advertising agency the usual commission, then the only other costs you might incur are those associated with the production of the advertisements. If the medium does not allow advertising agency commissions —and newspapers often do not—then you would be expected to pay the agency the equivalent of the commission. This fact explains why travel agencies frequently handle their newspaper advertising direct with the paper, while farming out the commissionable radio and television ads to an advertising agency.

How Do Ad Agencies Make Their Income?
There are two principal sources of income in the advertising profession—commissions and fees.

Commissions usually amount to 15% of the money expended in the media and, with the exception noted above, are paid by the media to the agency. Let's say, for example, that you plan to spend $1,500 for radio during a given time period. If you go directly to the radio stations, you will pay $1,500; if you go through an advertising agency, you will also pay $1,500, but the radio stations will bill the agency for $1,275 (which is $1,500 less 15%, or $225). Commissions form the greatest proportion of any agency's income.

Fees are also charged for special services. If you want public relations help for news releases, feature stories, special events, or other activities, you may pay an hourly fee (anywhere from $25 to $60 an hour and up), a monthly or annual retainer, or a set price agreed upon for a specific assignment. Fees might also include charges for research, for photography and artwork, or for manual chores, like preparing mailings, which are turned over to the agency.

There are some additional ways in which agencies may earn money. Collateral materials—printing, photography, artwork, and the like—may be plussed 17.65 percent. If the photographer charges $100 for photo services, the agency will bill you for $117.65. Why? Because the agency personnel also spend time meeting with the photographer, accompanying him, reviewing his work, deciding on usage and so on. Why 17.65%? This is a figure arrives at by calculating the equivalent of 15% of gross.

A final, though minor, source of income stems from agency discounts which are sometimes allowed if bills are paid within a specified time limit, normally 10 days. This may amount to 2% of the net charge. Reputable advertising agencies will pass along this discount to the client if the client also pays within this 10 day period. If the client chooses not to do so, then the advertising agency may pay the bill and pocket the 2% commission.

This may bring up a few questions:

- *Why are the media willing to pay commissions to advertising agencies instead of retaining the 15% themselves?* The media assume that they are going to get material that is in a more professional state, that payment is assured, that direct contact with the client is unnecessary, that time is saved in meetings and in billing. They may also see the advertising agency as a source of new business, since agencies locate and convince clients about media placement.

- *Why don't most newspapers pay commissions then?* They do pay commissions on national advertising, ads like those for Lifebuoy or Budweiser which are national in scope. Travel agencies would generally be looked upon as local clients within that newspaper's community and they therefore earn a lower local rate, which presumably saves the client some money but cuts out the advertising agency. Agencies don't like this practice but can do little about it. If a travel agency wants to employ an advertising agency to create and place local newspaper ads, they must be prepared to pay an add-on cost for this service.

- *Do radio or television stations ever work directly with the travel agency? Do they rebate the commission an ad agency would get?* Many stations work directly with clients. Generally, however, their creative efforts can't match those of ad agencies, although there are exceptions. Some also rebate part of the costs to a travel agency client, but most media would find this unethical. There should be no under-the-table deals.

- *How can I be sure in advance about ad agency charges?* Ask! Most agencies will spell this out for you anyway, and a good number have printed standard operating procedures that are given to clients. There should be no secrets and no surprises.

Finally, on the subject of money, if we take the hypothetical case mentioned earlier of the $1,500 expenditure for radio which results in a profit of $225 to the advertising agency, you should realize that this is hardly a windfall. It would barely pay a week's wages for a secretary in many agencies. That's why large agencies can't even bother with such accounts. Their people are so highly salaried, they lose money on such transactions.

So why would they bother with a travel account at all?

Perhaps the billings are substantial enough to whet their interest. Perhaps there are attendant public relation fees. Perhaps they just like the variety of working with different accounts, and travel agencies are generally considered one of the more "fun" accounts. Perhaps, too, they see some growth potential in a small account and want to get in on the ground floor.

It should be noted that some advertising agencies are experimenting with different methods of compensation, feeling that the straight 15% commission doesn't allow for the variables of the business. It may take as much time, for example, to prepare a full page ad for *Travel Weekly* as it does for *Newsweek* but the commission on the former would be a few hundred dollars and, on the latter, six thousand dollars or more. Spot television costs more to buy than other media, in terms of time, so clients who use a disproportionate amount of TV are more expensive to handle.

Travel agencies, of course, are familiar with this. Some money comes relatively easily, some breaks out at a nickel an hour.

Again, if the agency suggests another form of payment—such as an hourly basis for its work and you getting to keep the agency commission—be sure you understand it.

What Should I Look for in an Advertising Agency?

First, are you *compatible*? Do you like these people? Can you work with them comfortably? Arrange to meet the agency personnel, particularly that person who is likely to be assigned to your account. Does the style of this particular agency, its philosophy, fit yours?

Second, you'd want to take a look at the agency *size* to see if you are going to get sufficient attention. If you are a minor concern, you can't count on much service.

Third, does the agency understand the travel business? Having previous experience in this field would be a plus but, if the personnel don't have that, have they worked on similar accounts, or do they grasp the peculiar nature of your work? Even without such foreknowledge, the agency might still function very well for you, but some familiarity is a big time saver.

Fourth, what do other clients say about the agency? Are they satisfied? Would they recommend it? You can request a list of the agency's current clients and make a few phone calls. Also, does the agency have any clients who would be in direct competition with you—another travel agency in your market?

Fifth, what type of people does the agency have? Are they creative, innovative, dependable? Do they have sufficient depth so that you aren't left stranded when your account executive is ill or out of town?

Sixth, what kind of services does the agency offer? Are these what you need? How will it charge for them?

Seventh, is the agency's credit rating good? Does it pay its bills? Is it stable? Does it have a good reputation with the media and with other advertising agencies.

Eighth, ask to see some of the agency's work, particularly work that comes closest to your needs. You might even ask agencies to compete by making presentations based on your campaign needs. If your proposed budget is small, however, as most travel agencies' budgets tend to be, such a presentation might be an imposition. Perhaps a written statement of how the account would be handled would suffice.

There are other considerations, of course, from proximity to the makeup of the agency (an old conservative group or a young radical group?), and these must be sorted out according to the requirements of each travel agency manager.

How Is an Advertising Agency Structured?

Agencies differ according to size, specialization, type of management, type of personnel, type of accounts, location, and other variables.

A moderate-sized agency—say a $1,000,000 agency—would have the following departments:

- *Management.* Senior officers who may also handle some accounts in addition to running the business.
- *Account Executives.* Those individuals who work directly with clients. These persons may also do some creative work, particularly copywriting.
- *Creative Department.* Headed by a creative director, this department pools the talents of writers and artists to develop campaigns and create advertisements.
- *Production.* There will be someone (or several people) in charge of print production, seeing that print ads and brochures are produced properly and on time. Another department might handle radio and television production, supervising the production of spots at local studios.
- *Media.* This person or department is responsible for knowing the pros and cons of the media, the top rated television shows, the best magazine markets, and so on. The media buyer deals constantly with media salespeople and can advise on the most efficient use of a given budget.
- *Traffic.* In this division, the print ads, tapes, and video tapes are recorded, mailed, and collected. This individual keeps tabs on these items and sees that they get where they should go and get back again.
- *Accounting.* Because of volume, the number of suppliers, and employees who may be more creative than careful, this department is a busy one. All costs are captured here and billed out to the proper client.
- *Other.* Some agencies may have public relations departments, marketing departments, research departments, or other adjuncts. This depends somewhat on size, somewhat on demand, and somewhat on the availability of the proper personnel.

What Is My Responsibility in This Partnership?

Clients are an important part of any advertising campaign. They should know what they want and know when they see it. That means they must do some thinking prior to the involvement of the ad agency, and they must then communicate clearly to the account executive what they have in mind. It is up to the agency then to express this idea creatively or to solve the problem effectively.

The travel agency manager must also have a reasonable system of ad approval. Keep the approval list to one or two people; don't involve all of your travel counselors on every ad. This only leads to confusion. If they have a reason for passing judgment, okay, but don't circulate the materials just to bolster your own indecisiveness.

When you are reviewing ads, keep in mind your own goals. Don't be misled by the pretty pictures. Give sufficient time to this discussion and don't have the appraisal meeting punctuated by phone calls and counter conversations. Be open to new ideas, even if you didn't initially see the campaign this way. Be specific with your criticisms. Comments like, "Well, I really don't like it. It doesn't do anything for me," don't help the creative people at all. Give them something to go on. And don't be a nitpicker. If you keep making minor changes, the agency personnel will get discouraged, and will finally produce something safe and colorless.

What Are Some of the Pitfalls in This Relationship?

Client complaints about agencies include:

- Lack of sufficient staff
- Inexperience
- Inflexibility
- Lack of interest in travel business
- Carelessness in meeting deadlines and other obligations
- Poor communication
- Lack of fresh ideas

Agency personnel sometimes find these travel agency flaws:

- Expecting too much for too little money
- Lack of direction and communication
- Inconsistency of planning and funding
- Indecisiveness
- Too many critics involved
- Lack of candor
- Failure to have its own house in order

No relationship is perfect. The more communication you have with your agency, the more you understand each other's problems, the better the partnership will function.

A time may come when you feel you must change agencies. This could be because you've outgrown the previous agency, because it has gone sour on the account, because it keeps changing personnel on you, because it ignores you in the pursuit of new business, because it won't listen to your problems, because it can't handle finances, or because it can no longer deliver what it promised.

When this day arrives, you must ask yourself whether the rift is terminal or not. Can it be rectified with a change of personnel, or a change of strategy? Remember that you have lived with this agency for some time and you know each other—much as married people know each other.

Do you want to start over?

Should I Consider Operating My Own In-House Agency?

An in-house agency is one in which the client, probably wanting to save the agency commission, decides to incorporate into an agency. To do this, you must have sufficient volume to make it worthwhile, and you must add two more accounts. Some automobile dealers who spend a few hundred thousand a year on advertising do handle their own account, contracting out some of the services, and they take on two smaller accounts, like a pet shop or a boutique, to meet the letter of the law.

For a few travel agencies this might work; for the vast majority, it makes no sense at all. There isn't enough money in it, and the result will be poor advertising.

The best solution might be a combination of agency and your own handiwork. Some travel agencies, of course, do everything themselves; others do their newspaper ads in-house, and use an advertising agency (if they can get one) to do their radio and television.

The next few chapters assume you'll be doing most of the work yourself. Even if you aren't, it doesn't hurt to know what you're paying for.

Questions and Exercises

1. Why is most newspaper advertising for travel agencies handled by the agencies themselves?

2. List three ways that advertising agencies are compensated.

3. If you were looking for an advertising agency, what are some of the factors you'd consider in screening prospective agencies?

4. List some of the complaints travel agencies have about travel agencies. And list some of the complaints advertising agencies have about travel agencies as clients.

5. Visit a local advertising agency and ask them to describe in some detail the process involved in the development of any campaign.

Case Problem

You decide you want to put together a radio campaign that will be carried by two dozen radio stations in your section of the state. You have no advertising agency but decide to employ one to assist you in creative work, production, and media placement. How would you go about finding an agency? What would you tell the agency you selected so that it would understand your needs? What would you expect of it?

CHAPTER FIVE

Understanding Media

The first thing to remember about the various advertising media is that no one medium is the perfect answer for everything. For a number of years, television has been the darling of ad agencies, sometimes to the detriment of other good media. TV is a powerful advertising tool—but it isn't everything. Like all the media, it has its strengths and its weaknesses.

Let's look at the many media options the travel agent has, and examine their good and bad points.

Newspapers

This medium is one of the oldest forms of mass communication in this country, and, for travel advertising, remains one of the best. The survey by the Midwestern agency cited in chapter two showed that *two-thirds* of the customers of that chain of 14 branch offices were attracted by newspapers or direct mail, with the direct mail approach having a slight edge (34% to 33%). Magazine advertising accounted for another 15%; television nearly 8%; and radio just under 3%. Other media accounted for the remaining 7%.

Keep in mind once again that this is a survey in only one area of the country and percentages would differ elsewhere. Keep in mind, too, that this question dealt only with *advertising*. When all sources of information were included, giving the respondent ten choices, here's the way they responded to the question of *WHY they selected this particular agency:*

- A friend referred me (25.2%)
- Know an agency employee (21.7%)
- Newspaper ad (13.3%)
- Direct mail (6.9%)
- Radio (6.6%)
- Employer does business with agency (6%)
- Yellow Pages (3.7%)
- Television (1.3%)
- Travel folder (.9%)
- Other (14.4%)

These figures are a bit confusing when you compare them to some of the numbers cited earlier but they do point out two things:
Personal referrals and contacts are important.
Print advertising surpasses other forms.
(In fairness, television salespersons might point out that few travel agencies ever buy a decent TV schedule, so the ability to attract customers is slim.)

Of the print advertising opportunities, newspapers rate very high. Much of this is due to the psychological factor we mentioned earlier—you find what you're looking for, and people are used to looking in the newspaper travel section for information on travel.

Newspapers are the nation's biggest advertising medium, although television might challenge that honor in terms of dollars spent. But between 50% and 60% of retail businesses—like travel agencies—use newspapers as their first choice.

The number of newspapers in the United States has declined steadily in the last 60 years—from a high of nearly 2,500 daily newspapers in 1915 to nearly 30% fewer today. The remaining newspapers, however, do a higher volume of advertising business than did the 2,500 newspapers years ago.

Studies show that newspaper readership is high, with around 80% of the people in the United States seeing a daily paper. Involvement is also high. Readers clip coupons, write letters to the editor, talk about items with friends, or respond to classified ads.

While local or retail advertising is the mainstay of newspaper advertising, national ads also figure strongly in total income. Of these national advertisers, the top three categories are automotive, foods, and transportation. Under transportation are listed airlines, bus service, trains, tours, and cruise lines. Hotels and resorts rank in the top ten among national advertisers.

Totals for all newspaper advertising amounts to about $10 billion a year, which makes this print medium a pretty healthy business.

What are the *pros and cons* of advertising in newspapers?

• For the national—or even statewide—advertiser, the ability to select markets based on geography is a plus. There are many towns and cities where the local newspaper really dominates. You can buy space in these papers without having to purchase papers in areas you don't want.

• Compared to magazines, for example, or billboards and other print media, the frequency of publication of the newspaper is a plus. A daily paper is usually described as one which publishes four or more times a week; a weekly comes out less than four times a week. In either case, the newspapers represent an opportunity to reach an audience many times during a limited period.

• It is relatively easy to change newspaper copy—compared to television copy, for example, or billboards, or magazines. In some areas you might even be able to change a word or a line between a morning and evening edition, and most changes can be made within a day. For special sections—like the travel section on Sunday—there is a longer lead time, perhaps a week or more.

• It is also easier to schedule newspaper advertising. You don't have to

wait until a certain time segment opens up, as on television. Television and radio are locked into a certain number of commercial minutes per program hour. Newspapers have no such restrictions. If they secure an unusual amount of advertising, they merely add pages.
- Cost for newspaper advertising is relatively low—again compared to media like magazines and television.
- Newspapers are used for reference; they hang around a while. Prospects may keep the Sunday travel section around until the next one is issued.
- Newspapers are a good medium for co-op advertising. It's easier to work with print in fixing costs and in altering copy and illustrations to fit your own needs.
- A plus for many products and services—but not necessarily for travel agents—is that newspapers cover a wide economic range.

What about the drawbacks?

- There's a considerable amount of waste circulation. With fewer newspapers, each paper covers a wider geographical area. Many of the people who read the paper will not come to your agency simply because other agencies may be closer and more convenient. You also reach such a broad spectrum of the public, you take in a great many people who are not prospects at all.
- When you advertise in a number of different newspapers, you may run up against the problem of different sizes. That makes it difficult—but not impossible—to design an ad that fits all newspapers.
- If you plan to use color—and this would be a consideration for very few agencies—newspapers, although improving steadily, are not as good as magazines or billboards in reproducing color.
- Advertising agencies cite the difference between local and national rates as a problem with newspapers but this should have little effect on travel agencies.

Direct Mail

Despite the seemingly continual hikes in postal rates, direct mail, sometimes called "the quiet medium," remains on the increase. It accounts for better than 10% of first-class mail, a third of the postcards sent, 85% of third-class mail, and 100% of fourth-class mail. In a quarter century, it's grown from a $1 billion per year business to one that is nearly four times that great.

The largest users of direct mail are small businessmen, retailers, magazine publishers, catalogue companies, and pharmaceutical houses.

Small businesses, those doing an annual business under half a million dollars, account for two-thirds of the users of direct mail, and travel agencies figure heavily in this number.

There is an erroneous opinion that most people don't open direct mail, that they consider it junk mail and toss it without even opening the envelope. Not true. Three out of four people at least open the envelope, but 60% of these people merely glance at the contents. That's why you need a strong and attractive message to hold the reader's attention.

An A. C. Nielsen study done for the Direct Mail Advertising Association in the seventies also shows that 57% of the consumers make purchases through direct mail (7% frequently; 24% occasionally; and 26% rarely), while 38% of the people say they never make purchases through direct mail.

In terms of reaction to direct mail, the same survey finds that 22% of the people like it; 11% like it depending on the item; 28% of the respondents dislike it; 34% don't care; and 5% never received the mailing.

There are direct mail specialty houses that have the capability of designing mailing packages, recommending audiences, checking returns, and performing other duties. Some of their charges can be far above the budget of most travel agencies but local sources, like mailing houses, might be worth investigating. Among other things, these mailing houses broker lists of individuals according to a multitude of categories. You can buy lists of people by location, income, occupation, age, and other variables. The cost is so much per thousand and good mailing houses update their lists regularly, catching changes of address, deaths, and other alterations.

The Direct Mail Advertising Association lists these reasons why direct mail works well:

1. You can aim direct mail at a target audience better than you can with any other medium. If I have a special farm tour, for example, and I advertise in a regional newspaper or TV station, I'll be addressing more nonfarmers than farmers. With direct mail, I can select out the farmers and mail only to them. There is far less waste circulation.

2. Direct mail can be personalized more than any other medium. Many of today's mailing pieces are so well done, you can't even tell if the signature is genuine or printed. With banks of automatic typewriters cranking out thousands of mailing pieces daily, these, too, have a first copy appearance.

3. There is no competition for attention as there might be in another medium—no TV or radio commercials butted up against your message, no cluster of billboards, no page full of ads. If the reader opens your mailing piece, it's the only thing he sees.

4. There are far less restrictions on space and format in direct mail. Ads in magazines and newspapers are limited by things like page size and balance with editorial matter; television and radio have the ten, twenty, thirty and sixty-second time limits, with rare exceptions. Direct mail can be any size and shape you want, as long as it conforms to postal regulations. Even when it doesn't, you can usually have your way by paying an extra fee.

5. Production is more varied and flexible. You can use the kind of paper you want, insert little novelties, even have things pop up. And you can suit production to your schedule rather than tailoring it to that of the medium.

6. It can be mailed according to your needs and schedule, so that it reaches the consumer almost exactly when you want it to reach him—providing the postal authorities cooperate.

7. Direct mail gives consumers their best chance to take action, by returning a postcard, or using a prestamped envelope, or sending along a coupon, or bringing in something to be redeemed. It's an effective way to get people to write for brochures, for example.

Figure 5-1 Direct mail pieces take many forms.

8. If you want to check on results, direct mail makes this sort of research much easier. You can key envelopes in a certain way to check response from small or large groups.

Since no medium is perfect, what are the handicaps of direct mail?

1. It often has a poor image.
2. It can be quite expensive. All of the elements of direct mail—paper, printing, postage, and other items—have risen considerably in cost over this past decade.
3. There are relatively few people who really understand direct mail and who can get the most out of it.
4. There are many restrictive mailing regulations covering things like size, number per package, weight, even width.

Television

There are solid reasons for TV sales representatives to tout their wares. For one thing, people spend much more time in front of their TV sets than they do with their newspapers or magazines. The average household watches television seven hours a day. National manufacturers use it more than any other medium. Its total dollar volume for advertising exceeds that of any other medium. TV is *big business* for advertisers.

In many ways, television would appear to be a natural for travel agencies. The ability to show and tell, to put the prospect in the setting, has to help. So does the excitement element of TV, and the association with entertainment. However, except for some local travel shows and some sporadic local campaigns, travel agencies don't use television much. The reasons are cost, lack of experience with the medium, and even tradition.

Here are some of the good points about TV as an ad medium:

• It combines sight, sound, and motion. You can *show* the Hawaii tour, in color, play ukeleles in the background, show tourists enjoying a luau, even superimpose the dates and prices, if you want.

• Because the message is immediate, there is believability to it. People may not believe everything they read, but they believe what they see—or think they see.

• There are huge audiences for TV programs, often several people gathered around a single set.

• Because of the combination of sight and sound, there is a good opportunity for product identification.

• Television is popular. People go to it to relax and be entertained. Some of that pleasure can rub off on products or services advertised.

• There's a high impact to the message. As long as you are staring at the tube and paying attention, there's just one communication reaching you.

Disadvantages of television advertising:

• The message is restricted by time segments. If you have something that takes 2½ minutes to say, you have to cut it to a minute (unless you sponsor the whole show, but even then you have to cut to a standard time length). The most common length today is 30 seconds.

• The viewer has a hard time responding to the message. No coupons to clip, no return envelopes, and, since most travel agencies aren't open all night when viewing is heaviest, even listing a phone number isn't too helpful.

• It's also hard to arrange for time on TV. Many of the strongest time slots are already taken by larger advertisers. You have to take what you can get on the less popular shows and at less popular hours.

• Costs are very high for both time and production, with the latter being a major cost factor. Some of the McDonald spots, for example, cost over a quarter of a million dollars to produce. And a one minute spot in a program like the Super Bowl could cost double that figure for time alone. In a medium-sized local market, the best (or "prime") times are going to run from $300 to $500 for a 30-second spot. These may drop down to under $100 for some of the less popular times—when there are fewer people watching.

• There is considerable waste coverage. Think of the number of people who might see one of your travel spots compared to the number that would actually be prospects for that trip. The percentages would be overwhelmingly negative.

Radio

In the past ten or twenty years, radio has made a real comeback. Some media observers thought radio was washed up once television entered the scene, but radio found its own niche and has been doing well. A good part of its success stems for its role as "background" entertainment and information, a medium you don't have to watch or read to enjoy. The universal use of car radios has helped, as has the advent of FM radio, and the production of small transistorized radios. Its reach is everywhere.

If figures impress you, then consider that there are about 300 million radios in homes, 10 million in offices or plants, 100 million in automobiles, and some 40-50 million portable transistors. That's a lot of listeners.

Radio stations have also developed individual formats so that they can reach a certain type of audience. There are rock stations, country western stations, soul stations, all talk stations, middle-of-the-road stations, classical music stations and so on. Of the approximately seven thousand radio stations in this country, about two-thirds are independent, and the remainder affiliated with networks.

Both radio and television salespeople will give the prospective advertiser a demographic breakdown, telling him how many and what kinds of people are watching different shows or listening at specific hours. By using this information, you can make some general selections by audience type—usually male or female, and by age groupings.

While television's prime hours are usually defined as being from 7-10 P.M. (with 6-7 and 10-11 P.M. carried as prime time in some markets and "fringe prime time" in others), the most popular (and most expensive) radio times are "drive times," those periods, morning and evening, when millions of commuters have on their car radios. Morning drive time is frequently more expensive than evening drive time.

Both television and radio also have terms to describe the range of their messages. They talk about "share of households using television" or "program ratings," which represents that program's share of all the homes having TV sets. There are various rating services to determine how many people actually *are* watching a certain program or station—as against how many *could* watch it because the signal reaches them. The most current way of measuring TV's reach is by using *gross rating points* (GRPs). One GRP stands for 1% of the homes with TV sets in a given area. If you wanted 70 GRPs a week, you'd have the choice of buying 10 programs with 7 GRPs each, or two with 30 and one with 10, or any other combination.

Radio stations often talk in terms of their *coverage,* which means their potential reach, based on the strength of their signal. (Some stations are purely local, with a range of about 25 miles; others are regional and may cover an entire state: a few are *clear channel* 50-thousand-watt stations that may reach hundreds, even thousands of miles.) They also talk about *circulation*, which is the actual number of people listening in a given time period. (TV may also use these same terms with the same meanings.)

Travel agencies are concerned about circulation rather than coverage, except in unusual circumstances. If you own an agency in Fort Worth, you couldn't care less if the radio station gets into Tulsa. You have no potential there.

Okay, what are the advantages of radio?

- You can select geographical markets and isolate some kinds of listeners.
- It's an intimate medium, and some products are sold best by this means.
- In some areas where there is a single dominant station, you can really saturate the market.
- Radio is relatively inexpensive. Because sound has the ability to conjure up images, you can stage elaborate events with a little imagination and a few sound effects. A Strauss waltz puts the listener in Vienna; drums suggest Africa; a ship's whistle says "cruise."
- It is not too difficult to change copy. Given a willing radio station, you can alter a majority of spots the same day.

On the negative side:

- Radio has no visual appeal and may have waste coverage.
- No possibility of consumer referral to message.
- Messages are limited by restrictions of time.

Magazines

Few local travel agencies would use magazines, except for ads placed in regional editions of national magazines, and in local magazines (such as the growing list of city magazines).

Thanks to computers, it's possible for clients in many cities to buy a page in a special section covering only their limited geographical area. Magazine Network, for example, sells space in a combination of *Time, Newsweek, Sports Illustrated,* and *U.S. News and World Report.* Your ad appears only in the regional edition you want, so you get the prestige of association with a national publication, but at a fraction of the cost.

The big story in magazines over the past two decades has been the demise of many general circulation magazines (like the weekly editions of *Life, Look,* and *The Saturday Evening Post*) and the phenomenal growth of specialty magazines, catering to everyone from motorcycle riders to bottle collectors.

Travel is represented in this area by publications like *Travel/Holiday, Carte Blanche Magazine,* and *Diversion,* which contain a heavy sampling of travel pieces. For the travel professionals, there are trade journals like *Travel Weekly, The Travel Agent, ASTA Travel News,* and *Travel Age* with its regional editions.

Like newspapers, radio, and television, magazine information is carried in a set of publications called *Standard Rate & Data Service.* In these pages

Figure 5-2 Both trade and consumer magazines feature travel ads.

you get details of mechanical requirements, deadlines, and sworn circulation for the nation's magazines. Data for purely local publications can be secured by calling the local sales representatives.

What about the advantages of magazines?

• Good selectivity of audience—next to direct mail—but this is more helpful to a national advertiser than to a local one, like a travel agency (unless you buy the regional edition). If you had a farm tour in Oklahoma, for example, you could buy an ad in *The Oklahoma Farmer* and reach a fairly select audience.
• Magazines reach more affluent customers. That doesn't mean that everyone who reads magazines is rich—but the level of income is above average.
• Magazines have long lives and are often kept around for reference. If you miss the ad the first time, you may see it at a second reading.
• Magazines offer prestige to an advertiser. You can also derive a spin-off benefit from this by ordering copies of the ad (as it "Appeared in _____") and mail these to prospects. You need editorial approval for this, however.
• Color reproduction, a facet which doesn't affect much travel advertising, is also good in magazines.

There are some drawbacks:

• Long lead time for advertising. Some national magazines want your ad three months ahead of publication. Even local magazines, like city magazines, may request six weeks to two months.
• If you advertise in more than one magazine, you take the chance of duplicate circulation. The same person sees your ad in two or three different magazines. This isn't all bad, of course, but it does cut down on the number of people you are presumably reaching.
• Despite the advent of regional editions and inserts, magazine advertising cannot normally dominate a local market the way newspapers or radio can.
• Production costs can be high. This, of course, affects the larger, full color ads, rather than the small black and white ads.

Out-of-Home Media

This category is used to describe all those message you see only outside the home—billboards, transit signs, taxi signs, and so on. The most common of these is the outdoor poster.

Like direct mail, the outdoor advertising media have taken a great deal of criticism, from both the government and private citizens. It's easy to sympathize with environmentalists who protest the marring of our landscapes, but outdoor media people feel the size of their operation is greatly exaggerated. They say that, if all the legitimate outdoor advertising billboards in this country were placed end to end, they wouldn't cover one runway at O'Hare Field. They also claim that, when photographers take those telephoto shots to show the clutter of signs, the majority of these signs are *on-site* signs, erected by the owners.

There are varieties of sizes in outdoor posters, generally from about 5' high and 12' wide, to 10' high and 23' wide. They also vary according to special features, such as painted versus posted, illuminated or not, or with or without moving parts. The more you do, the more the cost. A 30-sheet poster (10' x 23'), painted in full color, with a trivision panel that exposes three different scenes at intervals as a pyramidal device rotates on a pivot, and in a prime location, would cost considerably more than a junior board (5' x 8'), in 1 or 2 colors, in a less desirable location.

So cost is based on production and location. The wise advertiser drives to the location and checks the way the board is facing and estimates the traffic flow and looks for obstructions.

Audience reach with outdoor posters is expressed in *showings,* and GRPs. A "100% showing," for example, would be equal to the number of outdoor posters you would have to purchase in a city (or locality) in order to reach 100% of the car-owning households in a 30-day period. A GRP is reaching 1% of the population one time. A "100% GRP" would be equal to the number of outdoor posters you would require to yield a daily effective circulation equal to the population of the area.

One other term used by out-of-home media people is a *rotary* board or *rotary* (or *rotating*) plan. Under such a plan, an advertiser might buy a single board for six months but have it moved to a new location every two months. Or he might have three different boards and rotate them in different areas every couple of months. This is one way to achieve variety and exposure at a reasonable cost.

The advantages of outdoor posters are:

• Selectivity of geographical markets. You could locate a few boards in the area of your travel agency, or you could place them where you feel your best prospects will pass them.

• Large physical size. This, however, can be deceptive. On fast thoroughfares, distant posters are postage-stamp size, loom large momentarily, and are gone. Obviously, a location near a stop light is a prime site.

• There's a high repetitive value in outdoor posters. A commuter who travels the same route daily may see a specific poster 20 or more times a month.

• Costs for outdoor posters are relatively low, and color reproduction is good.

On the other hand:

• There's a lot of waste circulation. Many thousands of people drive by your sign who may never be your prospects.

• The message must be short. You can't use outdoor for lengthy or complicated copy.

• Billboards sometimes have a poor image—and there are not too many creative specialists who can handle them properly.

• Changing copy isn't easy; weather can deteriorate your lovely creation; and, even though you are on a good corner, you might be the bottom inside sign among four, and be partially obscured by a building.

Other Media

There are many other ways to advertise, some of which may be used by travel agents, and some of which would be unlikely tools. There are movie trailers, sky-writing, signs on bus benches, and messages on match boxes.

There are also these media:

Yellow Pages
Travel agents find this medium a must. Even when you have been advertising in other media, the prospective traveler may have no other reference material in front of him except for the phone book. You have to at least be listed and you should also consider a small space ad which is purchased on a yearly contract. These ads are sold by sales people for the telephone company.

For purposes of commercial travel, you may also want to be listed in the city directory, or in other directories which have an audience that matches the profile of your best customer.

Booklets and Brochures
Unless you can do a decent job with printed materials, it pays to employ someone who can. Sending out something that poorly represents any business only detracts from sales.

In addition to the usual collection of travel brochures, many travel agencies also issue quarterly newsletters or similar publications, and they may print up general brochures about their services. These are handy to have and should be kept current.

It isn't necessary that everything that is printed be full color and on slick paper; but it is imperative that it is neat, attractive, interesting, and informative.

The great value of printed materials is that the client or prospect has something to take away, something to savor, a reminder of the agency's presence. Like every other advertising tool, it seeks to replace the salesperson when personal contact is impossible or impractical.

Point-of-Purchase Materials
These are signs, posters, easel-type cutouts and other items which serve as reminders in the travel agency itself. Virtually all of these are supplied by outside agencies. Too many of them, however, are haphazardly arranged, so that they merely clutter up the office decor. Don't use too many; make them as compatible as possible; change them periodically; make them work for you; and don't let them get in the way of efficient salesmanship.

Novelties
Businesses use thousands of giveaway items—pens, tie clips, matches, rulers, shoe horns, caps—all with some printed reference to the company name. The trick is to find things which also remind the recipient of the product or service.

For travel agencies, items like calendars, flight bags, cards showing conversion rates of money overseas, pens and pencils, and other related novelties are used. Frequently these are handed out when the agency opens and may not be used in the future. Even calendars are used much more infrequently because of the high cost of paper and printing.

Donation Advertising
Every small business is the target of appeals to advertise in high school yearbooks, college newspapers, opera or theatre programs, anniversary editions of publications, and many other periodicals.

To most of these, the agency should be polite but negative. There are perhaps only two times when you should use such advertising:

1. When it reaches an audience you want to reach. Programs for various artistic functions may be good—opera, ballet, community theatre, symphony—particularly where you have reason to believe that the people who attend these affairs are prime prospects. If you have special events that appeal to special audiences, finding the right vehicle is a plus—a golf club membership booklet for a golf tour, or a college directory for youth tours, or a Saint Patrick's Day dinner program for a trip to Ireland.

2. The other reason for considering such advertising is the possibility of good public relations. Even though it's unlikely you'll get any direct business from the ad, its appearance in a high school annual may enhance your image as a good citizen and lead to future contacts.

A Proper Media Mix

This subject was mentioned in the initial chapter in a slightly different way. There we had a look at the relative values placed on all marketing activities. For most travel agencies, however, these activities amount to advertising—except for special events and newsletters, which are not far removed from advertising.

Within the advertising framework, you also try to effect a proper mix. Again, when you are dealing with budgets that are quite limited, this is not a great burden. Firms that spend millions on advertising have a lot of tough decisions to make as to where they'll place these dollars.

Travel agencies still perform a miniature version of this planning, as shown in chapter one, assigning dollar amounts to a number of promotional areas. The object is to make this money work for you as efficiently as possible.

Even among the largest advertisers, the media mix varies from year to year, depending in part on the way their research tells them people are spending time with the different media. If there is any constant trend in this decade, it's toward more use of television, even among local advertisers.

In planning, the travel agency manager should sit down with staff members and, if he or she employs an ad agency, with agency personnel. If there is no advertising agency in the picture, perhaps the manager can lure or pay a consultant to sit in. In these sessions, all concerned should examine past performance in all media for their agency, look ahead at what they will be selling, consider the advantages of the available media, and put some price tags on the media packages. When the total cost seems in line, and they seem to have a good media package that meets their individual needs, they circulate it to others who might be involved, for their approval, and then check with the media representatives to be certain of what is available. They may need to make several revisions.

Most Productive Media

It's worth repeating after that lengthy list of media pros and cons that most agencies find *newspapers* and *direct mail* their most productive means of reaching prospective clients.

Part of this is attributable to the phenomenon of the prospect looking in the travel section, just as someone planning to attend a film checks the amusement section. Keep in mind, however, that the movie patron may also have been influenced by TV promotional spots, magazine reviews, and other factors. So, too, might the traveler.

Direct mail succeeds for all the reasons listed earlier.

It would be a rash travel agency manager who would ignore these two media, or award them a low budget position.

Media Placement

As we noted in chapter four, advertising agencies have individuals who are specialists at media placement. Chances are you'll have to do your placement on your own. However, there are guides.

Television and radio stations issue periodic breakouts of their audiences by age, sex, and other factors, and they also indicate listening and viewing audiences by program or time of day. You can go over these with their sales representatives, trying to match your needs with what these folks have available.

Once you agree on what you want and they can supply it, they will issue a contract that spells out their obligation to air the commercials at a certain time and on certain days (or they may give you a range of times and days) and indicate your obligation to pay.

Newspaper also have their representatives and you can talk with them about how often you want to run ads, what size and what location. You can learn a lot by listening to these people and by observing what other agencies do in other papers in other cities.

If you want to buy billboards, the sign company will supply you with a list of available sites or, perhaps, with a map on which these sites are indicated. Get in your car and drive these sites, looking at the exact locale where your message will appear.

Obviously, the people who sell time and space are in business to make sales—just as travel consultants are. That doesn't mean they can be expected to pressure you into an unwise decision. They'd like to make you happy because they are counting on repeat business. So, know what you want, but also pick their brains.

Media Charges

In general—but not always—you pay for what you get. If you want programs or publications with the largest audiences, you pay top dollar. If you opt for a smaller but exclusive audience, you also pay a premium. If you want a special place in the newspaper or magazine, a special location for the outdoor poster, you can anticipate an add-on charge.

Let's examine some of the ways the media charge.

Newspapers

Newspapers charge by the line or by the column inch, although they also have some full and half page quotations in many newspapers.

There are fourteen lines to an inch, meaning that, if you bought a 2-inch (1-column) ad and the rate charged was $1.10 a line, you would have 28 lines x $1.10, or $30.80.

If the rate quoted is a *column inch* rate, that means you are billed on the basis of each inch in a single column in the paper. Take a look at your daily paper. You'll note that it has anywhere from 6 to 9 columns of type across the page. These columns, which are often about 2 inches wide, are used because, if the human eye had to scan across the entire page, reading the newspaper would be a laborious job. The 2-inch wide columns are easily and rapidly read by a subscriber.

Take your ruler and measure up 4 inches on a single column. That's a 4-inch ad—an ad composed of 4 column inches.

You could also use 2 columns of 2 inches each to get a 4-inch ad but this preference would have to be spelled out. Most newspapers won't allow you to buy wider than you buy high. For example, you couldn't buy a 3 column x 2-inch ad; they'd insist it be at least 3 x 3.

If the charge per column inch is $11, that means a 4-inch ad will cost $44.00.

There are extra charges assessed for *preferred* position (such as on the run-over news page, or the society page) and for extra color—one or more.

The reason some papers charge more for exactly the same space as another paper is simply because they have more readers. Their circulation is larger.

To review, then, the factors that affect cost on newspaper ads are: size, circulation, position, and color.

If you have the newspaper perform other services, such as allowing you the use of their artwork, or doing the layout, or setting the type, they may also bill you for these items.

Magazines

Magazines charge much like newspapers, but with some differences.

Instead of dealing in column inches or lines (although magazines may do this, too), the magazine typically sells a portion of a page—full, half, quarter, sixth, eighth. You have a limited amount of leeway in the way you can set up your space on the page.

Because you are dealing in huge circulation figures when you get to the top national magazines, like *Reader's Digest, TV Guide,* and *Time,* you shouldn't be surprised to find that the rates are considerably higher.

Perhaps a full page black and white ad in your daily paper runs $1,500-$2,000 (much less in smaller towns, higher in the largest cities). The same ad (but smaller to fit the format) in a magazine like *Time* would run you *twenty times* that much. If, however, you bought the Magazine Network mentioned earlier, settling for regional circulation, you might find the newspaper and magazine costs not too far apart.

Magazines also charge for position. The back cover, center spread, and inside front and back covers are generally the highest-priced. Premiums may also be charged for pages adjacent to a popular columnist or section, or the page adjacent to the index.

Color would be another factor, and so would any other extraordinary instructions, like tipping in a coupon, or arranging a special fold.

The magazine would not normally provide any of the services a newspaper might—no artwork, layout, typeset. You supply them with the ad ready to run.

Direct Mail

There are a number of costs attached to direct mail, depending on how extensive the mailing is and how sophisticated the methods used.

To begin with, you have the cost of printing the materials to be sent—the mailing package. You might have a brochure, a letter, and a return card, plus an envelope to contain these elements. Type must be set for these, photos taken or illustrations obtained; you decide on weight of paper, colors to be used, the way the brochure lays out, and any other mechanical factor. Each of these decisions involves financial considerations.

You need a list of people to whom the mailing will be sent. If you use only the list of your clients, no problem. If you need to buy a list from a list broker, you are talking about another $35-$50 per 1,000 names, depending on the value of the particular list. These names can be furnished on labels, or envelopes addressed, or a straight printed list. In the case of a travel agency, for example, you might buy a list of individuals who live near your office, or who are in a certain income bracket, or who have travelled in the past three years.

Then there is the handling of the mailing. If you turn this over to a mailing house there will be a charge for their efforts of sorting, labeling, stuffing, tying and so on—perhaps $5-$10 per thousand.

Finally, there's the postage—both the cost of mailing, either bulk or first class, and the cost of return cards or envelopes.

Even when you do all of the handling yourself, you have to figure in the value of employee time.

You may, of course, be able to use a brochure supplied by a resort or carrier. If so, that cuts back on printing charges. Any savings you can realize makes the mailing that much more efficient.

People new to direct mail methods always want to know what percentage of return is a good one. This is impossible to say, since it depends on so many external elements. If, for example, you represented a missionary activity and bought a "cold" list of 50,000 names—names you selected because the category (let's say—"Those Who Contribute to Humanitarian Causes") seemed a likely one—you would be very happy with a return of 2%. If, however, this same missionary activity had built up a list of donors over the years and did a special mailing to them, they might look for a 25%-40% return.

Travel lists would be the same. You'll get a higher response from mailings to clients than from mailings to "cold" or unknown lists. The nature of the information, the value it represents, the timing, the design of the package—all these would affect returns.

Out-of-Home Media

As already indicated, the cost of billboards depends on things like size, location, and type. The larger billboards cost more; the prime locations (those with heaviest traffic) cost more; things like illumination, moving parts, extensions from the board, and other variations cost more. It is also more expensive to buy a painted board than a posted board, where a series of sheets of paper are pasted on the billboard surface.

You can't normally buy outdoor media for short periods, like a week. Most companies would like two months or longer. Obviously, if you take out a long term contract for a year or more, you have a better chance of tying up a choice location.

It's dangerous to give ball-park figures for any costs in advertising, but here are some very general figures for billboard costs. To these should be added production costs.

In a modest-size city (like 500,000 population) you'd pay about $50-$60 for the smallest size board, a junior board, in an average location, without painting or illumination. The larger boards (24 or 30 sheet—which indicates size, and not the number of sheets used in posting) would run from about $200 on up, with the top price for a painted-illuminated board coming in at something like $750 a month.

Radio

What radio and television sell is *time*.

As previously stated, the best radio times are during the driving hours to and from work, mornings and evenings. That's for AM radio. For FM, the evening hours are most expensive and there are some valuable weekend slots.

You might be able to buy a 30-second radio spot on midday AM radio for under $10, even on a station with a pretty good audience. The top radio station in your area might want $35-$40 for that same spot. From then on, thinking only of AM radio in an average market, you could get into the $150-$200 range for the very best times.

If there are radio shows which bring in an unusually large audience, even outside drive time, you also pay a premium. Suppose that Notre Dame football was being broadcast exclusively over a South Bend station and picked up by one Chicago station. Assume, too, that the game was not being televised. A 30-second spot in that program would be very expensive.

You also pay a premium for special placement, like within the morning news or market reports, or adjacent to the evening weather.

The radio sales rep will show you what is available, tell you what type and size of audience the station has for each time frame (based on national research ratings), and give you the price for the time you choose.

Television

Television also has its prime time—the evening hours which were mentioned earlier in this chapter. And, of course, weekend afternoons are more expensive than weekday afternoons because they deliver larger audiences. If you check your local listings, you'll note that Saturday morning is programmed for children and Sunday morning revolves a good deal around religious services. Some travel programs find Sunday morning a good buy, since that type of show fits the quieter format and offers the viewer an alternative to a religious program.

Within those broad time frames, the price of a spot is measured by the audience it plays to. Top-rated shows, like *Laverne and Shirley* and *Mork and Mindy*, cost more than *Movie of the Week* or *The Rockford Files*, because they are riding the top of the heap, with the most viewers. These change, of course. It wasn't too many years ago that shows like *The Beverly Hillbillies* and *Gunsmoke* led the lists.

Specials, like *Roots*, or the Olympics or the Super Bowl, call for special rate sheets. The Super Bowl is about as high as you could go in buying national coverage.

Locally, you might be able to purchase a 30- to 60-second spot (and the minute spot doesn't cost twice as much as the half minute spot) for anything from less than $100 to more than $400. Perhaps a good average for a prime-time program might be $300 plus.

The media representative from your local station or stations will show you a series of pages on which are listed all the programs they offer. The audience totals will be given for each, plus the cost of time. Some will not be available to you because they have been sold in advance. You may scatter your buys through a week or month, buying commercial time on different days and at different times, or you can concentrate in a certain time period. A client interested only in women might want to focus on daytime soap operas—although these reach only housewives, not the growing female work force. One interested in men might buy into sports programming.

Remember that you also have to add on the production costs, which can be high on television. Whether you like it or not, you are competing with commercials which cost hundreds of thousands to produce and yours can't look schlocky by comparison. It must have a look of professionalism, even if inexpensively produced.

* * *

A few additional facts on buying space and time:

- Salespeople for the media have rate cards which give you the basic costs for their print and broadcast prices. There are also books (like *Standard Rate & Data Service*) which supply such figures, but the rate cards will be more current.
- When you buy in quantity, you save money. If you purchase 200 radio spots over a 6-month period, you'll earn a discount; ditto for television. In the print media, the discount goes by lines. After you use a certain number of lines (or inches) you are entitled to a discount. It's good to be aware of these since, if the cost-break point were 1,000 lines and you budgeted for 900, you could probably add the extra 100 lines and actually save money.
- Discuss these and other cost factors in detail with the salespeople. Make certain you know what you are buying.
- One category—called run of paper (ROP) or run of station (ROS)—also saves money. This means they can fit your ad or commercial into any time or space slots they have available. A good paper or station will try to give you a decent blend of good and weaker positions. You can monitor newspaper placement yourself and the radio and television stations will give you a report on where the commercials aired. You may have to request this.

Cost Per Thousand

There's a formula, used primarily to compare magazine rates, called the CPM or cost per thousand formula. What it tries to determine is the cost of delivering one full page, black and white, ad to 1,000 homes. Here's the formula:

$$\frac{R \text{ (Cost of one page)} \times 1{,}000}{C \text{ (Circulation)}} = \text{Cost per Thousand (CPM)}$$

If the rate (or cost) per page were $10,000 and the circulation 650,000 for magazine A, the CPM for magazine A would be $15.38.

Magazine B tells you that you can buy a full page in their magazine for a mere $6,000. Their circulation is 180,000 subscribers. Looks like a cheaper deal but, using the formula, you see that the cost per thousand in this case is $33.33—better than twice as high.

It's another way of looking at what you get for what you pay. Obviously, you should be comparing publications that have some similarity. It's not quite accurate to compare *Newsweek* with *Montana Farmer*; *Newsweek* versus *Time* or *U.S. News and World Report* would be a more realistic comparison.

This formula is also used on occasion to balance one newspaper against another (again assuming they are similar in scope), using the cost of delivering a 1,000 line ad to 1,000 homes or, in another form, the cost of delivering 1 line of advertising to a million homes. This latter formula is called a *milline rate*. In both instances the circulation is the divisor.

You can, of course, compare radio and television costs in the same way, figuring out how much it costs you to reach 1,000 viewers or listeners with a 30-second spot.

If rates are in line, the cost of space or time should rise with the audience reached, except where there are special reasons for charging a higher rate—such as the ability to reach an audience in a high income bracket.

Working With Media People

Get to know the representatives of the various media. Listen to them, but make up your own mind. Read and understand their rate cards, watch for special deals, use as many media services as you can get for nothing.

If you have a conflict with a certain media rep (and this can happen), ask for a different person. It's easier to switch, of course, when you're a big advertiser, but no medium really wants an unhappy client.

Anticipate your needs and allow yourself plenty of time to make your media buys. This will enable you to get a better selection and will give you ample time to thoroughly check copy and production. If you can schedule months ahead—at least in terms of space and time needs—that will be an asset to everyone.

Keep your own calendar of advertising buys and keep a careful record of everything purchased and scheduled. In a sometimes hectic business like the travel business, it's easy to forget deadlines. You don't want to be rushing to get an ad out at the eleventh hour. This is where mistakes are made and advertising dollars wasted.

Questions and Exercises

1. Name three advantages and three disadvantages of newspaper advertising.

2. Find two examples of effective direct mail; and two examples you feel miss the mark. Explain your decisions in all cases.

3. If you were the sales representative for your college newspaper, what arguments would you use in selling space to a travel agency?

4. If the line rate for the *Alaskan Eagle* is 94¢, how much will that newspaper charge me for a 2-column x 6-inch ad?

5. What is the major factor in the rate structure for any medium?

6. Figure out the cost per thousand for your daily or weekly newspaper.

Case Problem

Taking your own community and your own potential client population as the base, assume you have an exclusive tour of China, including parts not seen by foreigners in thirty years. You're the only agency in your state to be allowed bookings. It's an expensive trip and you feel there should be a good strong market because of the mystery and exclusivity. You feel you can spend more money than usual on advertising. What media would you choose, and in what relative proportions? And why?

CHAPTER SIX

Constructing the Advertising Message

Once you know what you'd like to say, and to whom you'd like to say it, and the manner in which you'll convey the message, you still have to know how to present the information in an interesting, even compelling, way. That's where creativity comes in.

Advertising agencies succeed and prosper when they have people who possess unusual creative skills. They are able to turn a phrase, to render a concept in a visual manner, to convince the individual to read, listen, or watch. These creative geniuses command high salaries and work on major accounts. Their connection with travel would be in the handling of large carriers or resorts or tour companies; they will not be available to the average-size travel agency.

There are still some very good creative services to be found in smaller advertising agencies. It definitely pays to use these when working with commissionable media, like radio and television. With print media, however, most travel agencies do their own work. To accomplish this, they try to identify someone within the company who has some creative flair.

How do you recognize this?

The creative mind is curious. It wants to know things, to learn things. It enjoys expanding on the possible solutions to a problem or the possible extensions of an idea.

The creative person may be a trifle insubordinate, may not take well to rigid office rules, may require a long time to come up with an idea, and may be hard to budge once this idea arrives. That's why it's wise to set some guidelines for creative people to work within—not a straitjacket but some reasonable estimates of budget and deadlines.

We all know, too, that you may work on something an entire day without getting a single idea. Then, when watching television that night, a great idea hits you. The creative mind often works best when open and uncluttered, or when thinking of something entirely different.

The travel manager should look around the office. If you are blessed with several employees, then try to determine which one has a little style in writing, or who has a facility to describe travel experiences, or who possesses a little artistic skill. If no one emerges, or if you run a one- or two-person shop, you may have to tackle the advertising writing yourself.

One consolation. You don't always have to be deucedly clever. Some of the best ads are pretty simple. If you have something good to sell and the price is right, all you have to do is get this story into words and pictures. No funny headlines or powerful photographs. Just the facts, interestingly stated.

The person who has the responsibility for creating the advertising should be given enough time to do the job, and some relative quiet to complete it. Perhaps this may be a chore for after hours. In any event, it shouldn't be something a consultant does between phone calls and counter duty.

Research Precedes Writing

Any good writing requires research. Even in our novels, we expect the details to be authentic; we want the author to do his or her homework. In non-fiction, this is even more essential. That's why writers spend time in libraries, or interviewing, or traveling. Before they can tell their readers something, they must first know it themselves.

When copywriters in advertising agencies set out to describe a new product or service, they try to live with that item. They want to know how it's made, and how much it costs, and how it compares to the competition, and how durable it is, and what it does for the consumer. They may need to know how it's shipped, what its drawbacks are, whether it appeals more to women or to men, how it can be identified, what age of purchaser dominates, whether an occupational factors influence purchase, and any other facts that help them understand what they are selling.

When writing travel copy, that means you must have some idea of who the person is who will be reading your ad, or viewing it, or hearing it. You must also understand the specific package you are selling.

Suppose, for example, you are advertising an Alaskan cruise. If you've taken this cruise yourself, that's a great start. If you haven't, you can read about it in travel and other literature, or you can talk with someone who has taken the trip. In reading and interviewing be alert for key words or phrases that fire the imagination. These form the language of advertising.

You must also know how this Alaskan cruise is priced. Is it higher or lower than competition? If higher, then how do you justify the extra expense? If lower, you can concentrate on savings.

What you develop in your mind is a mental picture of a prospect in contact with your ad. Who is this person? What sort of questions does he or she have in mind, and how can you answer them in your copy? Perhaps all you can do in a limited space is arouse interest and get prospects to phone, write, or drop in for more detailed information.

It's a good idea to list all of the good points on a sheet of paper before writing the ad. Pull out the key phrases, too, and set them down: "Sail beneath towering glaciers," or "Cruise the ice blue fjords," or "Experience a fantastic northern world," or whatever other phrases seem to sing a little.

Focus Your Attention on the Prospect's Needs and Wants

Sometimes a travel agency has a tour it knows is superior in every way, from hotels and meals, to sightseeing and price. But, when it is written up, the language appeals to other agents, not to the consumer. There are things about the tour that may make *you* feel good, but what do they do for the *prospect*?

Perhaps you're proud because your office has some fancy new computers for ticketing. Great; but what the client wants to know is "what does the computer do for me?" Tell him. It makes processing faster, saving you time. It enables us to find travel options quicker, making your flight plans more efficient and direct.

Perhaps you managed to get a very low tour rate to Las Vegas, even though occupying a first-class hotel. Better be sure the client knows what a good deal this is, and why.

Talk, then, in terms of his interests, and not your own.

Some Copy Tips From a Top Agency

Ogilvy & Mather, one of the nation's top advertising agencies, has placed nearly 200 million dollars' worth of travel advertising. They've worked with Lufthansa, Air Canada, American Express, Cunard Line, the United States Travel Service, and others. A few years ago they took out a full page ad in such publications as *The Wall Street Journal* and *The New York Times* to expound on what they had learned about writing "travel copy that sells."

Here are some of their suggestions:

1. Spotlight the Unique Differences. Let people know why they'll experience something different on this particular trip. This stems from doing a good job of research. Ogilvy & Mather mentions discovering that Europeans weren't really interested in mountains and beaches when touring America; they have their own. What they want to see are sights like San Francisco and Disneyland and the Grand Canyon and Indian reservations and New York City.

For every tour description you write—or for any general description of your travel services—try to ferret out the reason this offering is different.

2. Facts Are Better than Generalities. In this age of inflation, this is more true than ever. People want to know what they are getting for their money. Spell it out. Some ads go into great detail on what the trip includes; others even get into such details as the exchange ratio for the American dollar. It's a lot better to say, "As Low as $760" than to write "Reasonably Priced."

3. Give Your Advertising a Big Idea. This ties in with the first point. The Ogilvy & Mather ad points out the great number of ads competing for attention in some of the metropolitan travel sections and adds that "if your advertisement isn't based on an idea that stands out from the crowd," you won't have a chance.

4. Don't Shy Away from Long Copy. Most ad copy tends to be short.

Sometimes, however, you have a message that needs more time and space. Give it this time or space. If it's interesting, people will read it.

5. *Copy Should Allay Anxiety About Going to a Strange Place.* Good point. Travellers worry about the food and water, the political situation, about how they should dress, how much they should tip. If you have space and time, set their minds at ease. Or at least have them write for other materials which will do the job.

6. *Use Research to Test Provocative New Ideas.* David Ogilvy once advertised tours to France by doing headlines in French. Everyone thought this was a dumb idea—except David Ogilvy. He was right. Readership went up twenty-four percent.

7. *Give Your Product a First-Class Ticket.* Take a look at some of the local travel advertising. Does it demonstrate quality—or ineptness? You wouldn't do business with a firm whose correspondence was sloppy and unattractive. Ugly advertising also repels.

8. *"Newsbreak" Advertising Can Make News of Its Own.* If you have some announcement that is really news, feature it. If yours is the first trip to the interior of China, or if reduced fares have just been approved, make that the focus of the ad. The energy crunch, for example, gave rise to a number of ads stressing the saving of gas—everything from home-state vacations to backpacking trips.

9. *Bargains Are Still Irresistible.* Note the headlines in many travel ads—"LAS VEGAS $99"—"EUROPE FOR ONLY $1,174"—"THE INCREDIBLE (BUT TRUE) MINIVACATION IN VAIL AT $14.95 PER COUPLE." Ogilvy & Mather once ran an ad for QE2 which began: "Sail to Europe regular fare—Sail home free." A unique way to announce half fares. In just over a week, they had sold out two round-trip crossings.

10. *Make Your Coupon the Hero.* This is an interesting idea. Instead of putting the coupon at the base of the ad, Ogilvy & Mather sometimes placed it elsewhere—including the top. They claim it tripled business for one client, American Express. There are some mechanical problems with this, of course. It makes it easier for people to cut out coupons when they are on a bottom corner—if you have the corner of the page. Newspapers should also take care that they don't run coupons back to back on two sides of a newspaper page. What Ogilvy & Mather has to say, however, has merit because it is *different,* and therefore attention-getting.

11. *Make the Coupon a Miniature Advertisement.* Since many people read only the coupon in an ad, why not put some sell into the coupon, rather than merely allow space for the signing of a name and address? Even a line like this is helpful: "Please send me all the exciting details of the 36 Winter Cruises now available." On occasion, travel agencies have made the entire ad into a coupon format.

12. *Go the Whole Hog.* This top advertising agency recommends de-

voting the whole ad to a description of what is being offered. If you are advertising a new brochure on Great Britain, for example, you might say: "Page 9 includes pictures and values of all British currency" and "Page 10 gives a capsule history of London."

13. Don't Scorn That Grand Old Word—"Free". Even though it's used often, the word *free* still gets attention. So do old standbys like *new* and *save*.

14. Caption Your Photographs. If you use a photo in an ad, a brochure, or a newsletter, give it a descriptive caption, telling what it represents. Twice as many people read captions as read the rest of the body copy.

Ogilvy & Mather have other tips, too, but those are the ones relevant to copywriting.

Writing Copy

This is no easy chore. Some of this nation's literary greats couldn't write a decent line of copy to sell a product or service. It's a different way of writing. The sentences are usually short. Sometimes incomplete. Advertising copy moves rapidly and packs a lot into a short space. The trick is to be conversational in tone, while including all the essential information, and to do both in an interesting and provocative manner.

It's easy to get corny. Some people think good advertising consists of selecting cute lines from other ads and adapting them to their own use. Wrong! Good advertising writing is that which grows out of the special qualities of your product or service. You know all you can about the thing you wish to sell; you decide what you want to say; and you learn to say it well.

It does help to read other ads. These stimulate thinking and give you a feel for the language. It also helps to have a decent vocabulary, one that can think of other ways to describe mountains besides "snow-capped."

And it takes practice. Like everything else, you learn by doing, and the writer who's willing to keep at it will certainly improve.

Here are some additional general tips on copywriting—from people who do it for a living:

- Be honest.
- Be consistent. If you have good campaign going, stay with it.
- Be sure the reader, listener, and viewer get the name of the company and don't remember only your witty premise.
- Reason with the consumer; don't pound at him.
- Dramatize consumer benefits.
- Visualize the entire ad as you write the copy.
- Humanize the writing.
- Don't let your own ego get in the way of objectivity when critiquing an ad you've done.
- Get used to writing against deadlines.

- Remember that much of your copy may not be completely understood and much of the rest will be forgotten. So make it simple and memorable.

Constructing the Print Ad

There's a formula for writing ad copy that has been around a long time—but which is still valid. It's called the AIDCA formula.

In this formula, the acronym stands for the following:

A	Attention
I	Interest
D	Desire
C	Credibility
A	Action

What the ad tries to do is, first, get you to look at it; second, to provoke enough interest to get you to continue to read; third, to create a desire for the product or service; fourth, to convince you that the offer is genuine and fairly priced; and, finally, to provide some means of acting on your impulses—a coupon, phone number, address.

Actually, this schedule of items works for any kind of ad, not only print advertising. If you think through the ad you have assembled, you might check to see that all of the above are covered.

Elements of a Print Ad

Most print ads contain four parts: *headline, illustration, body copy,* and *signature.*

There are ads, of course, which get along with less than all four elements. Sometimes, as in certain cigarette advertising, you may have only a large illustration and the brand or company name. Sometimes the ad may be all headline and copy, without an illustration. Leaving off the signature (the brand or company name) would be rare, but there are some ads—Sunkist, for example—that include the name in the illustration and see no need to repeat it.

We'll examine illustrations later, and not much needs to be said here about the signature or logo, except that it should be in evidence, and that it should work together with the rest of the ad. Let's concentrate on headlines and body copy.

Headlines

There are many ways to write headlines. There is even a monthly service which ad agencies subscribe to that lists, by categories, a number of the best current headlines.

The aim of a headline is to get you to notice the ad. However, it must relate to the illustration and copy and can't merely be a trick to gain attention. Readers will resent being fooled by a headline that really has nothing to do with the subject being advertised.

Here are some of the types of headlines you might encounter:

1. News. Anything that has a legitimate news look to it works well in a headline. For example:

ANNOUNCING AIR FRANCE "VACANCES." THE FIRST $363 ROUND TRIP PARIS FLIGHT WITH EVERYTHING YOU WANT!

LAST CHANCE FOR TUT!

2. Benefit. The reader is promised something that will benefit him or her. These should be real benefits and not merely advertising jargon.

THIS SUMMER LET FINNAIR GIVE YOU MORE VACATION FOR YOUR MONEY.

MORE LEG ROOM ON ALL OUR FLIGHTS.

WHERE ELSE CAN YOU TRAVEL THROUGH HISTORY AND COME HOME WITH A TAN?

3. Challenge. Wake up the casual reader with a direct appeal.

IF YOU DON'T SHOW YOUR KIDS WHERE AMERICA BEGAN, WHO WILL?

WHY SETTLE FOR MERE HAWAII?

4. Command. State your proposition boldly.

DON'T JUST CHOOSE A CRUISE. CHOOSE AN ITALIAN FESTIVAL.

COME TO A PRIVATE ISLAND RESORT.

5. Curiosity. The headline makes the reader want to know more.

IF YOU'RE SIX FEET TALL, LOOK AT YOUR TOES—THAT'S HOW FAR YOU'LL BE FROM THE BEACH.

IF YOU WANT TO STAY AT KANSAS CITY'S FINEST HOTEL, IT'LL COST YOU LESS.

6. Make a promise. Tell the consumer something you'll accomplish or something about your company. El Al, Israel's airline, had a good one:

WE DON'T TAKE OFF UNTIL EVERYTHING'S KOSHER.

And here's a headline promoting Western vacations:

FOR THE PRICE OF A STAMP, WE'LL SEND YOU THE WEST.

7. Offer advice.

MAN DOES NOT LIVE BY TENNIS ALONE.

HOW TO GET TO THE HEART AND SOUL OF BRITAIN.

8. *Single out a special group.* When you've organized a tour for a certain segment of the audience, make sure they get the message.

SPECIAL RAFT CRUISE FOR AMATEUR PHOTOGRAPHERS.

FOR LOVERS ONLY—A POCONOS HONEYMOON.

There are other ways to make headlines catchy. Most of these play on words, counting on the reader to be stopped by the way the headline is constructed. Here are some of these methods in use—but, remember, they're harder to write than they look.

1. Headlines that *take off* on book or song titles, or popular phrases. There is a slight variation which provokes interest.

PALM SPRINGS! IT'S A NICE PLACE TO VISIT BUT YOU WOULDN'T WANT TO LEAVE THERE.

OUR SUN THE DOCTOR.

WIND YOUR WAY THROUGH GARDENS FILLED WITH SAGE, ROSEMARY AND TIME.

2. Headlines that have a *double meaning.*

EASTERN HAS A WARM SPOT JUST FOR YOU.

YOU'RE INVITED TO TAKE OUR SNOW IN STRIDE.

3. Headlines that produce a *double take,* just as in the old movies. You have a delayed reaction—but a pleasant one.

ALL I WANT IS A LITTLE PEACE AND—NOISE.

WE REALLY WORK AT KEEPING BEHIND THE TIMES.

WHEN YOU'RE IN NEW HAVEN, SLEEP IN THE PARK. (The Sheraton-Park)

COME TO BERMUDA FOR A GERMAN FESTIVAL.

4. Headlines that give you two *contrasting* ideas

WHAT'S DOWNHILL AND ON THE LEVEL? Our Winter Sports plan gives you 17 downhill runs plus 45 miles of cross country.

LIFE'S TOO SHORT TO GET THERE TOO FAST.

5. Headlines that employ *modern speech* or *ideas.* You have to stay current with slang, however, because it's dated rapidly.

COME TO OUR ISLAND. THE NATIVES ARE FRIENDLY.

VISIT OUR FANTASY ISLAND.

GET THE LOWDOWN ON DOWN UNDER.

TRY OUR LOVE BOAT.

Writing the Body Copy

This is the real test. Even a beginner might get lucky with a headline; it takes experience to write decent body copy. This is the copy that makes up most of the information block in the ad. It doesn't have to be literary, or even grammatically correct (remember "Winston Tastes Good Like a Cigarette Should"?). What it must do is involve the reader quickly and keep him interested. Subordinate clauses become sentences; punctuation is for emphasis rather than propriety; single words become sentences; paragraphs begin with "and" or "but."

The best way to get a quick education in copywriting is to spend a few evenings reading the good ads in some of the better publications. Note the way these people handle sentence fragments and the methods they devise to keep the copy flowing.

Dick Jackson, of Altschiller, Morgan, Reitzfeld, and Jackson, published a list of *bridges* in *Ad Age* (July 24, 1978) which he says are designed to link thoughts and ideas. Some are cliches, but all have value at times. Among these are such phrases as:

To begin with . . .
Frankly . . .
Another reason . . .
For one thing . . .
You'll find . . .
Not to mention . . .
You also get . . .
Chances are . . .

So you carry the reader swiftly through a message, making it easy for him to digest, understand, and recall. Note how the following pieces of copy work.

The party's never over on The Dolphin! The Dolphin is the exciting new way to cruise to the Bahamas. And there's no other 3- or 4-night cruise like it.

Paquet chefs. A French, American and Continental menu. Free red and white dinner wines. Roomy, modern cabins with every comfort and convenience from private bath to wall-to-wall carpeting.

The gracious Barbizon Restaurant. The colorful Rendez-Vous Lounge. The spacious Cafe Miramar. The lively Cine-Disco.
And more.

Notice the short and incomplete sentences, the use of colorful foreign names to cause excitement, the inclusion of words like *spacious* and *lively* and even our old friend, *free*.

Here's another example:

Eurailpass is a single convenient rail ticket good for First Class travel in 15 countries. On trains that are fast, frequent, comfortable, often luxurious.

*Sleep on a train, gain extra daylight hours for sightseeing. Stop off, if you like, at some intriguing spot and continue later. You also get free or discount rates on many boats, ferries, buses, all over Europe.
All this at an unbeatable bargain.*

Just count the bits of information contained in these 66 words. At least a dozen are conveyed in this short space.
And a final example:

*In Goa, watch the women, silhouetted against a bronze sky, take their bright fish to market.
In Udaipur, eat in a palace. In Kashmir, live on your own houseboat. In the Himalayas, breathe the thinnest air on earth. In Agra, walk through the most beautiful building ever built.
India is huge and varied. And magical. You will not be the same after you see it. Air-India would like to take you there. On one of our many tours.*

Some of the copy tricks mentioned before are also found in the above copy—plus a more colorful language that paints pictures for the prospective traveler. These tours are made to sound like adventures. You might quibble with a few lines. Will readers know that the beautiful building in Agra is the world famous Taj Mahal? The copywriter is gambling that the audience he or she wants to attract will have this information, or look it up.

Here are some capsule tips about copy:

• *Be clear.* Even if you are wildly creative, the copy is no good unless it makes sense. Read it over a number of times to be sure nothing is left out or ambiguous.

• *Be current.* Your style has to be in the language of today. Notice how some of the phrases and concepts of World War II seem overly sentimental to us today.

• *Avoid cliches.* Stale phrases impede reading. Strive for something fresh. You *could* say:

Lush fruit trees grow near a gleaming sandy white beach stretching in front of rows of tiny white houses.

Not too bad, but the way Gerri Trotta describes Portugal's Algarve in a *Travel Holiday* article is much more effective:

Imagine orchards of almond and fruit trees interspersed with brilliant geraniums that slope down to miles of immaculate pale sand along the locally unpolluted Atlantic Ocean; clusters of perpetually whitewashed sugar cube houses reminiscent of North Africa . . .

At any cost avoid things like *bunny-soft* and *pearly white* and *foaming tide* and so on.

• *Use the active voice.* Don't say "Exciting seascapes can be experienced by the voyager." Say: "The voyager will experience exciting seascapes."

• *The key words come at the end of sentences and paragraphs.* Don't hide

Jamaica's Elegant Hideaway.

Sans Souci Hotel. Jamaica's easy elegance.

Just 5 minutes from exciting downtown Ocho Rios nightclubs, shopping and hotels, there's a remarkably romantic little hideaway resort built on hillside terraces and framed by dramatic architecture. And surrounded by tropical flowers, tennis courts and the clear waters Jamaica is famous for. It's near golf, shopping and spectacular sightseeing. And yet it's as intimate and private as a moonlight cruise for two. A small number of luxurious rooms and suites, with every amenity, including personal housekeepers, available. Private beach, superb food, lounges and pools. And an exclusive North Shore setting out of a James Bond movie.

For reservations, contact your travel agent. Or call Ray Morrow Associates, exclusive representatives, toll-free at 800-243-9420 or the Jamaica Reservation Service at 800-327-2054 for more information. (In Florida call 800-432-6550.)

Figure 6-1 Good copy conjures up vivid pictures.

important ideas in the middle of sentences, put them at the end. Not:

Our tour to the Caribbean and three southern ports, available at the lowest price ever offered, will sail on alternate Saturdays, with connections to South American air and sea transportation.

Here's the way that could go:

Sail on alternate Saturdays to the Caribbean and three southern ports. Connections to South American air and sea transportation. All for the lowest price ever offered.

Sometimes, for emphasis, you may mention the key idea at the beginning of the sentence or paragraph and repeat it at the end.

• *Write for the individual.* Don't visualize a mass audience reading your copy. Think of one or two people whose reactions you can trust.

• *Write tightly.* No unnecessary words. Every word must carry its share of the communication load. Avoid long sentences.

• *Rewrite.* Someone has said that "there is no great writing, only great rewriting." That may be true. Go over your copy. Trim where you can. Substitute a better word. Polish.

The Close

Advertising copy must have a close—a windup. Just like a personal sale. Note how the insurance or car salesman tries to get you to sign before you separate. An ad must accomplish the same thing.

> See your travel agent for details.
> Mail this coupon to us today.
> Write for a free brochure.
> Call your travel agent. Or call us collect at _____.

You may find more attractive ways to state this information but don't get too clever. The important thing is to give the reader a reference for action.

Different Styles for Different Media

Many things affect the way a smart copywriter puts an ad together. An ad in your Sunday newspaper would be written a bit differently than one in the symphony program. Or it should be. An ad for a Mediterranean cruise would use different language than an invitation to the Calgary Stampede. You make the feel and look of the copy fit the message.

In addition, you write differently for radio and television than you do for print media. We'll look at some scripts in chapter nine but here are some things to remember about writing for the broadcast media:

• *Radio copy is written for the ear.* This means many things. It means you should avoid words that are hard to distinguish (*chief* may sound like *cheap*); avoid words that give announcers trouble ("A tour treasure of unforgettable instances."); choose language that evokes pictures.

• Radio commercials should have strong openings, to attract attention, and strong closes, to reinforce the memory. Important words or phrases should be repeated.

• Don't try to crowd too many ideas into a short message. Concentrate on one or two ideas and get them across. And don't scream at the listener; use conversational tones.

Television also has its peculiar writing demands.

• You must know the technical possibilities of this medium before you can write. You must know what the camera can and can't do. You must

develop a sense of how long the talent must hold up the brochure, for example.
- Take it easy on the viewer. Not too many scene changes. Don't make your spot like those amateur slide shows which hurry through the weaker visuals. Simplify the spots.
- Let the visual or video portion carry the weight. Avoid wall-to-wall words. If the screen can show it, you don't have to say it. Someone suggested that scriptwriters and TV ad writers should be charged $2 a word. That would force them to be terse.
- Keep the time in mind. If you have thirty seconds for your spot, don't write one that takes forty seconds to deliver, forcing you to rush. And don't write forty seconds of copy for a sixty-second spot and drag it out.
- Finally, never forget that a television commercial is an interruption. The viewer didn't turn on his set to see it. Therefore, you should make it as interesting and entertaining as possible.

Other media also have their own copy restrictions. For outdoor billboards the message must be short—perhaps five words or so. Ditto for messages on novelties. Direct mail, which we'll examine in more detail in chapter ten, must do the whole job, anticipating and answering all the prospect's questions.

So, know the medium, its assets and liabilities, and learn how to handle the different challenges.

Varied Formats

Take a look at your local travel page or section. Most ads look the same, right? You'd think there was only one way to write an ad—start with a headline, add some body copy, stick in a coupon. Perhaps you'll insert some clip art from a mat service; or get really daring and put in a headline extender, or subhead, beneath the main headline.

There's no need to be this rigid. There are many ways to look at copy, particularly if you have a little space to work with. A copywriter, in fact, should be able to handle everything from catalogue copy to poetry.

Consider these possibilities, for example:

1. An advertisement could tell a story.

Harry and Rita Walker missed Spain when they honeymooned in Europe. That was 40 years ago. They knew where they wanted to go on their 40th anniversary. This time they had company—their 3 children and 4 grandchildren . . .

This story would then lead into the selling copy about Spain and its beauties and values.

2. An advertisement could feature two characters talking to one another. Their statements could be in comic strip ballons or captions. You might start with a comic drawing or photo, then move into straight copy.

3. You could use a series of pictures and captions. A lot of national travel ads use this device.

4. You could come up with some gimmick approach—a bit of verse, humor, pseudohistory.

Obviously, these suggestions won't fit every case. They may not fit most cases. The point is, you shouldn't be afraid to experiment a little, if you want the reader's attention. See what other agencies do—in other cities—and see if you can't learn something.

In fact, you should keep a *swipe* file of ads, articles, and brochures you admire. All creative people do this. There are very few totally original ideas; most of them are adaptations from something else. You'll discover you can derive inspiration from the work of others and that their ideas could provide a clue to your own needs.

Ads Built Around a Personality

There are two concepts here—one national (or international) and the other local.

A number of travel-related firms use recognizable people as spokespersons in their advertising. Hertz has O.J. Simpson; British Airways features Robert Morley; various resorts have their headline acts issuing promotional welcomes. You'll note two things about these ads. First, the particular personality ties into the specific advertising goals. Who could be more British than Morley? And, if you want to say *speed*, Simpson has to be a prime choice. The second fact about these ads is that the copy has to sound like the spokesperson. Morley doesn't talk like Simpson, and vice versa. Of course, you can give the star a few lines and then depart to the regular selling message, but even that should be somewhat compatible.

The local use of personalities is widespread in the advertising of special tours. The personality may be a travel consultant who's built a following and whose name means something because the prospective traveler knows he or she will have fun and be expertly handled. Another type of local personality is the individual who has some special expertise in an area, either geographical or professional. A person who teaches a wine-tasting course might be a natural choice to lead a trip through the vineyards of France; a professor of Slavic mythology might be just right for the Transylvania tour; and the director of the community playhouse should attract attention with a New York theatre week. Some persons are also associated with an area because of their own heritage or their ethnic associations. Tourists would enjoy traveling with them because they feel they know the territory.

A third group of local personalities could be those men and women who have no particular knowledge of travel, or the area, or a specialized profession, but who offer prestige to the tour. The mayor or governor, perhaps; or a local television personality; or someone prominent socially.

In selecting the tour personality, the travel agent assumes some natural following and figures others will sign on as the result of promotion and conversation. Don't be misled into thinking *everyone* knows these individuals. The copy needs to explain why they are such good choices. Perhaps a brief paragraph about their qualifications is in order, or, at least, a title and come-on line.

The personality should also be willing to promote the tour, by writing letters, or making appearances or cooperating in other ways. Advertising alone should not be expected to carry the full load.

Again, in the copy, try to capture the personality of the individual and don't merely stick a name or picture in the ad.

Combining Tours in Ad Copy

You can get an argument from many travel agents as to the relative merits of featuring each tour individually or buying a larger space and combining offerings. Using one ad for one tour certainly saves confusion and, if you purchase several smaller ads in one edition of the newspaper, it also adds repetitive value. On the other hand, with so many small space ads in travel sections, the larger ad has a chance to dominate. It may also indicate to the reader that you have a comprehensive agency with multiple choices.

If you do opt for the combination ad, there are some things to look out for. Most of them deal with layout and will be covered in the next chapter, but some pertain to copy. First, you need some headline that embraces all of the items included; second, you need individual copy that is different but consistent. Frequently, one trip or service will dominate, and the others cluster around it. Third, the copy should have a theme. Are you selling price? Or featuring diversity? Or talking about seasonal options?

If the combination ad fails to work together, either graphically or copy-wise, you end up with a mess. And messy advertising never helps.

Selecting a Feature

As we'll see when talking about layout, something must dominate in every ad. The same is true of copy. Occasionally, this decision is easy to make. You may have an exclusive tour, or a special personality, or a reduced price. This factor gets prominence.

When such features aren't obvious, you must do a little thinking. This is when knowledge of the prospects helps, and when it's good to be attuned to all of the outside elements that affect travel. There are tours which focus on an escape from winter, or energy saving, or attendance at an event like the Olympics. Then there are those you offer every year and you are strapped to think of something new to say. This is when you get back to the basics; *read, listen, think.*

Bone up on the travel area itself, and read the professional journals for travel trends. Often an idea will just pop out. "Dance a Hornpipe in Killarney" might be a good way to lead into an Irish tour that features tourist participation. "You've Seen the Exhibit; Now See the Original" would be an attention getter for an Egyptian visit.

Those who write copy should also be good listeners. What are your clients and your friends talking about? What ideas and concerns are uppermost in their minds? What sort of adventures are they looking for? In retail sales, the advertising department people always check with clerks who sell the merchandise, to learn what customers are saying. Travel agents should do likewise, particularly if charged with writing other advertising copy.

After you've absorbed this information, take a little time to think. If you're always saying, "Is it Tuesday already? I've got to get that ad copy together before noon," you're just wasting money.

Coupons

Coupons are bigger than ever. Virtually every business uses them at one time or another. In travel, they are indispensable. You rarely have enough space to tell your whole story. You need to provoke sufficient interest to get the prospect into your agency, or to move him to write for further information. And you have to make this easy for him.

Coupon copy is fairly standard. You have to have room for name and address and, sometimes, a phone number. You may also need a lead-in line requesting a certain publication or even a checklist if promoting more than one brochure. It's a good idea to put your own name and address on the coupon, too, since the reader may cut it out, separating it from the ad, and then be unable to remember where it should be sent.

Some maddening things are done by inept advertisers when it comes to coupons. They are so small that even the smallest type won't work effectively within the space given. They are located in the middle of a page and can't be readily extracted. Some advertisers, dominated by an unthinking artist, have produced coupons in *reverse,* white on black. You'd need a white pen to fill them out! Others, who are more aesthetic than rational, give coupons all sorts of shapes, from hearts to national outlines. These are the devil to cut out.

Keep in mind that the reason for the coupon is to make it *easy* for the individual to respond. Everything you do to diminish this ease just cuts down on returns. Think of this copy and layout feature as being very *functional.*

Tell 'Em Who You Are

Those advertisers who produce white-on-black coupons have cousins who forget to tell the reader who sponsored the ad or how you can get in touch with them.

Every ad must have the name of the travel agency, its address, its branch offices (if pertinent), and its phone number. You might also include office hours, logo or design that identifies the firm, and any slogan that is part of the agency's image.

Tower Travel superimposes its title over a drawing of the Eiffel Tower; World Tours uses a globe; Travel and Transport displays a kiosk; others have crowns, planes, tickets, or a monogram made of their initials.

Slogans include such lines as:

"We know the territory" or "Ready When You Are" or "Unrivalled for Quality Service" or "Go with the People You Know."

CONSTRUCTING THE ADVERTISING MESSAGE

Some of these slogans aren't great works of art but constant repetition gives them a real value; the aspect they promote becomes associated with the agency. You immediately think of Campbell's Soup, for example, when you hear "Mmm Mmm Good!" and United Airlines has taken control of "The Friendly Skies." There's no reason a local travel agency couldn't come up with a memorable line that would accomplish the same purpose.

Questions and Exercises

1. Find the following:
   a. Two travel print ads with copy you admire; and two with copy you think fails. Comment on each.
   b. Two clever headlines in travel advertising.
   c. Four different styles of coupons, all in travel ads.
2. Respond to three different travel offers of brochures and information and compare and evaluate replies.
3. Select a specific tour or specific country and draft a research plan for getting information preparatory to developing an advertising campaign. Using some of these resources, type or write out a *copy platform,* spelling out what you are going to say.
4. List five tips for writing travel copy as outlined by Ogilvy & Mather and explain what each means. Bring in an example to support each point.
5. What is the AIDCA formula?
6. List five different headline concepts.
7. What are some of the differences among writing copy for print, radio, and television?

Case Problem

Select a travel brochure from a local travel agency—or your own agency—and assume you are going to feature this tour in a 2-column x 2-inch advertisement in your local paper. Come up with a headline and write a description of the tour in 25 words or less. You don't have to include prices or dates or agency information in these 25 words.

CHAPTER SEVEN

The Design of Print Advertising

In addition to being able to write sparkling copy, the person who handles advertising for a travel agency must also be adept at visualizing the ad. This person must see how the ad will look and not only how it will read or sound.

In fact, even as the writing is being done, there should be some concept of the physical structure of the ad. Both elements should work together to produce an appealing message.

The Principles of Design

Some aspects of design are natural. The careful hostess arranges her table in a pleasing pattern. Pictures are arranged on a wall in a manner that looks right. We do many things unconsciously which are really the result of an impulse toward decent design.

In laying out an ad, we stick with the same principles. What layout means is the attractive arrangement of all elements within a certain space. That means the headline, illustration, body copy, and signature. All must work together.

This text can't make an artist out of you but it can introduce you to some basics which can be employed in doing at least a rough copy of an ad which can be shown to an artist for his finished work, or given to the newspaper's art department to complete.

Line

There are no lines in nature. The horizon, for example, is purely an illusion and distant objects that appear to be sharply defined by lines are really three dimensional.

In art—and in layout—the line is the first element. It's the basic tool. Horizontal lines are generally restful; vertical lines aspiring; wavy lines indicate growth or beauty; diagonals show stress or tension. A stack of lines of the same dimensions is boring; a stack of different length lines is more interesting. Lines, then, can do many things. See Figure 7-1 for examples.

Tension Growth Dignity Repose Excitement

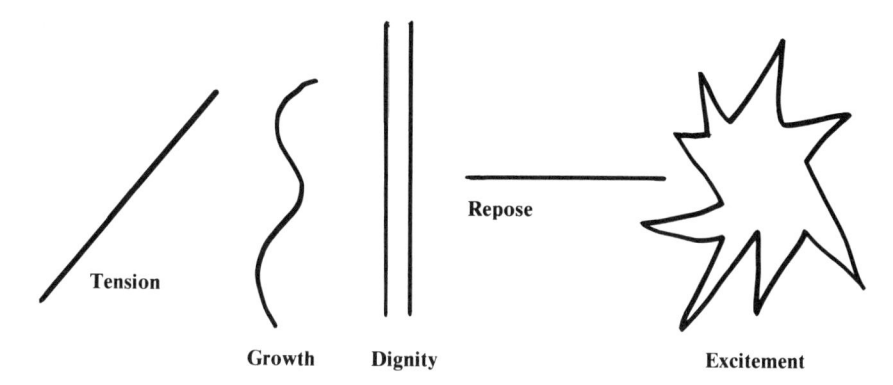

Figure 7-1

Shapes

Three basic shapes are used in all design: the *rectangle, circle,* and *triangle.* These can become boxes, tubes, stars, ellipses, TV screen contours, pyramids, or any other shape you can think up, plane or solid.

Look at any work of fine art. In it you'll note that, although subtly rendered, the basic forms are the three mentioned above. These shapes are interwoven, overlapped, balanced, repeated—and they make up the artistically pleasing effect.

When layout artists begin their design, they often experiment with these shapes, placing them in different relationships, then flesh them out into the results they want. See Figure 7-2 for examples of travel ads in which you can see the trio of basic shapes.

Harmony, Sequence, Balance

The lines and shapes must still be arranged in a way to attract and delight the reader. This takes some talent, and a lot of practice. If the designer fails to execute this task properly, the result looks cluttered, or uneven, or disconnected.

This is where the artistic principles of harmony, sequence, and balance come in. They characterize music and literature, as well as oil paintings and sculpture. They also characterize good layout.

Harmony means a pleasing relationship among all the elements. We are used to this as a musical term, meaning that the various voices work together for a unified effect. In art (and layout) this term means that colors blend, type faces work together, everything looks as if it belongs in the same ad.

Sequence refers to the flow of an ad, the way our eye travels through the space. Generally speaking, our eye first lights on an area about a third of the way from the top of the ad. Notice how many good ads feature something in that spot. From here you might move through the copy to the coupon or logo.

After a lifetime of vacations, have a vacation of a lifetime.

**AFFORDABLE ORIENT,
15 DAYS FOR $1,599.**
JAL's exciting Affordable Orient tour lets you explore the mysteries of five cities in Japan: Tokyo, Kamakura, Hakone, Atami and Kyoto. It will then take you to Taipei for two fun-filled days, then to Hong Kong, the shopper's paradise. Stay in Deluxe hotels, enjoy full American breakfasts, lunch or dinner daily and comprehensive sightseeing.

For more information, send in the coupon, see your travel agent, or call Japan Air Lines.

Please send me details on the Affordable Orient tour, plus JAL's free Orient Tour Buying Guide.
Japan Air Lines
P.O. Box 618, New York, N.Y. 10011

This year, the Orient.
JAPAN AIR LINES

☐ Affordable Orient (#3001)
☐ Other Happi Holidays Tours

Name_____
Address_____
City_____ State_____ Zip_____
Telephone_____
My travel agent_____

TM0379

STEAMBOATIN' It's still the only way to travel

Cruises from 3 to 20 nights.

Delta Queen STEAMBOAT CO.

Please send me your 1979 Delta Queen® and Mississippi Queen® Deluxe Cruise Schedule.

Name_____
Address_____
City_____ State_____ Zip_____

The Delta Queen Steamboat Co., Dept. TV03, P.O. Box 2000, Addison, Ill. 60101

Figure 7-2 The three geometric elements (circle, triangle, and rectangle) are seen in these two print ads.

If there is something exceptionally appealing in another part of the ad—a photo, a large price—we could go there first. Our eyes would then follow a different route. But there should be some logical flow from one element to another.

The average person spends more time (sixty percent) looking at the top of a page or the top of an ad than he does at the bottom (forty percent). And the area with the longest attention span is the upper left quadrant. Obviously, if everyone laid out ads based on this principle, it would be a dull world. Ads succeed because they are different, but it's still wise to be familiar with readers' habits.

Balance is an element we're all familiar with. We look at pictures on a wall and see that they are out of balance. We align magazines on a coffee table.

Think of a teeter-totter in a park. If two persons of equal weight sit on each end, the teeter-totter is in perfect balance. However, this arrangement is not too interesting. More interesting would be a lighter person on one end, balanced by a heavier person closer to the fulcrum.

We call the first situation *symmetrical* balance—meaning that all elements on one side of a painting or layout nearly mirror those on the other. *Asymmetrical* balance occurs when a heavier object on one side is balanced by an interesting item on the other, or by a blob of vivid color, or some other device. Good design uses both methods, but the asymmetrical is preferred. See Figures 7-3 through 7-7 for samples.

Four Seasons Hotel
TORONTO
Avenue Road at Yorkville
Toronto, M5R 2G1

For your Travel information kit, please call Director of Sales at 416-964-0411, in Toronto.

Figure 7-3 In this ad, which uses white space well, all elements combine to produce a delicate *harmony*.

88   TRAVEL AND TOURISM MARKETING TECHNIQUES

Figure 7-4 Note how this ad is based on a "S" curve design, with the *sequence* moving the eye from head to logo.

THE DESIGN OF PRINT ADVERTISING 89

South Carolina.
It's a lot of great vacations.

Whatever kind of vacation you're looking for, you'll find it in South Carolina.

And to help you plan your vacation, we'll send you the new South Carolina Trip Kit—free! It'll tell you about things to do and places to stay. And there are maps to show you how to get there once you get here.

Wherever you go in South Carolina, you'll find a lot of great vacations. Just clip the coupon to find out how they can all be yours.

FREE SOUTH CAROLINA TRIP KIT

Name _____

Address _____

City _____ State _____ Zip _____

South Carolina Division of Tourism, Room 685, Box 78, Columbia, S.C. 29202

Figure 7-5 Note how the sequence of this ad takes you from the headline through the illustration to the coupon.

WEEKEND SUN SALE

$43.90
ITCATM-RHGP2

Granada Royale's "SUN-SALE" weekend package is a 3 day-2 night holiday complete with sight-seeing tour of the Valley of the Sun! At every Granada Royale you always receive • 2 ROOM SUITE, living room/dining, galley-kitchen, bedroom and bath • FREE full hot breakfast—cooked to your order—EVERY MORNING! • FREE 2 hour cocktail party—EVERY EVENING! Call now for your "SUN-SALE," 800-528-1445. In Arizona call collect 957-9767.

Granada Royale Hometels
Phoenix, Tucson
El Paso, Omaha,
Kansas City

Offer good through Sept. 30, 1979

Figure 7-6 An example of symmetrical balance.

PHOENIX
HOLIDAY HAPPENINGS
3 days, 2 nights, $76 per couple

Our **Holiday Weekend** package includes a spacious two-room suite, free, hot breakfast each morning, unlimited cocktails from 4:30 to 6:00 pm each evening and complimentary airport transportation. In addition, there's a multitude of recreational activities — tennis, swimming, volleyball, golf, racquetball, bicycling and horseback riding.

Extra Nights   **$60 Single**   **$70 Double**

Additional nights available for the December holidays at $50 single, $60 double.

Make your get-away to The Pointe. For reservations call collect (602) 997-2626... subject to space availability.
Offer good through December 31, 1979.

The Pointe

Resort, Restaurants, Riding and Racquet Club.
7677 North 16th Street
Phoenix, Arizona 85020
(602) 997-2626

Figure 7-7   An example of asymmetrical balance.

Some Layout Principles

1. Don't forget that the copy is part of the layout. Squint at the copy block, seeing it as almost a solid. It should fit right into the ad in terms of harmony, sequence, and balance. Usually a rectangle, it could also be a triangle or circle.

2. Something must dominate in the ad. Perhaps it's the illustration, or the headline, an oversized price tag, even the logo. If every element in the ad is given equal emphasis, nothing stands out and the ad is monotonous.

3. The rules of composition come with practice and with study of the work of others. If you can learn how to take good slides of your trips, you can learn to apply these same principles of composition to ads.

4. The rules of proportion also apply to layout. We talk about well-proportioned people and well-proportioned design. A 3" x 3" ad, for example, is blocky and dull. Better to do a 3" x 5". The proportion is more pleasant. In fact, the ratio of 5 to 3 is supposed to be the *most* attractive relationship. Part of this, like other things in layout, comes from experience.

5. Remember that people read from left to right. That's how the comic strips are arranged. Ads usually read this way, too. If you have a person's face in the ad, for example, the eyes would be directed into the copy and not away from it. Heads would also be moving into the copy and not seeming to pull away from it.

6. Don't be afraid to leave a little white space—an area without any copy or illustration in it. That helps set off the other elements, and also gives the eyes a little rest.

7. Avoid the following:

   a. Visual cliches, like piggy banks for "save," and mortar board for "smart" and a policeman for "stop." These are corny and mark you as old fashioned.

   b. Headlines that run vertically or diagonally are very hard to read. Don't fool around with these odd angles. Ditto for coupons that slant sharply.

   c. A cluttered look with too many items in too small a space.

From Rough to Finished Ad

The professional layout person doesn't start by carefully drawing in every line in the ad, or in the brochure. He or she does what is called a *thumbnail,* a quick, small sketch, just to see how the main elements in the ad might look. The artist will do dozens of these within a very few minutes, to get a feel of what works and what doesn't.

Once the artist has something that looks promising, he or she will do a *rough,* a more finished sketch in which the elements are more well defined. From here, the layout moves to the *comprehensive* or *comp* stage, which is a finished rough, a quality piece of art with the illustration clearly indicated, and the copy lines drawn in. This is ready to show to the client.

If the client approves, the ad then moves from here to the final stage.

Type is set, the photo taken or illustration drawn, and the whole thing pasted up, *camera ready* to be shot and made into a printing plate.

Retail advertising may not be done this way. The large drug store and department store ads you see may be laid out full size, and various drawings and prices moved around and pasted down in what look like the appropriate spots.

You might do this with a travel ad, too. Suppose you were using the same general format week after week. There would be no real need for a rough. You'd just see what copy fit the design you had adopted.

The travel agent would not go to finished art, either—not like the professional layout person. If the travel consultant has any talent, he or she might get the ad to the rough stage, supply the copy and art or other elements, and turn the whole thing over to the newspaper ad department. They then do the finished ad, pull a proof for the client's approval, then make the finished plate for reproduction.

It's not wise to change an ad every week. There is great value in continuity and familiarity. At the same time, an ad that hangs around for a year or more begins to look old. Experiment with different formats and vary your ad from time to time.

Some Ad Formats
There are any number of ad formats, but most fit into one of nine basic layout patterns. Not all of these work for travel agency advertising, primarily because of limited space, but aspects of them can be used on occasion, either in print media or direct mail.

These nine designs are:

• *Picture Window* (Figure 7-8). This format features a large photo onto which copy or heads or logos are superimposed. Many beer and cigarette ads use this style. It is, in fact, the most common layout format for national advertisers.

The nature of the picture determines where the type goes, and there is usually very little copy.

When superimposing the type, don't put black type on a dark background or reverse (white) type on a light background. And don't put any type on a busy background, so that it can't be read.

• *Mondrian.* (Figure 7-9). Named after the famous Dutch painter, this format follows Mondrian's technique of using different sizes of rectangular patterns in his art. More common in magazines than newspapers (but suitable to both), this format relies on good proportion.

The uneven blocks may contain illustrations, type, headlines, or mere color blocks. Sometimes the blocks abut each other; sometimes they are divided by light or heavy lines.

When setting something like this up, just pencil in the horizontal and vertical lines lightly until you get the effect you want.

The Mondrian layout can sometimes be useful in featuring a number of tours, as in the example in Figure 7-10.

- *Frame.* (Figure 7-11). This is also a common format, particularly in newspapers, and is a favorite of travel agencies. It consists of the usual ad elements encompassed by some sort of border. While a handy design, the border does confine copy and limits the overall space.
- *Typeface.* (Figure 7-12). In this format, large headline type is the star. Not too common for travel agencies because it leaves little room for details.
- *Multipanel.* (Figure 7-13). Unlike the Mondrian format, the panels in this ad are all the same size, much like most comic strips. These panels can be used to tell a story in sequence (with balloons or captions for copy) or can show different features of a product or tour. The panels usually run left to right, but can also run vertically.

The multipanel layout is also used to repeat elements of an ad, or even to repeat the ad itself. This has its own eye-catching effect.

Some advertisers have long favored the idea of running the same small ad throughout a publication, to gain the advantage of repetition. This format can attain some of this goal within a single ad.

- *Copy heavy* layout. (Figure 7-14). This is one in which the copy dominates. This may be because there is a lot to say, or because the message is complicated. Insurance companies and realtors use this format a great deal. So do many travel agencies.

While not a particularly attractive way to go, even a copy heavy ad can have style. Small illustrations may break up the copy or there may be subheads or other dividing devices.

The copy heavy ad may also stand out on a page where all the other ads are picture window or Mondrian layouts.

If the subject is of interest and the writing good, a prospect will read long copy.

- *Silhouette* layout. (Figure 7-15). All of the elements form a silhouette. You may have to squint your eyes to see this. An irregular silhouette works better than one which is regular.

The silhouette ad may be an actual silhouette or it may just resemble this shape when viewed overall.

Often, one of the edges of the silhouette will touch the side of the ad, just to keep the form from slipping away from the viewer, and from invading nearby white space.

To gain the effect, imagine all of the areas blacked in, including the type.

- *Circus layout.* (Figure 7-16). This never wins any advertising prizes—but it can sell goods and services. It's loud, brash, full of reverse blocks, starbursts and other features. Price is often the focus. A grocery store ad is a prime example. There's a great deal of variety in a circus ad, but there still has to be some rationale to the design, and something has to dominate.
- *Rebus* layout (Figure 7-17). This gets its name from its similarity to those old puzzles where a picture substituted for a word. Of course, the ad can't be a puzzle; it has to communicate. So the text is sort of wrapped around the illustrations, which may be of varying size.

On occasion, you'll have only pictures and captions.

* * *

Many of these formats are used in combination. You'll see a picture window ad combined with a typeface ad. Or a frame with a copy heavy. The nature of the message should have some influence on the choice of format. So will the space and the character of the surrounding ads. It's fun to experiment with different ways to solve the layout problem, just as it's interesting to try various copy styles.

Figure 7-8 *Picture window* layout.

96 TRAVEL AND TOURISM MARKETING TECHNIQUES

Figure 7-9 *Mondrian* layout.

THE DESIGN OF PRINT ADVERTISING 97

Travel and Transport
Winter Getaways

Dick Walter
London Theatre
Tour
Apr. 7-19

Taking in the season's hits in London and at Washington DC's Kennedy Center. Escorted by Omaha's foremost impresario.

CANCUN
Jan. 31-Feb. 7

- Swim
- Sail
- Snorkel
- Skin Dive
- Golf
- Tennis

Enjoy some of the Caribbean's best beaches. Via round-trip charter from Omaha.
Prices start at

$524
from Omaha

KIEWIT PLAZA
3555 Farnam
344-4877
WESTROADS
Italia Mall
397-0968
SOUTHWEST
96th & L
592-4100
NEW TOWER
BLDG.
7764 Dodge
397-5171
COUNCIL
BLUFFS
Midlands Mall
328-1531

Cruise
Headquarters
Travel &
Transport

The perfect way to get away
Caribbean
Trans-Canal
Mexico
South Pacific

Quit dreaming about it ... do it ... take a cruise.

South America

Holiday
Jan. 26-Feb. 10

Hustle on down to Rio ... Buenos Aires ... Lima where it will be summer.

Tour also offers optional trip to Cuzco and Machu Picchu, site of the spectacular Inca ruins.

Aloha Hawaii Tours
Aloha Hawaii

14 days—13 nights
- Oahu • Kauai
- Maui • Hawaii

Saturday departures
Occasional seasonal supplements apply

GOING SOMEWHERE?? Whether your trip is short and simple ... or long and complex, one call to Travel & Transport is like separate calls to all the airlines. Save yourself time and get the best possible connections. Give us a call.

Contact any of our offices for free color brochures.

Travel and Transport

Royal Viking Sky
Panama
Canal
Cruise
Jan. 25 — Feb. 12

Mal & Millie Hansen, hope to see you on board.

The Hansens will escort this elegant cruise sailing from Ft. Lauderdale to Los Angeles

Calling at
- St. Thomas
- Aruba
- Acapulco
- Puerto Vallarta

Stella Solaris
Panama
Canal
Cruise
Jan. 16-29

Enjoy Sun Line's famous Greek hospitality

Best of the Western Caribbean ... plus

double transit of Panama Canal

CARIBBEAN
Cruise

Feb. 23-Mar. 1
The perfect winter escape. Sailing from San Juan

M/S CARLA C
Curacao — Venezuela
Grenada — Martinique
St. Thomas
MTS DAPHNE
Curacao — Venezuela
Grenada — Guadeloupe
St. Thomas
From morning 'til night ... includes everything to make each day special.
Fully escorted

Figure 7-10 Another version of the Mondrian layout.

Figure 7-11 There's an endless variety of *frame* ads.

OUT OF A TREASURED PAST COMES A BEAUTIFUL BEGINNING.

The magic begins as you enter the cool vaulted halls of Hotel El Convento, the romantic hotel in Old San Juan that brings the charm of long ago to a Puerto Rico vacation.

At a time when so many hotels seem alike, El Convento is an original. Distinctively old world, it's the small and personal hotel many discriminating travelers like to return to again and again.

Three hundred years of beauty and tradition are reflected in the authentic Spanish colonial setting, the famous Flamenco evenings and dining by candle light in the splendour of the original convent chapel. It's a beautiful experience, one you may enjoy now at substantial seasonal savings.

Please call your travel agent or (212) 541-6630, extension 44. Outside New York State, call (800) 223-0151.

El Convento
THE HOTEL THAT PUTS ROMANCE INTO YOUR VACATION.

Figure 7-12 Example of a *typeface* ad.

Give your clients the time of their lives. Rendezvous Time in Bermuda!

Our temperate Rendezvous Time weather is *made* for tennis on almost 100 meticulously cared-for courts—many lighted for night play.

British flavour everywhere—from cozy "darts 'n ale" pubs, to the pomp and pageantry of the Bermuda Regiment.

Free Rendezvous Time special events daily—Market Day, Festival Day, golf and tennis tourneys, even a witch hunt.

Exciting night life! Calypso or steel bands, jazz or waltz, and discos—where the beat goes on until 3 a.m.

BERMUDA FESTIVAL 1980

January 16th through February 23rd. Bermuda's 5th Annual Festival of Performing Arts. 32 exciting nights of international stars. Arlo Guthrie, Cleo Laine, The Ballet Repertory and Juilliard Theater companies, Brandenburg Ensemble, puppeteer Philippe Gentry...and more!

More golf-per-acre than any place on earth! 9 great oceanview courses—at their greenest during Rendezvous Time.

December through mid-March is Rendezvous Time ...when our island is lush and green...and our golf and tennis weather superb.

Bermuda's delightfully mild Rendezvous Time climate is ideal for active sports, motorbike touring, and strolling on our world-famous pink beaches.

There's also fabulous international shopping, our authentic and fascinating 17th-century town of St. George's, superb restaurants, and gentle turquoise waters for sailing or ferry-boat sightseeing.

So much to see, so much to do. And all less than two jet hours from the East Coast—so your clients won't waste precious vacation time getting to their vacation. Bermuda!...where your clients can get away to it all!

Bermuda Department of Tourism
630 Fifth Avenue, New York, N.Y. 10020 • Suite 1010, 44 School Street, Boston, Mass. 02108
300 North State Street, Chicago, Ill. 60610 • Two Bloor Street West, Toronto, Ont., Canada M4W3E2

New! Colourful 12-page Bermuda Rendezvous Time brochure

Please send 5 ☐   10 ☐ brochures.

Name _____ (Please Print)
Agency name _____
Address _____
City _____
State _____ Zip _____

Mail to the Bermuda office nearest you.

Figure 7-13 *Multi-panel* layouts may run horizontally or vertically, and may contain drawings, photos, color blocks, or copy.

THE DESIGN OF PRINT ADVERTISING 101

Holy Land Pilgrimages

Fully Escorted Group Tours

One FREE For Each Five Paying Passengers and Agency Commissions of 10% or up to 25%

If your clients are thinking about a trip to the Holy Lands, you should thin[k] about *Travelink Tours International*.

Ones and twos can joi[n a] group that's already established...and yo[u] can earn 15% commis[sion.] Or, we'll show you how [to] organize your own gro[up] and earn from 10% up to 25%.

Write or phone today f[or] details of our itinerarie[s] and scheduled departu[res.]

Our standard tours i[n-]clude...round-trip air v[ia] SCHEDULED carriers, a[c-]commodations at fir[st] class hotels, extensi[ve] sightseeing in delux[e] motorcoachs, profe[s-]sional escorts/guides, [all] transfers, baggage hand[l-]ing...and more...

Travelink Tours International, Inc.
9575 W. Higgins Road
Rosemont, Illinois 60018
(312) 692-5790
TOLL FREE NUMBERS:
800/323-2102
In Illinois 800/942-0174

Some **of our standard tours...**

☐ **8 Day Bible Lands Seminar**
Tel Aviv, Jerusalem, Jericho, Massada, Hebron, Bethlehem, Galilee, and Capernaum. **From $968.**

☐ **10 Day Holyland Pilgrimage**
Tel Aviv, Jerusalem, Bethlehem, Hebron, Jericho, Dead Sea, Massada, Galilee, Capernaum, Golan and Haifa. **From $1068.**

☐ **10 Day Tour From Dan to Beersheba**
Tel Aviv, Jerusalem, Bethlehem, Bethany, Jericho, Dead Sea, Ein Gad,

"Why you should send your clients to a dive."

"Did you know one of the best scuba diving schools in the world is in Freeport/Lucaya, Bahamas? And where do you think some of the world's best diving is found? Same place.

If you have clients who are bored with the usual Bahamas vacation, send them to us. We've got a sensational Learn to Dive Package. Plus two other special packages, a Honeymoon and a Family Package, that let you book your clients into either of our Freeport/Lucaya hotels at the same low price.

The Lucayan Harbour Inn & Marina. And The Lucayan Bay Hotel.

For confirmed reservations, call toll-free (800) 327-0787. In Florida, (800) 432-5594. Miami, (305) 443-3821.

My name is Jack Gold, General Manager. Your clients will have a super time. That's a promise."

CP Hotels
30 fine hotels in 6 countries around the world.

Figure 7-14 *Copy heavy* **layouts may sometimes be combined with other formats.**

Figure 7-15 In the *silhouette* format the elements form a pattern—usually an abstract pattern.

Figure 7-16 *Circus* layouts win few awards but sell products and services.

Book your clients into the President Hotel. You'll be sending them back again and again.

There are many reasons why your clients will be coming to Taiwan for the first time. Taipei's importance as a business capital, its exciting nightlife, and the unique Taiwanese cultural attractions are just a few. If you book them into the President Hotel, Taipei, on their first trip, they'll be coming back again, both to Taiwan and to you. Because every year more and more visitors return to the President Hotel, where hospitality, service, and cuisine are an ongoing tradition.

It's one of Asia's best addresses, for its convenient location, its restaurants and nightclub, its four-hundred-plus rooms and suites, and reliable quality that keeps guests satisfied whenever they return. Keep your clients satisfied. Book them into the President.

President Hotel

Teh Hwei St., Taipei, Taiwan, 104 ROC.
Cable address: Presdent Taipei Phone:595-1251 Telex: 11269 IP
Instant reservations through T.C.I. HOTEL DIVISION Los Angeles (213) 461-3541
Tel: New York (212) 953-0590 and Eastern Canada (416) 363-5321

Figure 7-17 *Rebus* layout.

THE DESIGN OF PRINT ADVERTISING

Black Mountain Ranch

A working ranch with guest accommodations. 3,000 acres amid the colorful Colorado Rockies. An unmatched setting, conveniently located between Vail and Steamboat. Offering both summer and winter adventures.

BLACK MOUNTAIN RANCH
Crossroads Center, 141 E. Meadow Drive, Suite E-209, Vail, Co. 81657
303/476-1200.

BARBADOS

Fashionable St. James — the beach. And directly on it, the impeccable Colony Club. Small, chic, with the easy style of relaxed Indies living. All rooms have patios looking out on verandahs and gardens. The best in dining with buffets, barbecues, patio dancing. Yachts for cruises and parties. Glass-bottomed boats, fishing boats. Pool. 7 miles from Bridgetown's dutyfree shops.

COLONY CLUB
See your travel agent or call
David B. Mitchell & Co., Inc.
777 Third Avenue, New York City 10017
Phone: (212) 371-1323
Toronto & Montreal call ZEnith 3-2030

GRAND CAYMAN
Caribbean Club

Caribbean Club is a small group of delightful one and two bedroom villas right on world-famous Seven Mile Beach. Always considered the finest in accommodations and service, The Caribbean Club also boasts superb candlelight dinners in elegant surroundings.
For reservations, see your travel agent or call **9-2593**.
Caribbean Club • Box 504 • Grand Cayman • B.W.I.
Tennis and Sailing available on premises.

JAMAICA
WE'VE GOT IT!

Opposite world famous Doctors Cave Beach. You can play shuffleboard, volleyball, tennis, swim in our rooftop level pool or golf, horseback ride, scuba, sport fish or sail nearby. High-rise luxury studios and suites.

Montego Bay Club
For reservations: Wolfe International
212-730-8100 or 800-223-5695

HALF MOON
HOTEL, COTTAGES, GOLF, TENNIS & BEACH CLUB
Heinz E.W. Simonitsch — Managing Director
Rose Hall, Jamaica, W.I.

3000 ft. private beach, Robert Trent Jones championship 18-hole golf course, eleven tennis courts, sailing, 18 freshwater pools, sauna, massage, shopping arcade, luxurious cottages, suites and rooms. Exclusive vacation plans available.

Call TCI 800-423-2922 or see your Travel Agent.

A Touch Of Europe
On Florida's West Coast

Enjoy continental service, hospitality and cuisine in a casual beach-front setting.

far horizons *Beach Resort*
2401 Gulf of Mexico Drive
Longboat Key, Sarasota, Florida 33548
For reservations: Area Code 813/383-2441

GOURMET
WINE TASTING TOUR TO
South America
LIMA • SANTIAGO • BUENOS AIRES • RIO

$731 PER PERSON DOUBLE OCCUPANCY PLUS LOW ITX AIRFARE VIA LAN CHILE
16 DAYS FROM

ASK YOUR TRAVEL AGENT FOR THE COLORFUL "GOURMET SOUTH AMERICA" BROCHURE OR WRITE

TRAVELUXE
150 BROADWAY, NEW YORK, N.Y. 10038 (212) 233 6580

PAVILIONS & POOLS
Star Route, St. Thomas, U.S.V.I. 00801
(809) 775-1110

At our hotel everyone has a private guest house with its own private pool.

for reservations and information
Write Direct or call:
ROBERT F. WARNER, INC.
711 Third Ave., New York, NY 10017
(212) 687-5750

ESTES PARK

WEATHER & SKI INFORMATION
1-800-525-5616
DENVER: 573-3880

Hotel of Suites!
and all at "room prices"

Only 4 blocks from the State Capitol; 6-8 to business section, library, art museum. All suites have private lanai, living room, dining alcove, kitchenette, color TV. Full hotel services. From $23.00.

Hampshire House Hotel
"Hospitality"
1000 Grant • Denver 837-1200

SITZMARK SKI LODGE
European Rates • Packages • Chalets with Fireplace • Rooms • Dorms • Color TV
Free Shuttle Service • Free Color Brochure
Box 65 • Winter Park
Colorado 80482 • (303) 726-5453

Vail Reservations Inc.
ACCOMMODATIONS • TRANSPORTATION ACTIVITIES
1-800-525-8930
Toll free from Denver: 571-1833

Spend your perfect Caribbean holiday at
Simson Bay Beach hotel
P.O. Box 205, Philipsburg
St. Maarten, Netherland Antilles
• Write us or call your travel agent •

Figure 7-18

Working in Small Space

One of the difficulties with many courses in advertising is that students are invariably given large spaces to work in—full or half pages. Upon entering the profession, they may have to confine their creativity to a few inches. This is a tough assignment.

After all, if budget were no problem and you could hire the finest photographers and select the most distinctive type faces and purchase the largest available magazine or newspaper space, you should be able to come up with something that at least attracts attention. When you have to come up with a 2-column, 3-inch ad that contains all you want to say, and do it artistically, that's a challenge.

Working in small space means that you have to minimize copy. You learn to condense. Your headlines must also be brief, and any illustrations must be small. You'll stay away from photographs because, even on magazine stock, they won't show up well. In the newspapers, they'll be blobs. You may not always have room for a coupon and must settle for an address and phone number.

You'll probably try to reach the public either through a clever headline or an unusual shape. You could also opt for some white space, cutting down on copy, but raising readability.

Notice the way the advertisers in Figure 7-18 have used a limited space.

Make Your Ad Stand Out

Take a look at the travel pages of *The New York Sunday Times* or any other metropolitan newspaper. Or, for that matter, the travel pages of much smaller communities. What do you see? Ads crowded in together. Dozens of small space advertisements competing for attention. Imagine one of these on the artist's drawing board, alone. It looks great, attractive, eye-catching. Then it disappears in that sea of similarity.

What can you do about this?

One of the old advertising truisms is that "if you're standing and everyone else is dancing, you're noticed." That means you don't have to be flashy, just different.

If the page you normally appear on is full of ads with reams of copy, try an ad with lots of white space and an open look. If the ads are all black on white, experiment with the reverse. How about using some unusual type or giving your ad a border that sets it apart? Or an illustration that forces the scanning eye to stop?

Notice what others are doing and imagine your ad placed among them. Then devise a way to render yours just a bit different. Like the motionless dancer, it will stand out.

Typography

As mentioned earlier, copy is not only informative, it can also be decorative. It's an essential part of the layout.

Copy is communicated via type, such as you are reading in this book. In the next chapter we'll talk about measuring and fitting type. In this chapter we look at the various styles of type available to you.

While there are hundreds of different designs of type and varieties of sizes for each design, type is generally divided into four broad categories:

- *ROMAN.* The basic typeface which has the small serifs or extensions at the end of the major strokes. These serifs make reading easier, particularly for longer articles. This is an example of a *Roman* typeface:

$150* Round-Trip Miami - San Jose
Discover the beauty, the friendliness and the

- *BLOCK.* Sometimes called *Gothic* or *Sans-Serif.* The typeface has no serifs, making it harder to read over a long stretch, but giving copy a more modern look. Here's an example of the *Block* letter:

SCANDINAVIA
Rosy-cheeked wonderland, sparkling, clean, spectacular! Cruise Norway's

- *SCRIPT.* This typeface resembles handwriting and gives an ad a more delicate or elegant look. It would be good, perhaps, for a honeymoon ad but not so hot for a football excursion. You see this style used often in invitations. When the letters are not connected to each other, that form of script is called cursive. Here is an example of *Script*:

Cafe Chauveron

- *ORNAMENTAL.* This category has the most variations. It could be anything from the Old English Text found on parchments to the balloon lettering seen in displays. Here are some examples:

Kernwood At-Lynnfield   **hawaiian**

Singapore   **Central Asia and Siberia**

There are over a thousand different typefaces in use today and more are entering the market every day. This fact may not mean much to you unless you are in a major city where selection is vast. In most places, the variety will be limited. The travel advertiser should see what's available locally by requesting a type book or type specimen pages. If you absolutely need something else, you can try in larger nearby cities, or order type by mail. This, however, gets expensive. It's better to try to live with what you have, unless the choice is dismal.

As you'll note from the previous samples, and see even better by leafing through a magazine, each typeface has a different feel to it. This becomes quite important in travel advertising, since different countries also have a special feel to them. The type you'd choose for a headline for Mexico might be totally different than one for France. An American tour would look and feel different than an African safari. As much as possible, the type—particularly the headline—should support this feeling.

Figure 7-19 The type selected should look right for the subject of the ad.

Another caution is that the body copy should be compatible in type with the headline. This doesn't mean they must be the *same*—just *compatible*. You wouldn't normally use a Roman headline for a Block letter copy block, and you wouldn't use an Old English head for a Roman copy block. There are exceptions, of course, but this is the rule.

The advertiser should avoid mixing too many different typefaces. A couple of faces in one ad are usually enough. Five or six different faces stamp you as an amateur.

As with other things, keep samples of type that you like and see if they may be found in your hometown shops. After a while you'll get so you know what looks good and know what you can rely on. Typography, however, is a real science, and few people in advertising really master it. You don't have to get so good that you can immediately recognize size and family of type; all you really need to know is what looks right, and how it will fit your ad.

Illustrations

If you have someone on your agency staff who can handle art—commercial art—that would be nice. And rare. Most agencies must lean on newspaper art departments, art supplied by carriers and others, or on *clip art*. Clip art is furnished at a fee by an art service. These illustrations come in books assembled by categories—like holidays, or groups, or sports, or travel. Virtually all of these are *line* art, meaning that they can be reproduced without "screening" like you'd screen a photo; they are simply made up of lines.

In such a travel clip art book you might find familiar symbols like the Eiffel Tower, the Pyramids, a cruise ship, couples running with suitcases, exotic foreigners and other items. There would be several different books under the category of travel, and new ones are added periodically.

Even so, one of the detriments of clip art is that it begins to look familiar. Others can also buy and use it, so the originality is lost.

But it is cheap. You can buy a book full of illustrations for $5 or $10, which is far less than you'd pay for a single illustration if you had it drawn at an art studio. When you come to something like a logo, which is going to be with you for a long time, it makes sense to use an art studio and not try to find something out of a book.

Figure 7-20 is an example of line art from a book called *Instant Art for Travel Promotion,* reprinted through the courtesy of Forsyth Travel Library, P.O. Box 2975, Shawnee Mission, KS 66201.

You should also check to see what art is available from airlines and cruise ships and international tourist bureaus. They often have items you can adapt to your use. You'll also see travel agencies that lift sketches right out of magazine ads or brochures. You're not supposed to do this without written permission.

You'll also see references to *mat services,* which means that, instead of illustrations coming on regular coated paper, these will provide molds make of heavy paper (almost cardboard), or rubber, or plastic. They are used just

Figure 7-20 Some sample clip art.

as any mold. Metal is poured into them at the newspaper or magazine and the resultant metal plate is used in the printing process. The reason for using mats and not metal plates is because the mats are much lighter and more efficient to ship. The use of mats, however, has diminished, since most publications are printed by the offset method.

Photography

The first word to be said here is that, if the photography isn't good, forget about it. Don't wait for the terrific slides from someone's brother-in-law, and don't rely on an amateur to perform a critical photo assignment for you. Get a professional. It's cheaper in the long run.

Photography would be used primarily in feature stories, in magazine advertising and, rarely, in large newspaper advertising. Slides are also used in special presentations, television programs, and exhibits. Both slides and prints may be utilized in brochures or printed materials.

You've seen company publications where black and white photos were out of focus, poorly composed, or inexpertly cropped. While this may (?) look cute and please those who are featured, it leaves a negative impression on an external audience. *Anything you use should be the best you can get.*

In general, you want photos with high contrast, so that they'll reproduce. These pictures with grainy textures which sometimes win photo contests are no good for your purposes. Wherever possible, include people in the pictures. Ogilvy & Mather recommends: "Photograph the natives, not the tourists." Normally, this is good advice. Readers would rather see Croats in colorful dance costumes than look at Americans watching Croats in colorful dance costumes. There could be exceptions to this. If you wanted to show the variety of things a tourist might participate in, of course you'd show the traveling American.

If used in an ad, the photo, like the headline, must tie into the general idea. If it needs explanation—and most do—give it a terse and interesting caption. Try to avoid the show-and-tell caption where you depict the Leaning Tower of Pisa and say below: "This is the Leaning Tower of Pisa." Instead, put something like: "Begun in the 12th century, Italy's Leaning Tower of Pisa survived World War II virtually intact." And that line could be shorter.

When would you choose a photo over a piece of art?

First, you'd have to have enough space and be sure the reproduction would look good in the medium you chose. Then you'd want to be certain that the photo did what you wanted it to do and was not merely decorative.

Photos have more immediacy than illustrations and are more believable. Seeing a photo of Victoria Falls is better than looking at a drawing of that landmark. You can also do tricks with photos which have shock value, whereas the reader knows anything is possible with a drawing.

Most photographs you'll need will be available from suppliers. Some could also be in the newspaper or magazine morgue (file), and you may have compiled your own cache of pictures. In addition, just as with clip art, there are stock photo houses, where you can purchase photos in a variety of categories. These are not cheap—although they are cheaper than tackling most projects yourself. They also suffer from familiarity, a certain stiffness, and are often dated. Remember that things like dress and car styles change frequently, so the photos must mirror that change.

As with layout, try for something different in photos. Perhaps a different angle, or people doing different things (and not staring at the camera with a handful of souvenirs), or some exciting action. While the photo may also serve to illustrate or inform, its main purpose is to attract attention, like the headline.

The Logo

This is your signature, or company motif, or emblem. It may merely be your company name in distinctive type or it could be a piece of art which includes the company designation.

Whatever you choose should be pertinent, attractive, readable, and flexible. Consider how it will look in an ad, on a letterhead, on your window, on luggage, on television, on brochures, and even on novelties. If you intend to use color on occasion, reflect on how this logo will look in either color or black and white.

Try to be original and distinctive, and avoid being trite, imitative, or corny. Look at some of the travel agency logos. Some are good; most aren't much. With a little thought you can stand out in this field.

If possible, an agency should employ an artist to design this symbol. Before you take this step, however, do a little thinking on your own. The more direction you can give the artist, the more economical the assignment. If the artist has to doodle around for days, coming up with samples which you reject, the bills keep mounting. At $15-$50 an hour, it doesn't take long for a massive art bill to accrue. Explain what your company is and what it tries to do, suggest some concepts you'd like to see in the logo, and then let the artist do some roughs.

Some companies feel so strongly about their logos, they spend $25,000-$50,000 and more designing just the right item. This is beyond the reach of travel agencies but some expenditure is justified because of the long life and multiple use of this symbol.

The Use of Color

For nearly all travel agencies, color is not a major consideration. Few advertisers would use it in newspapers and not many travel agencies employ magazines as a medium. In brochures, direct mail, outdoor advertising, and other media, some color might be used. This makes it worthwhile to consider a few aspects of color.

Like type, color has its own properties, and its own abilities to affect the viewer. Note how major advertisers use color. Marlboro cigarettes employs darker, redder, warmer tones, to emphasize the masculine image of its product. Many filter cigarettes are heavy on greens, suggesting a cool, cleaner smoke.

Obviously, when it can be used, color enhances the marketing of travel. The reader associates color with both beauty and excitement. A mountain sunset, an Alaskan cruise, a night in Las Vegas—all demand color to truly show them off.

Color also gives a little glamor to a headline, or sets off a logo, or provides a tinted background on which copy or photos are displayed. When dealing with a photo, you have little choice of color—you normally try to capture the true colors. With other hues, however, you should try to select appropriate colors. Green has long denoted Ireland; Russia rates a red cast; cruises opt for blue or green. The color choice should fit the mood and subject.

There are three primary colors: red, blue, and yellow (or magenta, cyan, and yellow, in printing terms). These colors, mixed with each other and with black or white pigments, provide the full range of colors. These colors—or hues—may also vary in intensity, or in lightness and darkness. The latter quality depends upon where they fall on the scale of values, a tone scale going from white to black.

As with other elements of a layout, colors should also be compatible. Any smart dresser knows this. Work with colors that complement each other, rather than clashing with each other.

Also, avoid printing black lettering on a dark tint block. You can't read it. Neither can you read white lettering on a light tint block. Dark hues are also recommended for headlines rather than a light yellow or pink.

In printing, we talk about one-, two-, three-, and four-color work. Unless the printer has a four-color press, each time you add a color that means another pass through the press and, consequently, higher charges for press time. We'll see that in more detail in the next chapter.

Know the Effect of Paper

The weight, color, and finish of paper have an impact on the way an ad or brochure will look. You might also add "surface" and "grain" to that trio.

Paper, which is made from wood pulp, or, occasionally, from cotton or linen rags, comes in large sheets, like 17" x 22". There are 500 sheets to a ream and the weight of each sheet is expressed in the total weight of the ream. If you see a bond paper listed as 20# paper, that means the large sheets from which it was cut totaled 20 pounds to the ream.

Paper for the pages of books will typically be 60-, 70-, or 80-pound paper, and these weights are also used for brochures. For booklets, a heavier stock may be used for the cover—perhaps 90 pound or above. Many national magazines use 60-pound paper, even 50-pound paper. One hundred and fifty-pound paper is about the limit, and would seldom be used.

When deciding on the size of a brochure, it's wise to talk with your printer about the most economical way to make cuts in the large sheet. You may find, for example, that by tailoring your brochure measurements less than an inch, you could get another complete folder out of each sheet.

In fact, you should rely pretty much on your printer for advice on weight, color, texture—and availability. Paper has become difficult to obtain. You can't just find a sample of paper you like and go down and order it. It may not be in stock, and weeks could elapse before your order is filled. Better stick to paper that's on hand, or that can be readily shipped.

Newsprint, which is used by newspapers, is made of groundwood pulp, and serves well for a short period. Eventually, however, when light and air get to it, it turns brittle and yellow or tan.

Offset paper has a flat (non-shiny) finish and is very popular because of cost and versatility. Coated stock is more expensive but provides a better surface for photographs, and also impresses many people as designating quality. You can also buy papers with antique finishes, or with ripple finishes, or a variety of fancy weaves. These should be used sparingly, and only when the occasion demands something special.

Paper also comes in many different colors. When printing on these colors, keep in mind the way the type will reproduce. A dark paper would call for *very* dark or *bold* type. Even then it will be tough to read. A colored ink on colored stock also alters the look of both elements. Brown ink on green stock, for example, will look much different than brown ink on white or tan stock.

Printers have paper samples they can show you, along with swatches of available colors. Match these two items by putting the swatch next to the paper and see how they look. Even this test is not perfect, but it gives you some idea of the final result.

The Travel Page or Section

Some travel sections are full size (about 14½" wide x 22" high) and others are tabloid size (about 11½" wide by 14½" high). It takes a larger ad to dominate the larger page, but a full page in one is really not much different than a full page in the other—in terms of attention-getting, not cost.

Check the section your ad will appear in and recognize the problems and opportunities. You may want special placement, like on the outside of the page, or near some well-read travel feature. The section may contain 20 pages and over 200 individual ads, or it may be a single page with a handful of ads. The former situation is tougher to combat, and more expensive to buy.

A really unusual ad will gain readership, even in a relatively small size, but when you are looking at bulk alone, it's going to take about a third of a page to dominate the other ads.

Miscellaneous Design Problems

The design possibilities are endless, so a list of things you *should* do is impossible to compile. If it works, it works, and that's the best test.

There are, however, things you *shouldn't* do. Many of these have been mentioned already, like ignoring the ad's balance or harmony, letting elements float around loosely, forgetting to have something dominate, printing so that people can't read the copy, mixing too many type faces in a single ad, failing to tie headline, copy, and illustration together, and so on. Here are a few more tips:

• Don't *harden* your thumbnail sketches. Let them be loose at first, then firm up the lines.

• Repeat some elements in an ad occasionally. This adds to the idea of simplicity and also keeps the reader's attention.

• When you run your ad across two pages, learn how to deal with the *gutter*—the space between pages. Running a headline across ties the ad together; or repeating an element on both sides; or carrying a tint block across; or matching large type on either side. There are many devices. Check several magazines and not how they handle this.

- Get all the information you can from printing and paper salespeople, newspaper and magazine salespeople, and other professionals.
- Save ads you like, type you find attractive, paper you'd like to try.
- Come to terms with your own art ability, or that of anyone in the office, and realize what you can and cannot do. If there is limited talent, your only hope lies in clip art, imitation, an art studio, or the newspaper's art department.

Questions and Exercises

1. Using travel sections of newspapers and magazines, find an ad in each of the nine format categories covered in this chapter.
2. Bring in three print advertisements for travel and isolate the basic design elements in each.
3. Working with larger travel ads, trace only the circles, rectangles, and triangles in three ads. Use a ruler, pencil and tracing paper for this.
4. Explain harmony, sequence, and balance.
5. What advantages does a photograph have over other illustrations?
6. What colors result from the following mixtures: Red and blue? Yellow and blue? Yellow and red?
7. What is meant by 80-pound paper?
8. Find five print ads for travel that violate any of the principles discussed in this chapter.

Case Problem

Using the same brochure you used for the case problem in chapter six, turn this into an ad that measures 3 columns wide x 8" high (or deep). Make this as attractive as you can, assuming you are going to show it to a client. Draw in the headline; indicate the copy by lines (but type the copy on a separate sheet); use an illustration or photo, either drawing it in or pasting something on your layout, and invent a travel agency name and logo to identify the ad. You can decide on format, on the use of coupon or not, and on other factors.

This ad will appear in the Sunday edition of your newspaper, on the travel page, or in the travel section.

CHAPTER EIGHT

The Mechanics of Print Production

Like so many other aspects of advertising, production of both print and broadcast material is a specialty. It's not necessary that the practitioner or the agency manager know how to produce the ads, but it is helpful to understand how they are produced and what steps can be taken in advance to make production better and more economical. Again, there is no substitute for talking with the experts and visiting the print shops or recording or television studios to see exactly what the process entails.

To appreciate what transpires from concept to finished product in print advertising, let's follow a newspaper ad from the time it is merely an idea until it appears in the Sunday travel edition.

What Happens to an Ad

First comes the need. Let's say you want to advertise cruises to the Bahamas. Here's the way this might go:

1. You'd collect all the information you can get, tie down the details, settle on dates, costs and other items.

2. You'd consider the budget and determine how much money you can afford to spend on advertising and still make a profit. This would affect the size of the ad and the number of insertions. (You might, of course, lay out an ad first and then see what it would cost, but this is a more sensible routine.)

3. You'd come up with a central idea and devise a copy platform for all the advertising.

4. You would do a number of thumbnail sketches to get an idea of what design might work. Or you might incorporate the new information into a previous ad format.

5. Once the copy and layout are approved, you would provide the art department of the newspaper (or your own artist) with your rough idea and the typed copy. Copy for ads is always typed on separate sheets and the ad layout merely indicates, by use of lines, where the copy will go. (Figure 8-1).

The typed sheet might look like Figure 8-2.

THE MECHANICS OF PRINT PRODUCTION   117

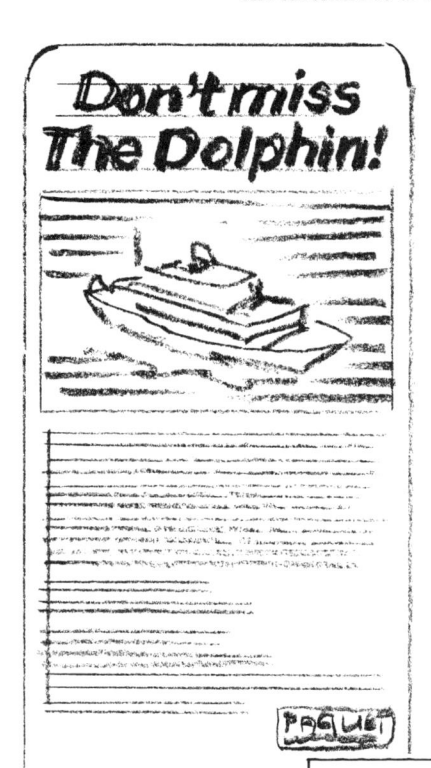

Figure 8-1

Rough of proposed print ad, without copy.

Figure 8-2

Copy should be typed on separate sheet, keyed for position in ad, and marked for type sizes.

Don't miss
The Dolphin!

HEADLINE:
20/20 Helvetica Bld. Ital.
2 lines centered

From French chefs to free dinner wines, this is the exciting new way to cruise from Miami to the Bahamas. 3-night cruises to Nassau any Friday from $170 to $370. 4-night cruises to Nassau and Freeport any Monday from $215 to $450.

TEXT:
8/9 Helvetica
Light
X 11½ picas
Rag. Rt.

Ask your Travel Agent.

Paquet Cruises, Inc.
1001 North American Way
Miami, Florida 33132 • 305-374-8100
Registered in Panama

(Paquet logo and S.S. Dolphin art to be furnished)

The pencil markings indicate the type families chosen—Helvetica Bold Italic and Helvetica Light and the size of each. The *u & lc* means upper and lower case letters. If you wanted all capital letters, you'd write *caps*.

Now, the average travel agent would not be familiar with typefaces or sizes. For that matter, neither would many advertising agency personnel. Your layout would indicate the approximate size you wanted the letters and you might include a sample of the type you wanted for each spot, and the art studio production person or, more likely, the newspaper art department, would *spec* (specify) this type, indicating style and size.

6. Once the type has been marked up (as in the example) it goes to the typesetter. Newspapers have their own composing rooms but there are also typesetters and printers who set type. The type is set to match and fit your layout and instructions, and a copy of this type, suitable for reproduction, is sent along to the art department.

7. Meanwhile, since you have decided you want to run a photo of the ship

Figure 8-3

in your ad, you will need this photo. It's likely that one may be furnished, or you may have to have the picture shot. A glossy print is supplied to the paper, marked up to fit your layout (as we'll see later). At this time you would also furnish the distinctive signature copy and logo.

8. The art department or studio then pastes down all the elements on a piece of bristol board (heavy paper stock), positioning the illustration and the typeset copy, then drawing in or setting in the border. This is the time to be certain all corrections have been made.

9. A proof is pulled from this pasteup (which is said to be *camera ready*) and a proof is run off. This is the first copy but looks just like the ad should look in the paper. The proof is for your approval. If you catch any errors, you indicate the changes. You might also correct sizes or alter anything else that doesn't look right, but as stated above, it's wiser and cheaper to make changes earlier.

10. After you've approved the proof, the ad department gives the go ahead to the printing department. Your ad is given a spot on the appropriate page and run as part of the entire paper. The end result looks like Figure 8-3.

Measuring Type

Let's retrace a few steps in the previous list of steps involved in the production of an ad, and examine them more closely.

Type, for example, has the artistic and psychological function we looked at in the previous chapter, but it also has mechanical properties.

The height of type is expressed in *points*. There are 72 points to an inch. That means that 72-point type is roughly one inch high, from the top of the tallest character to the bottom of the lowest character below the baseline. Thirty-six point type, then, would be half an inch. Eighteen-point type will approximate one-fourth of an inch. All of these sizes would be used in headlines. The normal body type would be 10-12 point, and this is the size type you'll find in newspapers and magazines.

Here are some examples:

10-pt. Times Roman Bold
DATA COMPILED FROM A RELIABLE SOURCE
Date compiled from a reliable source

20-pt. Times Roman Bold
DATA COMPILED FROM A
Data compiled from a reliable

If you want type to have a more open look, you may add a small amount of space between lines. Taking a cue from the days when this space consisted of a small strip of metal inserted between lines, this process is called *leading* (pronounced *ledding*).

Type is measured by *picas* when measuring lateral distance. We say that a line is so many picas long, or a copy block so many picas wide. Why picas? Because they are easier to work with than fractions of an inch. *There are six picas to the inch.*

The human eye will only span so much space comfortably. That's why most columns in magazines and newspapers are about 12-13 picas wide (2-2¼ inches). The copy below is 10-point type with an extra two points of leading, making it 10 on 12 (shown as 10/12) and measures approximately 13 picas wide.

> SNOW BALL gives you incredible discounts on hotels, meals, shopping and entertainment, as well as airport transfers or car rentals. Skiers get discounts on the slopes, tows and equipment rentals and convenient transportation from downtown Montreal. Get to Montreal by air, train, bus or drive.

Estimating type by eye is risky. Few people (if any) can spot the difference between 9- and 10-point type, or one or two points of leading, or even between headlines of 36 and 42 points.

You specify the type you want and, if it looks too small, you move up a size. If it's too large, you back down a size, or cut copy.

Another technique that is good to know is how to *copy fit* type. This works two ways—when you have something already written and are wondering how much space it will take, and when you have the space and wonder how many words you can write.

There are a number of ways of estimating this. The easiest way is by using charts which tell you the space required for certain sizes of type. Another way is to draw a square inch around the type and count the number of words in that square inch and then multiply by the number of square inches in the allotted space.

Both of these methods get a little complicated for the person who is doing this only periodically. A simpler (though longer) way is to just paste a piece of copy—any copy—that has the type size you want in the space you have to fill. Then count the words.

When you start with typed copy, count the words (or characters—with each typed letter and each space representing a character) and then determine how many lines you will need in the type size and block you have chosen.

In the type example above, there are approximately five words to a line and approximately thirty characters to the line. "Approximately" is used here because the copy block is really too short to estimate words and the spacing in these lines is irregular. However, assuming these figures worked, it would be a simple job to set your typewriter for thirty characters and then all you'd have to do is count the typed lines to see how much space you'd require.

When you are doing something regularly, like a quarterly brochure, you'll find it simple to use columns of type from back issues to paste on the *dummy* (which we'll explain later) to stand for copy in the upcoming issue. Here's the step by step way to do this:

1. Count the number of characters per line in the previous issue.
2. Set your typewriter for this number and type your copy.
3. Count the number of typed lines.
4. Count the same number of lines on previously printed copy, cut out this block and paste it in your dummy. If you've done everything right, this piece of old copy should be very close to the copy for the next issue.

You can, of course, do the same thing for an ad, particularly when you are using an identical format, but new copy.

A few final words on type.

In the last chapter we looked at the four general categories of type but mentioned that there were over a thousand variations, called typefaces or families, which can be selected. You see names like Garamond or Caslon or Stymie or Bodoni, and these denote type specimens which have different looks, sometimes obvious, sometimes subtle. You pick the style that seems to suit your message—but don't get too cute. Remember, it still must be read.

You'll also see the terms *series* and *fonts* used when referring to type. *Series* means all sizes within a single design, like everything from 6-point to 48-point type in Helvetica, including caps, italics, and bold face (heavier or darker letters) and light face (regular printing). A *font* is limited to a single size within that series—like 6-point Helvetica, again including all variations, like caps and lower case, bold face and light face, and italics, in that single size.

In addition to indicating spacing between lines, some designs also require spacing between letters or words, or they require that lines be tightened up. The first method is called *letter spacing* where you have a very open look; the second method is called *condensing,* and there are special condensed typefaces. When you condense, of course, this means you get more letters in the same space required for normal spacing. This should be taken into consideration when copy fitting.

Hot and Cold Type

All type used to be set via the use of hot metal. Machines, called monotype or linotype machines, served as small foundries, casting into metal the letters or lines that a typographer typed on the machine. This is called *hot metal* type or *hot* type. It is still in use today.

Cold type is normally the product of a photographic process. The characters are typed onto film or paper by exposing a negative to light, much as you would in developing any film. You have different faces to choose from and you can vary the size of type by changing the focal length of the camera. This is usually done automatically.

There are also typewriters which type your copy on a clean sheet which can then be pasted up and photographed. This is also cold type.

When the type is set—either reproduced on a page or, as metal, locked into a frame—it is made part of the ad or brochure by being pasted onto the layout, or included in the larger frame which contains all elements of the item to be printed.

This is what the printer works from.

Letterpress and Offset

While there are four ways to print: silk screen, gravure, offset, and letterpress, only the latter two methods have much use for the travel agency. Silk screening is used for posters and outdoor work, while gravure is employed for the printing of special color sections of newspapers or certain books. The choice is usually between letterpress and offset for ads and brochures.

Letterpress is the older method. In this form of printing, raised type is used, much like the rubber stamp printing sets youngsters enjoy. The raised portion is inked and it prints on the paper, which is pressed against it. Both hot and cold type can be used in this process, although hot metal characterized the first use of such a system.

Offset lithography is based on the principle that oil and water don't mix. Once the camera ready copy has been pasted down, a picture is taken and this is transferred, electrically or chemically, to a thin metal plate. The letters aren't raised as in letterpress printing, although all the images do stand above the plate an imperceptible distance. After being treated with oil, the plate is washed, removing oil from all but the image areas. These areas then accept ink, while the plain areas reject it. The plate is wrapped around a cylinder which transfers the printing to a second cylinder, which then prints it on paper.

Offset lithography has become the more popular because it is usually, though not always, cheaper, and because it is a more flexible system to work with.

Newspapers use both letterpress and offset techniques, with the latter dominating. No matter what process is used, the result will be only as good as the material supplied. A poor layout will remain a poor layout, and a dull photograph will remain a dull photograph. The only problem is that this ineptness is now made public. That's why it pays to supply the printer with decent copy and visuals.

Photographs

This field is a subject in itself and has spawned many books. Here we need only look at a few mechanical items.

The photograph you have chosen may not be the right size for your ad or brochure, or its composition may suggest the elimination of certain extraneous items. This means reducing or enlarging or cropping.

Normally, you'll be working with an 8" x 10" photo, although you could also have in hand a 4" x 5" print. Let's suppose you have ad space that allows for a photo that is 2 inches deep. You'll want to know the width. This involves setting up a simple ratio, thus:

$$\frac{4}{2} = \frac{5}{x}$$ x, then, equals 2½ (the width of the photo)

Actually, it is unnecessary to go through all this arithmetic, since a slide rule will provide the answer immediately. Many people who work with layout keep a circular slide rule handy, set up the ratio above, and just read over to the appropriate number. Some calculators also provide this function.

Another method for reducing or enlarging a photo is by laying a piece of tracing paper over the photo and carefully drawing a diagonal from the upper left to the lower right hand corner of the photo. You can then pencil in horizontal and vertical lines anywhere along that photo and where they meet you have your new dimensions (Figure 8-4).

One important caution. Be certain to use tracing paper and *never* draw lines directly on the photo, since you may need it again. Nor should you press down too hard with pencil or pen on the tracing paper, since this, too, could damage the photo. And don't clip things to the photo with a paper clip.

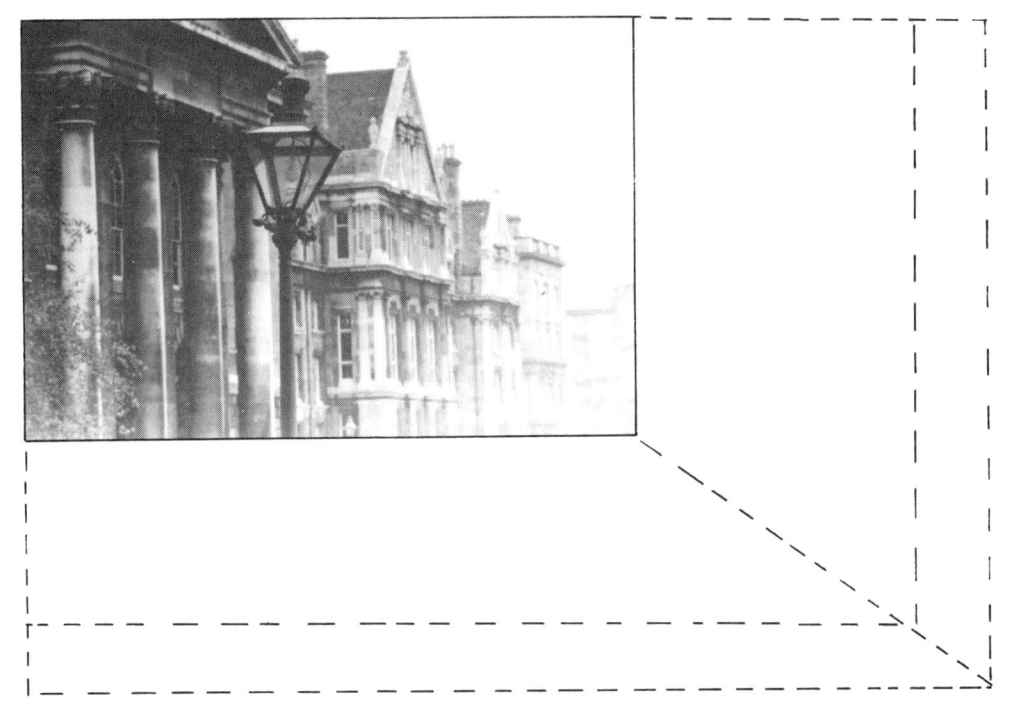

Figure 8-4

Once you have determined your new dimensions, you should write these instructions on the back of the photo, using a grease pencil or felt tip pen: *(Never use a pencil or ball point pen, since this could show through the other side.)*

Reduce to 2½" wide x 2" deep

or

Blow up (enlarge) to 7½" wide x 6" deep

Sometimes you may want to *crop* certain portions of the photo, to produce a more pleasing shot, to get rid of distracting background, or to bring one of the dimensions into harmony with the other when you reduce or enlarge.

In the latter context, suppose you had a photo that was 8" x 10" and you wanted it to be 3" x 3". There's no way to get that proportion without trimming a couple of inches off the width of the photo, or by making adjustments to both width and depth.

Sometimes a figure in the background will be out of place, or a sign will give away a locale, or a car will date the picture. You could remove the offending item in a variety of ways—like using an air brush, which sprays a fine coat of paint over the object, concealing it and creating a background that blends with the rest of the picture; or you could mask out the item with acetate. The easiest way, however, is to crop the picture.

You decide what portion of the photo you want (keeping in mind the final dimensions you need) and then place the crop marks, using a grease pencil, in the appropriate places on the *margin* of the photo (Figure 8-5).

This instruction would be written on the back of the photo, with grease pencil or felt tip, like this:

Crop to 3½" wide x 5" deep

If you intended to reduce or enlarge after you had cropped the picture, you'd state the cropping information first, and then the instructions about reducing or enlarging.

Be sure to double check all your figures before committing them to writing. It gets expensive when you have to redo photos and plates.

When there's a long caption for the photo, it's probably wiser to type this on a small piece of paper and attach it (using rubber cement or scotch tape) to the back of the picture. If you are identifying people in the photo, start left to right and say: "L to R: Mary Smith, John Jones etc." If the picture needs a credit line for the photographer or supplier, put that here. Ditto for any instructions about returning the photo and to whom it should be mailed.

You could, then, have a photo with all these details on the reverse side or on a separate typed sheet of paper:

CROP TO 3½" wide x 5" deep

REDUCE TO 2¼" wide x 3¼" deep

Figure 8-5

CAPTION: Fishing boat on Luzon

PLEASE CREDIT: Mabuhay Studios, Manila

RETURN TO: Philippine Tourist Board

(ADDRESS)

Drawings and paintings can also be marked up in similar fashion, including instructions about cropping and reducing. When cropping a work of art, however, it's wise to get a living artist's permission. He may conclude that you ruined his proportions merely to accommodate your mechanical requirements. This art work should also be credited.

The average travel agency manager is not going to have to worry about *screening* photos, but it should be mentioned briefly that photographs, if reproduced directly from prints, would look like dark smudges. To preserve the gray values in these photos, a copying camera equipped with a set of screens is used to reshoot the original photo. These screen break the photo into a picture made up of a series of dots, called a *halftone*.

The screens are designated according to the number of dots they produce per linear inch. For newspaper, for example, a 65-85 line screen is used, producing fewer dots further apart. This is because newsprint tends to blot and a finer screen would run together. For smoother paper, such as found in magazines, you use screens varying from 100-150 lines. Obviously, you can achieve more sensitive reproduction on the finer papers.

To see this, take a magnifying glass to any halftone in a newspaper or magazine and the dot structure becomes apparent.

The light and dark values in halftones are made possible because, in the photographing process, large dots are photographed on the negative where the light is strong and small ones where the light is weak. When ink touches these dots on the plate more adheres to the larger surfaces and this creates the illusion of tonal graduation.

The Brochure

If ads start with thumbnail sketches, then brochures begin with folding paper. You try to decide what size brochure you want and how you want it folded. Figure 8-6 shows a few of the options.

The size of the brochure is going to be determined by how much you have to say and how much you want to spend. You could end up with a twelve-page booklet, composed of three single-fold pages, or you might be satisfied with a single sheet, printed on both sides, and not folded at all.

Keep in mind that, when you go to larger booklets or brochures, you move by fours. You can't really decide to have 9 pages. You go from eight to twelve—unless you want to do something fancy, like a *gatefold*, which is an extra two pages that swing out as an extension of another page. Even then, you're at 10, and not 9. Better, however, to stick with multiples of four.

When a brochure is printed, the pages are not printed one at a time. They are probably printed eight pages at a time, maybe sixteen pages, sometimes four pages. These pages are assembled in a certain rotation that makes for proper final order after folding, and printed in one pass through the press. Ask your printer about this when you give him a job and he'll tell you how the pages lay out.

Why is this important?

Well, if you intend to use color on part of the booklet and not the other, it would be advantageous to know which pages worked together so that you could specify one form or the other. Figure 8-7 is one way that a sixteen-page booklet might be placed on the printing forms.

Obviously, it would be wiser to use all your color on Form A *or* Form B, rather than picking a few pages from each (unless, of course, economy was not your object.). This way, one side of the sheet need be printed in four colors. The other form would not require additional separations, plate, and press costs. Incidentally, even when you use a four-color press, there are still other color costs to consider, as we'll see in a moment.

Another thing to discuss with your printer, especially when you are considering doing an off-size brochure, is the question of the most economical use of paper. Remember that paper comes in large sheets, like 35" x 45", or

Figure 8-6

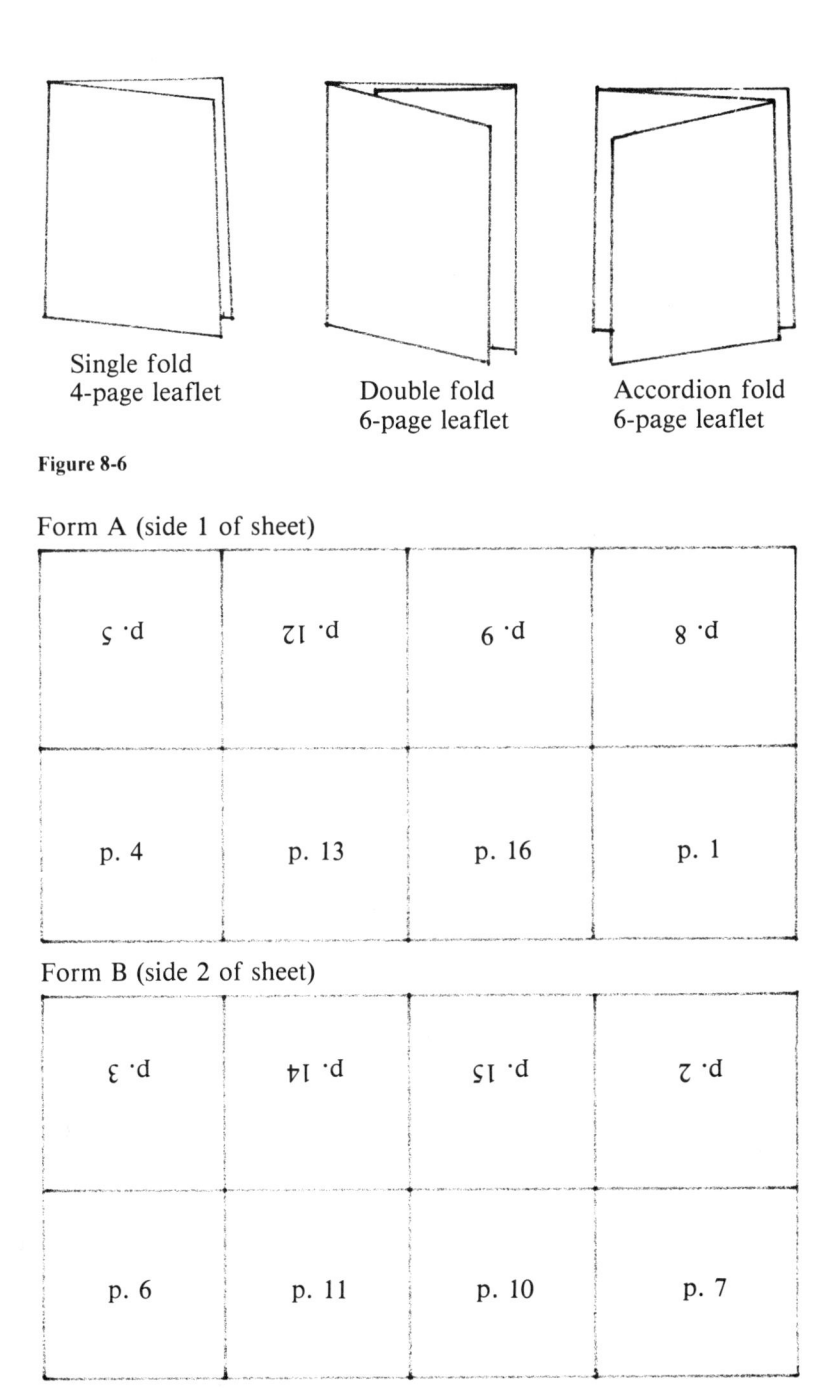

Single fold
4-page leaflet

Double fold
6-page leaflet

Accordion fold
6-page leaflet

Form A (side 1 of sheet)

p. 5	p. 12	p. 9	p. 8
p. 4	p. 13	p. 16	p. 1

Form B (side 2 of sheet)

p. 3	p. 14	p. 15	p. 2
p. 6	p. 11	p. 10	p. 7

Figure 8-7

25" x 38", or 17" x 22". Consider the number of pages of the size you want that will cut out of the large sheet, without leaving a lot of waste paper. If your page size were 8½" x 11", for example, you could get 4 sheets out of the 17" x 22" sheet, but if you increased your page size to 9" x 12", you would get only 2 pages out of the same sheet, and leave a lot of waste paper.

The Dummy

The layout for a brochure (or folder, or leaflet, or booklet) is called a *dummy*. The dummy is prepared so that you can experiment with different designs, and so that the printer will have a guide when he prints your piece.

Again, you might doodle on some small pages first, just to see what you might want to put into the brochure. Then, if you know what you're doing, you'd get a piece of the same paper you intend to print on, and do your sketching on that. If the dummy is for a small leaflet, you'd fold the paper first, and then indicate illustrations and type. If a larger booklet will be the result, you'll go page by page.

Anyone who begins working with dummies eventually devises some shortcuts. For those not gifted with artistic talent, for example, there is always tracing paper, which can be used to trace art or photos, or to serve as a guide for tracing typed lines. This traced page can then be photocopied, giving you a firmer paper to work with. Do this for every page, pasting succeeding pages back to back, and joining other pages with transparent tape.

For example, in a sixteen-page booklet, you'd paste the cover (p. 1) to page 2, and page 15 to the back cover (p. 16). Then you could join these two dual pages by scotch tape. Do the same for pages 3-4 and 13-14, and lay these on top. Piece by piece you build the book. If you wish, you can staple the entire booklet at the crease.

This isn't the way an artist would do it, but it works well for an amateur.

You can also paste on to the dummy any regular items you have on hand, like your logo, or a piece of art, or some standing type that can be used again. This, too, is the place to show samples of type or color.

The copy for the brochure, like the copy for an ad, goes on separate sheets, which are keyed to the proper dummy page. Artwork and photos are similarly keyed so that they can be properly positioned.

The important thing to remember is that the dummy is a *guide*. You're not going to print from it. It's just to show the printer what you want the brochure to look like. He'll provide you with a proof of the brochure before he prints it so that you can see if it resembles what you had in mind.

After the printer has the dummy, copy, and illustrations, he follows the same routine as in ad production—setting type, pasting up, showing a proof, making a plate, running the job. He also has to handle the illustrations and work within an color restrictions or paper requests that you submitted.

Final reminder: The more you can do and the clearer you can make your wishes known (by clean and accurate copy, and a workable dummy, and specific color and paper specifications), the less risk of disappointment.

Using Brochure Shells

Tourist offices, carriers, and certain resorts may supply the travel agency with a brochure *shell*, a folder with some photos or artwork already on some of the pages, but with space for the agency to add its own information or illustrations.

Let's say you planned a Rhine cruise. From one of the ship companies or from the German tourist board, you might be able to get shells which had color photos of Rhine scenes and, perhaps, even an attractive headline. You would then add your specifics, like dates, and day-by-day sightseeing, and conditions, and, perhaps, information on the tour leader.

You could, of course, receive a shell which had nearly everything in it, including the itinerary. You might then add only very little copy.

The advantage of using a prepared shell is that you save on paper, illustrations, and gain the advantage of color while adding only one color for your copy.

Creating the Brochure

Brochures should invite reading. Take a look at the racks of brochures in any travel agency. The good ones snap right out. That's a start—but the inside must maintain this same level of interest.

The cover of any brochure is something like a billboard advertisement, featuring a minimum of copy and a strong illustration. Its purpose is to arouse curiosity and get you to continue reading.

The initial inside page sets the theme, perhaps in summary fashion, or gets the story going. After that the details are communicated in logical and colorful fashion, using a lot of subheads or illustrations to break up the pages. You may proceed page by page or treat the entire inside as a single sheet and carry the copy completely across it. The prose must be terse, informative, and compelling. Just as a good salesman intrigues a prospect with product benefits before spelling out the cost, so a good brochure emphasizes the delights of any tour before adding such mundane items as price, baggage requirements, and passport information.

Again, like the sales pitch, there should be an unmistakable close, and a means of responding. A coupon could be enclosed, or a return envelope supplied, or at least a phone number and address featured.

Collect a handful of brochures that appeal to you—and analyze them. What makes them special? Is it the attractive graphics, or the crisp copy, or the manner in which the entire booklet flows? Figure out how they accomplished this effect—and try it yourself.

Color Reproduction

You need not be expert in rendering color or producing color, but you must be able to recognize the difference between good and bad color work. Notice, for example, how important color is in depicting food. A steak on the grill can't look too light or too dark; it must have just the right shades of red and dark brown. A washed out photo of a Mexican fiesta also loses its

130   TRAVEL AND TOURISM MARKETING TECHNIQUES

Figure 8-8   Some examples of the many shells available from airlines.

charm. And a brochure printed on a sickly green or deep purple stock is a certain loser.

Admittedly, color work is not a major concern of the individual travel agency. Few of their ads are in color and even the company newsletters tend to be just black on white. The color brochures are generally supplied, and their colored billboards rarely use more than a few basic colors. Still, it helps to have some idea of the way in which color is printed, and that's the reason for this brief section.

In reproducing a color photo, you start first with a good picture. If the slide or color print or color transparency is weak, regardless of dark room magic, the result will also be weak.

Assuming the original print is good, here are the steps that go into reproducing this in a color ad or brochure.

First, the picture must be separated into the three primary colors (magenta, cyan, yellow) plus black. This is because each color will be printed separately, using a separate plate, for a total of four plates.

You separate out the magenta or red by shooting the color transparency with a camera that has a green filter over the lens. Why green? Because it is a combination of blue (cyan) and yellow, so it filters out these two colors and allows only the red to seep through. The blue is achieved by using an orange filter; and the yellow by using a purple or lavender filter. The black plate is composed largely of highlights to achieve definition.

New developments in color separation, including laser beams, are becoming more common today.

On a regular press, then, the yellow is usually run first, the paper dried, then the red press run occurs, another drying period, then the blue run, drying, and finally the black. It's obviously important that, during all these press runs, the *register* be perfect, meaning that each plate fits perfectly with the previous one. Otherwise, you would get a shaky-looking result with garbled colors.

As mentioned earlier, there are also four-color presses which can accomplish all of the above with one pass through the press. And there are fast-drying agents to speed the drying process.

If properly done and printed on high quality paper, the end result should mirror the beginning photo.

The above explanation refers to four-color work. For two-color work—like black and red—you do two passes through the press, specifying the areas you want red, and those you want black. For example, you might set a headline in red, or a piece of art in red, and keep the type black.

You could also specify a *duotone*, a combination of black and one other color to give your halftone a different look.

Keep in mind that color is a sensitive medium. It may seem like an artistic idea to put one of your halftones in black and green but imagine how the faces of people in the photo are going to look. Also keep in mind that type must be *read*. If you put it in green or light blue, it may be difficult to read. Red could be hard on the eyes.

Tint blocks—a light color screen behind type and/or illustrations—may sometimes be very effective. For example, many companies, in producing their annual reports, find that a light screen behind some of the columns of figures helps to set them off and also relieves the monotony. Again, however, you must be certain you can read the copy. A screen that is too dark or type that is too light, or the use of two colors that disappear into one another—these destroy readership. You can specify how dark you want the screen by asking for anything from a 10% screen (very light) to a 90% screen—the next thing to a solid color, or solid black.

You can buy colored stock (paper) in many shades or you may also print the shade you want on the paper, producing the same general effect. You can then add other colors to this colored stock, using the same good judgment you'd use in papering your home. Lavender on tan is not very appealing, but dark brown on tan could be. Bright reds and greens are always going to look like Christmas so, unless that's the effect you want, better try something else. Collect pieces you admire and check with your printer about duplicating these color combinations.

But caution is the watchword. A poor color job is worse than a poor black and white job—and much more expensive.

Newspaper and Magazine Reproduction

As stated earlier, magazines normally use a paper that has a much smoother or glossier finish than newspapers. This makes you ad look sharper and your color look richer. It will also keep your ad around longer. After a certain number of uses in the newspaper, you'll see letters start to fill in or break down or look muddy. At that time, you should get a new cut, or plate, and furnish it to the paper.

Although newspapers have come a long way in the past decade in the use of color, they are still very much limited. Again, the porous paper is the reason. They must stick with primary colors and fundamental combinations. Even then, it's risky. Two-color work, however, often looks quite good, and is worth trying.

Some advertisers print their own ads on glossy stock and then supply them to the paper for inserting. This insures better quality color, but you have to have enough pages in your insert to make it worthwhile, and you still have to pay a fee for inserting. You'll notice that, in the past decade, the use of inserts in newspapers has increased significantly. There has been very little published research on this subject but some advertisers—like discount chains, and nationwide department chains, and film companies, and others—evidently find these very effective. Few travel agencies have tried this method, because of expense, but it might be worth experimenting with on an annual basis.

When considering reproduction in either newspapers or magazines, be certain you read their mechanical requirements for insertion. This information may be found on their rate cards or in Standard Rate & Data Service publications. You'll learn what sizes they want, how the publication is printed (letterpress or offset), what they need from you (plate, cut, velox proof, camera-ready copy), what their deadlines are, and similar data.

Some Final Print Production Tips

1. Develop your skills as a proof reader. If possible, catch errors in the initial typed copy. The further along you get in the production process, the more expensive it is to make changes. Read the printer's proof carefully. It's easy to miss words with transposed letters, words that read properly but are not the right words, and words which appear in headlines (which are often ignored). It's a good idea to have someone read the original copy as you check the proof. A "typo" which hides as you search for it, inevitably looms large when it's printed.

2. Be certain you allow sufficient time for the printer to do your work. If you ask him to work nights and weekends in order to meet your deadline, your costs escalate.

3. Be certain that everyone who has to approve the project does so in the beginning stages.

4. Be curious around production people. Ask questions; watch. See how they do things, what shortcuts they take, how they save money.

5. Realize you cannot attain the impossible triad of *price, speed,* and *quality.* If you want speed and quality, the price goes up. If you want speed and economy, the quality suffers. And so on.

Questions and Exercises

1. Define the following terms:
   a. Thumbnail sketch   d. font
   b. Impossible triad   e. dummy
   c. pica
2. How many picas are there in four inches?
3. Based on this chapter, list five errors that could increase printing costs.
4. Using a tour brochure, write 100 words of copy about a specific trip. From a type book, select a typeface and size you want. Determine how many lines will be required to fit those 100 words, in the typeface you've chosen, into a copy block 15 picas wide. (Incidentally, some type books run pica rules across the bottom of each page to help in measurement.)
5. Pick a photo out of a magazine, then show how you would enlarge or reduce this, making clear what you intend as the ultimate result.
6. Pick another photo and show how you would crop it to make a more effective picture.

Case Problem

Select a travel ad from a newspaper or magazine. Make a six-page dummy for this particular tour, indicating what will be on each page, but do not write any copy. You should indicate headlines, illustrations, where the copy blocks will be (using lines or a rectangle), and subheads or page breakers, and what the colors will be.

CHAPTER NINE

Producing Radio and TV Spots

Radio and television are two media that are not used enough by travel agencies and, when they are used, the commercials are often poorly produced and fail to take full advantage of the medium.

The assumption in this chapter is that the particular agency does not have a large production budget, so whatever it produces must be done economically. Obviously, if money is no object, you can hire the talent, create your own special music, and even shoot on location in some exotic tourist haven.

For most agencies, however, the production of broadcast and telecast materials has to be spartan. There are ways to produce acceptable radio and television spots without spending a ton of money.

The Idea

First you need a good idea—a good idea that fits with radio or television. It's not enough to merely translate print copy to these media and feel you have created another good advertisement. Each medium is different, and each requires it own *kind* of idea.

From this basic idea, you write the script, keeping in mind the *sound* qualities of radio, and the *visual* qualities of television.

Radio

Radio is written for the ear—and that can sometimes be a blessing. Bagpipes, for example, instantly suggest Scotland. You don't have to show Edinburgh Castle or the Trossachs. The listener creates his or her own images. Think of all the sounds that work for travel advertising: surf, a ship's whistle, sound of a plane taking off, roulette wheels, laughter, glasses tinkling, animal sounds, the San Francisco trolley bell, sports crowds, the sizzle of a steak, and thousands of musical items.

You can create pictures with sounds—and with words.

> Your Italian dining room captain makes a gracious host.
> His domain abounds with gourmet delights: Duck a la

Bigarade. Fettuccine Alfredo. Or, if you're in a hometown mood: a juicy, top sirloin. A vintage wine from our star-studded cellar makes a perfect companion.
(*Princess Cruises*)

To really see Mexico City is to be there on a Sunday . . .
to stroll the winding paths of Chapultepec Park . . .
to float along a canal in a flowered boat at Xochimilco . . .
to get up early and be the first to see the day's array
of funky junk on sale at La Lagunilla . . .
(*Travel & Leisure* magazine)

You try to create an atmosphere, a mood, and you sneak up on the listener with the practical information.

Radio Formats
There are a number of different ways to write a radio spot. Here are a few of the more common formats:

• *The Straight Sell.* This is a spot where an announcer merely delivers the copy, without any special effects or dramatization. With the right announcer for the right product, this can be quite effective. You've heard many of these.

"This week only—a chance to see an exciting new film on the Philippines—thirty minutes of lavish color, haunting island music, and unusual adventure. Your local Travel Mart invites you . . . "

• *The Testimonial.* Many advertisers find this to be a most effective method of advertising, but few travel agencies employ it. Obviously, the better known the person giving the testimony, the more effective it will be.

"Like many of you, I thought a cruise would be dull—that I'd be bored and itching for something to do. Let me tell you, I found that there's plenty to do. Like the first evening . . . "

The person giving the testimonial may identify himself or herself, or he or she might just remain anonymous. Identification usually adds to the credibility.

• *The Dramatization.* This format sets up the premise of a story. It may simply be a travel agency talking to someone on the phone, or two friends visiting about a trip, or a wife talking over vacation plans with her husband.

FRANK: What's so special about the Eden Club?
MARGE: Golf?
FRANK: Golf?
MARGE: Two 18-hole courses laid out by that one—you know, who won all those tournaments last year?

• *The Musical.* Sometimes the whole spot could be music, like Coca

Cola's eminently successful "I'd Like to Buy the World a Coke." Sometimes a jingle may be only part of the spot, with copy filling in.

OPENING JINGLE: *"It's More Fun in Fresno"* (8 seconds)
ANNOUNCER: Fresno even sounds like fun, doesn't it? And here's why!
....
So call Travel Systems today. 999-0830. That's 999-0830. Travel Systems.
JINGLE UP AND OUT.

- *The Promotional (or Institutional) Spot.* This is the sort of spot that talks generally about the travel business, or why you should use a travel agent, or what is happening to fares, without pitching a specific tour or other offering. It is supposed to garner good will, and help with name identification.

- *The Humorous Spot.* Humor is tough to write, but very effective. People like to repeat jokes, right? They also repeat funny commercials, and that's a big plus. The problem is that few people can write humor. Some ads think they're funny, but they're not. They age fast. Others are genuinely comic, and you turn up your radio when they come on. Stan Freberg, Bob and Ray, Stiller and Meara—these are the big names. You remember those Blue Nun commercials, or the Lanier Dictating Machine spots? Great Stiller and Meara routines.

You have to be careful when writing funny things about travel. There are ample opportunities for humor in travel but some aspects won't stand for much kidding. Stan Freberg produced a rare dud when he began a commercial for a West Coast airline with the line: "Hey, you there with the sweaty palms!" You may joke about your fears with friends, but you don't like to be reminded of them in connection with an appeal for flying.

There are all sorts of combinations of these spots, and there is also what is called the *integrated* spot, which consists of an advertising plug within a program. Arthur Godfrey used to do these, and some local disc jockeys also make what seem like spontaneous comments about a product or service. If the personality involved has a following, this isn't a bad way to go.

Some Tips for Radio Writing
1. *The opening and closing statements must be strong.* You want to grab the casual listener's attention. Imagine yourself in your car, with the radio on, or working at night with the FM tuned in. Because radio is a "background" medium, you may be completely unconscious of exactly what is being played or said. Consequently, you have to get the listener to pay attention. Some sound effects or music may do it, or some statement that produces an instant alert.

"Who said you can't afford to go to Europe?"

The closing statement must also have something memorable about it. What do you want this listener to take away from this commercial? A name, an address, a phone number, a date? This will probably be a repeat of some earlier information, given here to reinforce the message in the mind of the audience.

"So, don't delay. Send today for your free European booklet. Just write: Travel Management Inc., 300 North Arapaho, Kingston, North Carolina. That's . . . "

2. *Keep your sales points to a minimum.* Radio messages can't be complicated. Ask yourself what the basic information is that the listener *must* have. Be sure this gets across, and don't clutter the spot with too many details. Citing a long list of cruise options, cabin assignments, and prices is hopeless on radio. Sell the scenic and recreational aspects, and have them write or call for specifics.

3. *Keep a conversational tone.* You're not selling a potato peeler or circus tickets. Travel ads should normally sound relaxed, unhurried. The delivery should be personal, warm, and intimate, not frantic and hard sell. Talk to the individuals; don't shout at the mob.

One of the problems here has to do with *timing*. Don't write forty seconds of copy for a thirty-second commercial. This forces the talent to read rapidly. Write a little under, and give the announcer a chance for a more conversational presentation.

When timing a spot, read it aloud to a stopwatch. And ask one or two others to read it aloud. This way you'll be sure it works before taking it to the sound studio or radio station, and you'll avoid having to cut or pad while paying for studio and talent time.

Remember that your aim is *persuasion*—and you rarely persuade people by screaming at them, or pushing a string of words in their direction.

4. *Avoid cliches and superlatives.* Descriptions like "fun in the sun on the sandy beaches," and claims like "the greatest tour ever assembled" won't convince many listeners. Be believable.

5. *Create pictures with words.* This was mentioned earlier, and it's a tough discipline, trying to be picturesque without being trite, corny, or too ornate. Foreign words sometimes add color, and so do specific names instead of general names. It's better to say "motor beneath an arch of linden and aspen" than it is to say "drive underneath arching trees." Help the listener to *see* what you're talking about.

6. *Repeat important words.* One of the values of radio as a medium is its ability to instill memorable phrases or jingles. Don't be afraid of saying something more than once. Perhaps it's a deadline date for signing up, or a one-time price, or a phone number. Give it to them at least a couple of times. You'd be amazed at how many times you can mention a company name in a thirty-second spot without being obnoxious.

7. *Be careful of tough things to read.* Certain words are hard to read, particularly in combination with other words. Saying "underneath the arching aspen" might be a bit tricky for most announcers. Try this one: " . . . welcoming in the winter wonderland". Or this: " . . . a memorable

journey aboard this spotless twin-screw cruiser." Adverbs with *ly* in them can be difficult like *extraordinarily,* and so can words with *un* in them, like *unenviable* or *unavoidable.* Some good words are rough in themselves (*applicable*), or look like other words (*ingenuous*), or sound like other words (*health* for *help*). Some hiss—*sensational*—or pop—*power-packed performance.* Try your commercial aloud and get a substitute for those terms which sound bad on the air.

8. *Use short words and sentence fragments.* Not always, of course. But sentence fragments usually work. Short, terse statements. And short words. Better to say a "great tour" than a "stupendous tour."

9. *Indicate punctuation.* When you have words that are *particularly* important, and which need to be *stressed,* underline them. When you want to indicate a pause use a double hyphen:

"... but three days on Maui--now that's something special." Be certain that the person who will read the copy understands what it means, and the way you want it to sound.

10. *Dialogue must be credible.* If you have two or more people conversing, their speech must sound *something* like normal speech. You can't put hard sell in the mouths of ordinary folk, and you can't make the exchange too obvious.

FRANK: Oh, I see you are carrying a Travel Systems travel folder, Marge.

MARGE: Yes, I always go to Travel Systems because they have installed new CR2 instant retrieval ticket systems which save the customer a minimum of forty minutes on each ticket purchase, whether domestic or international, thus speeding up the entire ticketing process and providing for instantaneous confirmation at hundreds of carriers across the globe.

You want to reach through your radio and clobber people like this.

Some Other Attention-Getters
Listen to some radio commercials yourself and note the different methods they have of forcing you to listen. Kids' voices, for example, or unusual accents, or sound effects (like the Alka Seltzer fizz), or a familiar star's voice, or a tie-in with current events, or a real-life interview, or some different musical effects.

You can slow down or speed up the voices; you can set a familiar tune to a different tempo; you can be funny; you can hitchhike on a station feature. One travel agency has a standing order with a local radio station to broadcast a Hawaii commercial everytime the temperature gets below 20 degrees or there's a snowstorm.

Producing the Radio Commercial
Once you have the script in hand, you should determine what music or sound effects you want, and what kind of talent you want as the reader(s). If you can bring all of this with you to the recording session, so much the

better. The more you have set, the shorter the recording time should be.

Sound recording studios and radio stations also have talent pools and music and sound-effect libraries. You can call and ask if they have something that will work for you. The radio station announcer may also serve as your announcer. The problem with this latter idea, of course, is that it doesn't permit contrast, and the voice may be too familiar.

You bring enough scripts to give one to the talent and the engineer, at least. And you'll want your copy to check as the spot is being recorded. In the simplest of setups, the announcer may be in one booth, and the engineer (with the music and sound effects on record or cassette) in an adjoining booth. The engineer cues the music and the announcer, and puts the spot together, timing it, and adding the appropriate sound levels. When it's finished, it's played back for you. If you're not satisfied, you say what you don't like, and they try again. After you approve, as many *dubs* of the commercial will be made as you need to supply all the stations you will be using.

If you have enough money, of course, you get even fancier. You might have your own special jingle written. There are companies that specialize in this work, charging anywhere from $1,500 for a jingle based on a tune already in stock, to $7,500 and up for an original tune to fit your specific lyrics.

You could also have a live orchestra or combo at your recording session, for which you would pay the musicians' hourly rate, and probably double for the leader. You would also pay for rehearsal time.

The normal routine would be to bring the script, use the station or studio music and effects, and pay for an announcer and for the extra dubs. While the radio station may provide studio and engineering services free (if you are advertising on that station), the recording studio will bill you for studio time. The recording studio, however, normally gives you a superior product.

The Script

Script copy is double spaced, with the name of the character (or announcer) on the left and capitalized. Sound effects (sometimes written SFX) and music cues are also capitalized.

If you understand the technical jargon (like FADE UNDER when you want the music to go below the announcer's voice), that's helpful. However, if you can just describe the effect you want, the engineer will provide it.

Figure 9-1 is a sample radio script, intended for a thirty-second spot.

Actually, this script is fairly tight, so you see that you can't get a lot said in thirty seconds. If you have a longer message, buy a sixty-second spot.

You'll note in this spot these particular items:

• The talent is directed to read the spot in a "cultured accent." You would select this talent on the basis of his being able to accomplish this.

• The pronunciation of *Guinness* is given. This should be done for any word that may be unfamiliar to the talent. It's better to take a chance on

TRAVEL TOURS INC. JOB NO.: 112
(Address & Phone) DATE: 10/14/80
  TALENT: Rob Harris

DESCRIPTION: 30 SEC "LONDON THEATRE TOUR" (Radio)

SOUND: "RULE BRITANNIA" WITH LONDON SYMPHONY. UP, THEN UNDER.
SOUND: ADD APPLAUSE, THEN UNDER. CONTINUE MUSIC UNDER.

HARRIS: (CULTURED ACCENT) One of Travel Tours' most exciting and educational trips—the annual London Theatre Tour. See five plays, featuring such stars as Peter O'Toole, Vanessa Redgrave, and Alec Guinness (GIN'-ESS). Plus these Travel Tour extras—six nights at the palatial Roxbury Hotel, a "pub crawl," a sumptuous London Broil Dinner, and two days of sightseeing. The curtain's going up, so call Travel Tours, 666-4200, or visit the Travel Tours office in the Northroads Mall.
SOUND: APPLAUSE, THEN MUSIC UP AND OUT.

Figure 9-1

being too careful, than on allowing a mispronunciation to creep in.
• Remember that numbers take as long to read as words. The reading time for a phone number is the same as reading seven words.
• Note that Travel Tours was mentioned four times without annoying the listener.

And, Finally . . .
- Be careful of slang or cute language. It's dated rapidly.
- Clever music and sound effects don't replace good writing.
- You may sometimes get a radio tape from a carrier, tourist office, or resort, with room left at the end for your identification or *tag*. This can be recorded as above, or left to the booth announcer at the radio station to add each time the spot is played. You have to notify each station of this in writing, as accompaniment to the tape.

Television

It should be unnecessary to remind script writers that television is a *visual* medium, and not merely radio with pictures. You *think* in terms of pictures; you *visualize* the commercial. In fact, whenever you can let a picture do the work of words, let it!

Keep in mind that the average over-18 viewer sees about 3½ hours of television daily. A lot of commercials pass in front of his or her eyes. Many of them aren't even seen, not only because they've taken this opportunity to leave the room, but because they simply don't register, even when the person is watching the set.

Very little of most television commercials is retained. Half the time the viewers can't recall the sponsors of a commercial they admired. A fourth of the time they credit a favorite spot to the wrong sponsor!

What you have to say, then, must be interesting, compelling, and memorable. You also have to realize that you have interrupted the program the viewer was watching, so your commercial should be somehow rewarding and worth the intrusion.

Television Formats
- *Straight announcer.* While this may be okay on radio, it is usually dull on television. They refer to this as "talking heads" and there is little excitement in this approach. As with any statement, however, there are exceptions. And sometimes a straight announcer may provide a contrast with flashier commercials.

- *The testimonial.* Probably more effective on television than on radio. Now you can *see* the person giving the testimonial, and this has added credibility. To liven up such a spot, you can place the person giving the testimonial in some interesting setting.

- *The demonstration.* One of the major advantages of television is that it can *show* as well as tell. If you were doing a spot on how fast your computers can process a ticket request, why not show the computer in action? Or, instead of talking about cruise accommodations, show the viewer an animated chart. Contac shows the tiny capsules, and some antacids let you watch their product dissolving stomach problems. Travel has many things (and more appetizing things) to display.

- *The "slice-of-life" commercial.* This kind of spot features people talking about a product or service, like housewives discussing coffee or laundry. Or an agent and a customer visiting about travel options?

- *The story.* Some commercials tell a story. Some of the award winners from companies like Coca Cola and Kodak unfold a complete tale in thirty or sixty seconds, with very few words. Other stories take the form of a crisis (like stale sandwiches or spotted glasses) which is solved by a product (often presented by a company symbol, like Big Wally or the Man from Glad). Travel agencies can also use this approach to convince the viewer of the convenience of using a travel agent, or the ease of getting a car rental.

- *The Musical.* This is generally expensive and wouldn't be used much by the travel agency, although it could be effective for the cruise line or airline. In this commercial, the music is the star, and there may be a chorus line, or a pop singer, or some other talent. It's like thirty seconds from a Broadway musical.

- *The Special Effects Spot.* And here the star is the camera. You drop a man into a speeding car, or make a travel brochure appear suddenly in the hands of a would-be tourist, or freeze the character in midair. You've seen this often in commercials that feature expanding washing machines, tiny announcers walking inside car engines, or the Jolly Green Giant patting a cartoon child on the head.

Some of these are difficult and expensive; others are simple enough to be handled by your local TV studio. If you have something like this in mind, visit with the producer-director of the TV station, explain the effect you want, and let him suggest ways to accomplish it.

Take a couple of rather simple examples:

In the case of the would-be tourist who suddenly finds a travel brochure in his hand, all you do is tell the empty-handed actor to freeze in position, stop the video tape from rolling, walk on the set and put a brochure in his rigid hand, then start the camera again. Presto; the brochure pops into his hand as he registers astonishment.

To place a grown man inside a toy car, you'd use two cameras, one on the toy car, and the other on the man, who would be standing in a light blue *chromakey* area. The light blue disappears when you blend the two camera shots together, so all you see is the man. By varying the focal length, you can make him small enough to seem to be sitting inside the toy car.

Talking hamburgers and sprouting flowers, as in the McDonald commercials, however, are a more demanding assignment.

Some Tips for TV Writing

- *Understand the way the camera operates,* knowing what it can do and can't do. In fact, be conversant with the entire production technique.

- *Don't include too many shots or scenes.* The viewer can't handle multiple changes within the brief framework of a TV commercial.

- *Consider color,* and the way things will look in color, since a majority of American homes now have color television.

- *Favor close-ups over long shots.* Remember that virtually all television sets are relatively small. If the picture shows a distant figure, this makes it harder to catch expressions—even harder to understand. Use both types of shots, of course, but the close-up should dominate.
- *Remember that you can superimpose type over the screen.* Type can be used to identify people speaking, to caption a scene, to highlight a price, and, certainly, to feature a firm name, address, and phone. It doesn't hurt if the audio also repeats this information as it's being shown.
- *Match sound to the pictures* (or *audio* to *video*) *but let the pictures carry the weight of the message.* What is being said must tie in with what is being seen, but there is no need to explain something which is perfectly clear to viewers watching the tube.

The Storyboard

After the script is written, there is often another intermediary step before production. It's called the *storyboard*. This is a visual depiction of the commercial, much like you'd see in a comic strip. It enables the producer-director to better understand what you have in mind.

Sometimes the picture panels in the storyboard are drawings, sometimes they are photos. Polaroids, for example, work quite well. The storyboard may be rough or finished, depending on time, money, and who needs to see it.

You can buy special sheets which have a space for the picture and for copy under the picture. This makes the whole process simpler, since you can type the attendant copy into the space beneath the appropriate illustration.

The Television Camera

In a sense, the lens of the television camera does what the eyes does—only more. It can move up and down, the way the eye would examine a person from head to toe. This is called a *tilt* and instructions would be to "Tilt up" or "Tilt down." It can move from side to side (a *pan*) and you can write into the script: "Pan left to right" or "Pan right to left." You also have a *follow pan* where the camera follows a moving object, with the background blurred; or a *whip pan*, where the camera whips across the scene, causing a blur. This latter technique is sometimes used to show change of time or locale.

The TV camera also has a *zoom* lens which can move toward or away from a scene or person, either slowly or rapidly. This really replaces the *dolly* shot, where the whole camera was pushed forward or pulled back, but there could be occasions when you would also want to dolly.

A *truck* shot is one where the camera moves laterally on wheels, either following some action or covering a wide panorama. And a *crane* shot is one where the camera is overhead, on a crane or *cherry picker,* in order to shoot down on the subject.

The Shots

A number of different terms are used to describe the size of the subject you are viewing on your screen.

Beginning with the extreme long shot (ELS), which would encompass a whole panorama, like a chase scene in a western, the script can call for any of the intervening shots, such as: long shot (LS); medium long shot (MLS); medium shot (MS)—which would take in a person's whole body or most of the body; medium close-up (MCU)—a torso shot or closer; close-up (CU)—tight on head and shoulders; extreme or tight close-up (XCU, ECU, TCU) —face only, or even a portion of the face.

Directors also talk about full length shots and reverse shots (showing you what the actor is seeing, at 180 degrees from him), and *package two shots* which means an actor and a package (or brochure), and many other variations.

Again, the travel agent needn't be familiar with all this technology, nor does he or she have to write these directions into the script. As long as the script explains what is required, the director can call for the appropriate shot.

The Editing Possibilities
When the director sits in the booth helping you to put together your commercial, he or she can speak directly into the earphones of two or three (or more) cameramen who are on the studio floor. The director can also see what each camera is seeing. These images are shown on a bank of monitors in the booth. Transitions from image to image can be handled in a number of ways.

The technical term for these transitions is *optical effects*.

• *Fade In and Fade Out*. The director can start from black and then bring in a scene, or go from a scene to black, before introducing the next scene.

• *Dissolve*. Instead of going to black, one scene merges momentarily with another. The blending may be rapid or slow, depending on the mood or pace you desire.

You sometimes have a *match dissolve* where the object in one shot nearly matches the shape in the next. A globe, for example, may turn into a rotating tire.

• *Wipe*. There are dozens of variety of wipes. A new picture can come down like a curtain, across like a sliding door, explode from the center, sneak in diagonally, and so on. Some of these may be artistic; some are merely cute.

• *Miscellaneous*. You may use fast motion or slow motion; you can split the screen so that you see both ends of a phone conversation; you can have multiple images, like the reflections of a score of mirrors; you can use the chromakey mentioned earlier; you can superimpose type or other objects over the scene.

Sound
Although the visual aspect of television is the more important, sound remains a key element. You indicate this on the script just as you do with radio. The two most often used terms are: *direct sound* or *voice over*. Direct

sound or *lip sync* means that the person being shown is doing the talking, with his speech synchronized to his lip movements. The sound is usually recorded at the same time the film is shot. Your normal TV drama uses this technique. Voice over means that an off-camera voice is doing the narrating, such as you experience when watching many documentaries—or, for that matter, most travel films. This is added later.

You'll hear people say that something is "out of sync" when the lip movements don't match the sound exactly. And the expression "wild sound" refers to just leaving the mike on to catch things like traffic or cocktail party noises or jungle birds. These may be used later as background for other sounds.

Ways to Produce TV Shows
In the early days both television shows and TV commercials were done live. There was a certain spontaneity to this which was exciting, but there was also the possibility of error. Easy-to-open doors stuck; ice cream melted in the dish; actors missed cues.

Today, with rare exceptions like the occasional spot on the *Tonight Show,* all commercials are taped. Most shows are also taped, except for fast-breaking news and live sports.

When you tape a commercial, you can play it back immediately, to see how you like it. You can then make changes, running the tape back, and rerecording on it. Or you may just cut a second tape and compare the two spots.

Besides live television and the nearly universal tape, you also have film. Some commercials are filmed and then transferred to tape, because film is a bit more versatile and a bit sharper. Tape is improving every year, however, causing more and more shows and commercials to be made this way.

Film can be run on a separate projector and just integrated into whatever spot you are producing. Slides, too, are placed on a special slide chain which can also be made part of the tape during the production process. Before this was possible, the cameras would use photos which were placed on *tote boards* and illuminated, so that the TV camera could take a picture of it and transmit it live.

How Commercials Are Produced
As mentioned above, you could film an entire commercial and put it together in a film studio, using film editing equipment, just as they do to produce Hollywood films. Or you could take some film to the TV studio and have it transferred to tape. Or you could tape the whole show in the studio, using live performers, and integrate appropriate films, slides, art, or music.

For most travel agencies, the routine will be more like this:

- A script is produced.
- Talent, props, and music are obtained.
- A time and date are set for recording at a local TV studio.

- The director takes your script, rehearses the talent, cues the appropriate music and visuals, and puts the tape together.
- If you approve of the results, he can make you video tape dubs, just as the sound studio produced sound tapes.

If you use an advertising agency for your radio and television, it would perform *all* of these chores for you, from script to seeing that the right video tapes arrived at the right TV stations. You could go along to watch production if you wished, but the agency would handle the details.

The Script

While the script is the first thing that is done, it seemed appropriate here to discuss it last, since a knowledge of production must come before any sensible writing can be accomplished.

There are some variations on the way a television script might be written —particularly if film is involved—but the usual format is to place the *video* (or visual) instructions on the left of the script sheet, and the *audio* portion on the right, thus:

LONG SHOT OF MATTERHORN   ANNCR: One of the world's most talked-about mountains, the fabled Matterhorn . . .

Sound cues are also indicated under audio, are printed in capital letters, and underlined (at least this is one good method to use).

Figure 9-2 explains one way the previous radio script on the London Theatre Tour might look on television.

A Few Added TV Tips:

- If you are supervising production of the television spot, make certain everything is ready to go—AND rehearsed—before you go to the TV studio. Television studio time is expensive.
- When the producing is being done, the director is in charge. You don't stand over his or her shoulder making suggestions. When the spot is taped (and before it's taped), you can make your suggestions.
- You have to develop a sense of time. For example, how long do you want "Rule Britannia" to be up at the beginning of the previous spot? If the talent is holding up a brochure, how long does he have to hold it in order to have it register with the audience?
- You also have to develop a sense of timing. When you get experienced at writing a spot, you can get pretty close to the right time for a 30- or 60-second spot, without having to do a lot of cutting or padding.

There are some guidelines. You can figure about two words a second, straight talk. But there are so many variables. You may use a character voice that requires a slower delivery. Or you may want to leave a picture up with only music behind it. It may take only a few words, for example, to describe a film sequence that takes 10 minutes on the screen. If you write 60 words for a 30-second spot and 120 for a 60-second spot, you'll be close— but FULL.

TRAVEL TOURS INC. JOB NO.: 113
(Address & Phone) DATE: 11/30/80
  TALENT: Rob Harris

DESCRIPTION: 30 SEC "LONDON THEATRE TOUR" (Television)

VIDEO	AUDIO
NIGHT SHOT OF LONDON'S STRAND (SLIDE #1) Dissolve to: MONTAGE OF LONDON PLAYBILLS (#2) Dissolve to: HARRIS, IN TUXEDO, ON STOOL, IN FRONT OF PLAY POSTERS	SOUND: RULE BRITANNIA SOUND: APPLAUSE. FADE MUSIC UNDER HARRIS: (Cultured Accent) One of Travel Tours' most exciting and educational trips—the annual London Theatre Tour. See five plays, featuring such stars as Peter O'Toole, Vanessa Redgrave, and Alec Guinness. Plus these Travel Tour extras—
CUT TO SLIDE OF ROXBURY HOTEL (#3)	—six nights at the palatial Roxbury Hotel—
CUT TO SHERLOCK HOLMES PUB (#4)	—a "pub crawl"—
CU LONDON BROIL DINNER (#5)	—and two days of sightseeing.
CUT TO LONDON TOWER (SLIDE #6) Dissolve to:	—a sumptuous London Broil Dinner—
MCU HARRIS. START ZOOM PAST HIS HEAD TO PLAY POSTERS. SUPER SIG AND PHONE	The curtain's going up, so call Travel Tours, 36-4200, or visit the Travel Tours office in the Northroads Mall. SOUND: APPLAUSE, THEN MUSIC UP AND OUT.

Figure 9-2

- Remember that TV screeens have rounded edges, so don't put important things like a phone number or address in the corners.
- Any visuals you use must fit the dimensions of the TV screen, meaning that they must have a ratio of 4:3. So the artwork could be 12" wide x 9" deep, for example.

Another consideration when using slides is that slides on the horizontal axis work best. Those which are taller than they are wide either get cropped at top and bottom, or they have empty space on either side.

- The commercials you see for national products cost anywhere from $15,000 to $150,000 to produce; sometimes more, rarely less. While the travel agency can't compete with these types of expenditures, it still must produce something that doesn't look sick by comparison.
- Don't forget to figure production costs in your budget.
- Test your commercial before an audience before it airs. Take them to the studio to see it. Pick average prospects, not your own employees. See if they understand it; if they remember it; if they regard it favorably.

Radio and Television Travel Shows

There are few travel shows on radio—but that doesn't mean the package isn't adaptable to radio. With a little thought, a good radio show could be developed, built around interviews, traditional music, and straight information. This might not sustain for thirty minutes but a series of five-minute programs works well, and would not be difficult or expensive to produce.

The advantage of a show over a commercial is not only length, but, if done properly, a greater amount of interest and credibility.

Travel programs on television are fairly common. Some of them are expertly done; some of them are hardly more interesting than your neighbor's vacation slides. The secret is to minimize the individual or group conversation, and to show visuals that have impact. Coming up with an interesting topic is also a plus. The alert agent will tie the program into current news events, or into seasonal travel, or into a topic that has a high degree of appeal.

Many films are available, of course, but these should be screened in advance for their appropriateness. Slides can be used effectively, and it helps to bring lively people on the set for interviews. Generally speaking, it's wise to center each program on a specific topic (like shopping in Europe) or on a particular geographical area. This keeps the show tight and logical.

Some travel show sponsors have films and slides they've shot, or they use film and slides shot by friends and associates. These visuals must be good. You can excuse some poor photography when you are explaining your efforts to friends in your home, but this program is being televised to thousands (well, you *hope* there'll be thousands) of strangers.

The same principle applies to the question of who should host the show. If you're good at it—and some travel managers are—then you can run the program yourself. If not, then get a professional announcer. Think of the terrible work done by many used car dealers.

If you use a professional announcer, you or someone from your staff

Figure 9-3 Vacation America, Inc. uses a storyboard as the basis of a print ad.

should also be highly visible on the show. Perhaps you are interviewed at the beginning and end, or you help out with interviews of guests. The trained announcer then carries the show but the viewers get to see what you look and sound like.

A typical travel show on television *could* go this way:

1. Opening segment of introductions and setting of the stage for this specific program.
2. A film or slide sequence,
3. An interview.
4. More film or slides.
5. Closing segment and wrap-up.

You must be certain you get strong agency identification. This can be accomplished by designing a set which features your company name and logo as background, by occasional *supers* (type superimposed over an image) on the screen giving your name and title, and by periodic reminders by the announcer.

Most travel shows occur at hours when the audience potential is lowest—in non-prime time. This could be on Saturday or Sunday mornings, perhaps, or on early weekend afternoons. This is less expensive for the agency and the local station may also be quite happy to have this show aired—if its quality is acceptable.

You can help build an audience by doing some direct mail to your list of clients and prospects, informing them, perhaps monthly, of upcoming programs.

The show will likely be taped a few days in advance. As with commercials, the more you can do in advance to insure a professional look, the better off you'll be. Sloppy performances connote a sloppy business.

Questions and Exercises

1. List four tips each for writing radio and television spots.
2. List four formats each for radio and television commercials.
3. Find three print ads that contain colorful language which has the facility of conjuring up images.
4. Monitor television for a couple of nights, selecting two spots which run frequently. Jot down the number of scenes in each commercial; the types of shots used; the type of optical effects used; plus any other production problems or techniques you notice.

Case Problem

Select one tour brochure and do the following:

1. Write a thirty-second radio spot, using the format in this chapter, and indicating what music and sound effects you want.
2. Using the same basic material, write a television spot, indicating both audio and video. This, too, should be thirty seconds.

CHAPTER TEN

Those Other Advertising Media

Provided you have the money, there are dozens of other ways to advertise besides the regular print and broadcast routine. Some of these—like direct mail—could prove the best approach in a specific advertising campaign.

Out-of-Home Media

This category sums up all of the poster-type advertising, from illuminated billboards to taxi-top cards. Virtually all of these (with the exception of ads inside subway cars or on bus benches) share the problem of allowing little time for reflective reading. That's why all of these considerations must go into the creation of such posters:

1. *The background should be simple.* A background that is too busy, having a lot of conflicting elements, will cause problems for the reader. He or she will find it difficult to focus attention on the ad, and difficult to make sense out of the copy.

2. *Copy must be short.* Use as few words as possible. Many designers recommend keeping the number of words under five. In any event, this is no place for a long message.

3. *Use short words.* An occasional long word may be an attention-getter, but it's wiser to use crisp Anglo-Saxon prose, rather than long Latinized terms.

4. *Make the illustrations large.* Tiny, subtle illustrations won't work. You need SIZE! If you're advertising a flight to Hawaii, you want a plane that covers most of the board, or a huge palm tree, or a larger-than-life King Kamehameha. A few coconuts hidden in a corner will be lost to motorists or pedestrians.

5. *Make your colors bold.* There are exceptions to this, but pastels look washed out, and they fade quickly. Stick with the bright, vibrant hues.

6. *Employ readable type.* The few words you use must be in a typeface which is large enough to read, and in a design that is easy to make out. An

elaborate script, or an Old English type, might be impossible to interpret when you're driving past.

7. *Be sure your agency is identified.* Small logos and indistinct type are bad news. In fact, the two things that should emerge from any poster are—your name, and the reason to patronize you.

Producing the Poster

Although this may not be accurate for every type of poster, billboard, or bus card, you'll find that a preliminary sketch with a ratio of 1 to 2¼ will suffice. A workable size for such a sketch, for example, might be 4" high x 9" wide. When you come down to creating the art work which will be used to make the poster, however, you'll want to be certain what dimensions are more exact. Check this with your sign company.

To produce the large billboards you see on your highways, the original artwork is put into a projector which blows it up to the exact size needed, projecting it against the paper, wood, or metal surface on which it is to be painted. For painted boards, the painting can be done right on the surface which will be used. For paper posters, the drawing is used to make stencils, and the individual panels for the finished billboard are *silk screened,* meaning that paint is squeezed through the stenciled areas, much as you might stencil an article at home.

If a large number of boards will be used, it is usually cheaper to lithograph them, rather than using the silk screen process.

When the individual panels are finished, they are brought to the site and *posted.* Each panel is glued on, overlapping its neighbor, to give the appearance of one solid advertisement. The names of billboards are somewhat confusing, since a *30-sheet poster,* for example, contains not 30 panels, but only 12.

A Few Reminders

- At a distance of 100 yards, a 24-sheet poster (9' high x 20' wide) appears about as large as a postage stamp.
- Severe changes in weather affect outdoor posters, washing out colors and, on metal boards, popping out the paint.
- Be conscious of the placement of colors, since a little thought while laying out the poster may save several extra press runs.
- If a large photo is used in an outdoor advertisement, the local sign company may not be able to handle it. This may require the work of an out-of-town specialty shop, with a large enough camera to tackle this assignment.
- Perhaps even more than any other medium, the outdoor field demands early and close consultation with the ultimate supplier.

Transit Posters

Posters in subway stations, and cards ranged above subway car windows, have been staple advertising items for many years. Those inside the cars have the advantage of a captive audience who may have little else to do but read these signs. Those in subway stations get through traffic as well as local pedestrian traffic—but need to be larger.

Cards on the top or rear of taxis; on the side, back, front, and interiors of buses—all these have value, particularly as name recognition tools. Frequency of use is a major factor in creating a lasting image.

Displays and Exhibits

There are occasions when a travel agency may be called upon to locate an exhibit or display in a convention hall or shopping mall. The primary need for display materials, however, is likely to be within the agency itself.

Many agencies have a cluttered look. There are a hundred different items, from wall posters to ship models, all scattered about with no apparent sense of proportion or organization. The trick is to look exciting without appearing messy. This takes someone with as much courage at removing items as in adding them. Frequent changes are healthy and attractive.

The rules for organizing exhibits are little different than those for good layout. You want harmony, sequence, and balance. You want the proper proportions, an appealing mixture of colors and themes, but without any sense of confusion. The travel office should seem a warm, interesting, *and* efficient place to visit.

When exhibiting your wares elsewhere, keep in mind that a static exhibit is the least likely to attract a crowd. Something should be going on. Perhaps it's a continuous slide show, or travel films, or a contest in which the passer-by can participate, or some live entertainment. A display of pictures may attract an audience on a slow day, but not when there are other more exciting choices.

Novelties

Many firms specialize in the production of novelty items, from pens to shoehorns, and from emery boards to golf tees. There are literally thousands of items to choose from, and one of the desirable skills to have is the ability to select something appropriate.

You always want something that is useful, so that it will enjoy a long life, and something that allows for decent name identification. You may also have to consider things like cost and distribution.

Matchbooks are one of the more popular novelty items and certain match companies can produce a variety of containers, from the standard folder to cylinders (for products like Campbell Soup and Babo) to boxes shaped like trucks or buildings. Not much copy can be placed on these items, but, again, a strong agency identification is paramount.

Before ordering any novelties, the agency should also consider how it is going to distribute them. Will they be sent through the mail to regular customers? Handed out over the counter? Given away an an open house?

Failure to plan wisely can result in a large and useless inventory. Many politicians, for example, have invested in thousands of bumper stickers, only to discover that they can't get them circulated or used.

Directories

Directory advertising isn't usually too imaginative and perhaps it doesn't have to be. After all, when you use a directory, you're already looking for certain information. You've by-passed the attention and interest and desire factors, and are looking now for credibility and action factors.

You would tailor your ad somewhat to the directory. If you were advertising your agency in a Chamber of Commerce directory, you might want to stress commercial accounts more. In a telephone directory or city directory, you're appealing to a general audience and will include more general information. The ad should still be attractive, and it should anticipate the usual questions an information seeker has in mind. Obviously, it should also include a striking agency identification.

Check you ad and copy periodically. Advertisers have a tendency to repeat their directory ads year in and year out. This can result in stale promotional efforts. Keep the ad looking fresh.

Direct Mail

There's no question that this advertising medium has considerable potential for travel agencies—but they must know how to use it properly. The secret of direct mail is to pinpoint just the right audience, tailor a message that's perfect for them, and give them a means of responding.

Direct mail advertising isn't the same as *mail order advertising*. The latter term is used to define ads which sell goods through the mail and appear in newspapers and magazines, usually including a coupon. Those late-night record album offers on television are also mail order ads.

Neither is direct mail advertising synonymous with *direct advertising*. Direct advertising encompasses direct mail, but also includes merchandising across the counter, door-to-door giveaways, street vendors who distribute samples, and other forms of reaching the consumer directly.

Direct mail refers to advertising which reaches the consumer through the mails, instead of appearing in the mass media, like newspapers or television.

Since 1928, direct mail advertising (IF it meets the postal requirements) is entitled to a bulk rate. Generally, either first- or third-class mail is used.

Over 30 billion pieces of direct mail are sent to people in the United States each year, which means that every man, woman, and child receives over 140 individual pieces annually. Some days 5 or 6 pieces may be in the same mail. That emphasizes the need for a package that *stands out*.

Mailing Lists

The first consideration in the use of direct mail is the development of a workable list of recipients. You want a list of the *best* prospects, those most likely to be interested in that particular mailing piece. If you could do this with scientific precision, no other advertising medium could touch direct mail. You'd be able to talk only to those potential consumers who had the desire and the means to respond to the offer.

Such precision, however, is rarely possible, although experts in this field obviously do better than amateurs.

A West Coast educational TV station, seeking to raise funds for its programming, bought a list of Cadillac owners, since that group has traditionally been associated with affluence. Response was poor. Then they tried Volkswagen owners and the response was much better. In retrospect, there's a kind of logic to this. Undoubtedly, more Volkswagen owners watched (and, therefore, valued) educational television than did Cadillac owners.

If you are setting up a direct mail list for a travel agency, where would you begin?

For commercial accounts, you'd certainly want a list of the major business firms—preferably one which listed the chief executive, or his or her secretary, or the purchasing agent. If there were a purchasing agents' group in town (and if they typically bought travel packages), you might work from that list.

But how would you go about securing regular clientele?

You might be able to get a list of those who travelled anywhere during the past two years. Or you could get a list of subscribers to travel magazines. Or you might work on occupational lists containing people (like secretaries and teachers) who generally travel. Or you could build up a "Gold Coast" list of the city's wealthiest individuals.

If you were trying to sell a special tour—say, a two week tour of Ireland —you could direct your mail campaign at ethnic groups, like the Ancient Order of Hibernians, or Friendly Sons and Daughters of Saint Patrick, or members of the Irish American Cultural Institute. You might even do a telephone check of those with obviously Irish names.

For a tour of Europe's Catholic shrines, you might try to locate lists of the congregations in all the Catholic parishes. A trip to Israel would seem to indicate a list of synagogue memberships, plus members of the Jewish community center and B'nai B'rith.

Most of the larger communities have direct mail houses, and these firms both broker lists and perform all the mailing mechanics (addressing, stuffing, mailing). You can also buy lists from national firms, if they meet your need. Lists are sold for so much a thousand names (usually anywhere from $25 a thousand to $50 a thousand), and are available on magnetic tape or labels, or in some other form.

If the list is large, it's wise to buy a few thousand and experiment with them, before committing for larger numbers.

Let's say you have available, in a large city, a list of 50,000 persons who have purchased air tickets over the past two years. You should buy 5,000 of these and do a pilot mailing. If the response is good, buy another 5,000. If it remains good, then buy the list.

What do we mean by *good*?

Well, this will vary. On a *cold* national mailing for a charitable cause, sponsors might be happy with a 1.5% return; 2% would be very good. With a local mailing, returns could be higher, depending on what you were selling. This argues again for selectivity. If you could isolate the best prospects among the 50,000 above, that would be the thing to do.

These lists are *cleaned* regularly, meaning that they are checked for changes of address, deaths, and the like.

For a number of these lists, the sender is required to supply a sample of the mailing package.

The Direct Mail Package

Typically, a direct mail package would include a letter, a brochure, and some method of responding—either a return postcard, or a blank and a return envelope. These will be enclosed in a mailing envelope.

The *mailing envelope* should be attractive enough to encourage opening. Sometimes a window envelope is used, with an address or part of a message showing through; sometimes a provocative statement is printed on the outside envelope. The sender's first step is to get you to open the envelope. As more and more direct mail advertisers use up the bag of possible tricks, it gets increasingly difficult to be different. Many readers can quickly spot insurance plans or retirement plans or swatches from cloth coats, and they may discard the package without peeking inside.

Travel has a lot of romance and interest going for it—naturally. So the travel manager should not be too hard pressed to come up with a gimmick line or illustration that arouses curiosity.

WANT TO KNOW WHAT FRANCE HAS BESIDES POSTCARDS?

THE TRUTH ABOUT THOSE $5 A DAY EXCURSIONS.

LET ME TELL YOU WHAT HAPPENED TO ME IN NAPLES . . .

The *letter* may not have as many readers as the brochure but, if the prospect really gets interested, he or she will take time to read everything.

The trick to writing decent letters is to write to *one* person. After all, only one person gets each one. It must sound personal and human. Machines are available today that also make the letter *look* personal and individualized. So, have a typical prospect in mind and sell him, using the language that will excite and interest, and remembering to answer all his potential questions—or almost all of them.

Using a *narrative hook* to start a direct mail letter is a good technique. After all, addressing a stranger as "Dear Friend" is a little awkward, and "Dear Sir" is too formal, and often inaccurate. Many letters begin with some quote or statement to entice the reader to read on. For example:

"I'd never use a travel agent because they cost extra."

WRONG!

or

What's the biggest travel bargain
available today. It's Russia.
Surprised? Then read on.

The first paragraph in these letters is usually short, as are most paragraphs, but they should be varied for length. You don't want the letter to look like a child's primer, nor do you want any huge paragraphs which scare the casual reader. Break up the bulky paragraphs and use frequent subheads to separate the page(s) of copy. The idea is to make perusal seem simple and pleasant.

Sometimes you may center some of the information, like this:

>Here are three reasons to visit Russian NOW!
>- Fares are low.
>- The weather is perfect.
>- It's the festival season.

Like radio, direct mail features strong opening and closing paragraphs. Don't just wander into the reader's consciousness, and don't hang around after you've said everything. You must be truthful and factual, avoiding "advertisingese" and obvious exaggeration.

You must also keep the prospect's interests in mind. What are his or her possible motives for making this journey, or for using your other travel services? Speak to these. Emphasize the benefits. This helps build credibility along with desire.

Remember to convince the reader about the *differences* involved in doing business with you. There are always alternatives. Even if you are the only agency in town, there is the choice of going directly to the carrier. You must show the prospect why your route is better.

Generally speaking, you don't tell the prospect the entire story. You want to save something for the office visit or the follow-up brochure. Cramming *every bit* of information into the direct mail piece could turn off the prospect. Perhaps he or she thinks February is a bad month for a vacation, or reacts against a visit to the Berlin Opera, or fails to understand one of the expenditure items. You should not be devious, but you should leave *some* unanswered questions. A face-to-face conversation can alter many presumed biases.

The exception to this rule is when direct mail is used as *mail order* direct mail, meaning that it must do the whole job and get the order. This would be rare in travel advertising, since the prospect does have many things he or she wants to know, and because the cost of a trip is usually significant.

The format of the letter can take any form, just like an ad. It can be chatty and conversational; it can tell a story; it can be a testimonial; it can be humorous, flat-out factual, or very soft sell. You select the method which seems best for this particular story.

Finally, there are mechanical ways to get attention as well. Some letters are typed using different colored ribbons for emphasis, or they include the prospect's name (inserted manually or automatically), or they employ gadgets.

Gadgets are items which are stuck on the letterhead or somehow made part of the package. Many are corny—like a toothpick and the accompanying admonition to "Pick One of Our Sensational Tours." Or a tiny shoe with an adjacent statement reading: "You'll get a boot out of our low prices." You've seen swatches of cloth, paper clips, pennies, and other items used. If you go the gadget route, here are some cautions.

- You can't send unlit matches or sharp objects through the mail.
- Be sure the gadget is appropriate to your message and not just an unrelated gimmick.
- Be sure it isn't offensive to anyone.
- Be sure it sticks or stays in place.
- Make certain it doesn't overpower the message.
- If possible, make it something useful.

If there is a *brochure* as part of the package, it should complement the letter, but also have its own appeal. Remember, when printing, that the brochure, letter, and other inserts must fit whatever size external envelope you've chosen. Usually this will be a #10 envelope, the long envelope which measures approximately 9 1/2" long x 4 1/8" high. You also have to be conscious of weight, if mailing first class.

Brochures are sometimes mailed by themselves—as self-mailers—with the back page blank for the address of the recipient.

The *return card* or *envelope* needs to be convenient and comprehensive. The convenience is for the prospect; the comprehensive aspect for you. You try to make it as simple as possible for the individual to reply. A prepaid envelope is the usual choice. The respondent needs to put no stamp on the envelope; *you* pay the postman (1980 rates) 27¢ per returned envelope. While this is more expensive than a regular 15¢ stamp, don't forget that you pay *only* for those which are returned.

The 15¢ stamp on the return envelope, while more expensive and wasteful, might be better in some instances—such as with a small and tested mailing list. The stamp somehow seems more urgent than the prepaid statement.

You can also request that the post office notify you of changes of address, in order that you may make the appropriate change in your mailing list. For this service you pay 25¢ per change. This may seem like a lot of money but it's not when you consider what it costs to get a new and untried name. Most mailers would not make this request each time they mailed, but would confine the change-of-address request to one or two times a year.

The return card should have sufficient information on it to allow you to properly handle any further business. The name and address, certainly, along with the zip code, should be included, but you may also have a place to check for certain brochures the prospect would like, or tour dates he or she would prefer. On some occasions, you may request a phone number, and you could solicit other information as well.

Obviously, you must have an efficient system for processing all of the direct mail responses. If someone replies right away and then waits for weeks or months before getting the brochure or a call, you've probably lost that prospect.

There are many, many other facets to this complicated but effective medium of direct mail. Here are merely a few last minute reminders:

- Plan your printing well ahead, making sure that all pieces of the package fit together, and arrive together. If you are hung up waiting for one element, that's just as bad as having nothing ready.
- All of the principles we applied earlier to advertising and to good printing also apply here.
- Stay abreast of postal regulations, which change fairly often.
- You can build your own lists from directories, club membership lists, trade publications, distributors lists, government files, trade show registrants, and from many other sources, including your own mail responses. Or you can go to mailing houses, to list brokers, or even secure a list of lists from Standard Rate & Data Service.
- When examining a list for potential use, you'd want to know how it was compiled; how old it is; how often it's updated; how it's maintained; what selectivity you have; and how well it did for others.
- Certain trends, like more working wives, the move to suburbia, a larger senior citizen population, and rising income and educational levels all enhance the value of direct mail.
- Your lists must be zip coded.
- You'll need a system for keeping the names. Computer with punched cards? Metal plates? 3" x 5" cards?
- First class has prestige, speed, and a better track record for results. But it's expensive and might be impractical.
- Make direct mail part of your total advertising campaign, and not something separate. Each medium should reinforce the other.
- Remain attuned to timing requirements, attempting to have your direct mail hit when the prospect is in the most receptive mood, and when the other direct mail competition is lightest.
- Don't try to get too many items into a single mailing. You're usually better off if you concentrate on selling one major item, or on promoting one travel area.
- Take advantage of appropriate flyers and stuffers which are supplied by tour operators, carriers, and other suppliers. You may need to add only your name, address, and phone number. These serve well as interim mailings.

Questions and Exercises

1. On your next drive around town, take note of the billboards which attract your attention and try to determine why. Location? Color? Message? Illustration? Originality? Your own preconditioning?

2. List five tips for producing effective billboards.

3. List three novelties that would be appropriate to the travel agency business, coin a message for each, and tell why you selected these items.

4. If you planned to sell a raft trip down the Mississippi, from Minneapolis to New Orleans, what sort of considerations would you have in compiling a list? Set down five categories of individuals you feel might be prospects, and tell why.

Case problem

For the raft trip described above, write a direct mail letter which will be directed to the list you have chosen. Write the entire letter. Also *describe* (but do not develop) the other items which will be part of this package.

CHAPTER ELEVEN

The Advertising Campaign

No single ad ever does the whole advertising job. It would be a naive travel manager who would insert one small ad in the local paper and then sit back and wait for the business to roll in. As many professionals point out, the individual ad is like the tip of the iceberg; perhaps it's all you see, but, hopefully, behind it is a larger campaign and an entire marketing strategy.

Planning the Campaign

As with any enterprise, planning ahead—often *far* ahead—is the first step in an advertising campaign. Laurence Stevens, writing in *The Travel Agent,* suggests preparing a schedule of the products you know you'll advertise during the coming year.

> Prepare a schedule of what product you intend to advertise on a certain date; example: February 1: Cruise; February 8: Hawaii; February 15: Florida; February 22: Mexico; February 29: Europe OTC, and so on. You know your own market best, so plan the timing of your product advertising accordingly. By the end of January you should have prepared your complete advertising schedule through the end of April, and have made tentative schedules for May, June, and July.

Stevens' planning advice also includes allocating file space for advertising ideas—including those supplied by people like tour operators and cruise lines; better utilization of co-op advertising, where tour operators furnish materials which the agency then personalizes; better analysis of past performance, profiting from errors and lapses.

Here are some practical steps to be taken when planning for an advertising campaign.

1. *Determine the current marketing situation.* This means an analysis of ALL the factors affecting your ability to market an individual travel product. You look at the nature of the item, the receptivity of the potential audience, the competition, past performance, current factors which could enhance or inhibit sales, and anything else that will influence your ability to deliver that service to that prospect.

2. *Establish some advertising goals.* You should have some idea of what you hope to accomplish through your ad campaign. This may be expressed

in numbers of tour members who need to be signed up, or in the number of inquiries which should be generated, or in some other measurable form. You may have other advertising goals, too, like making customers aware of new office hours, or the establishment of a branch office, or the agency's ability to handle some new sorts of assignments.

If you get really scientific at this, you might even break down advertising expectations by media.

3. *Construct your advertising budget.* Once you have an idea of what you need to accomplish, then you can work on what it will take to get the job done. This balance is rarely ideal, since most agencies have to be a little thriftier than they should be. Agencies utilize a number of methods in arriving at a budget—some of them good, and some merely guesswork. You could build a budget around what you considered necessary to the success of the campaign; or you could construct it on the basis of competitors' efforts; or you might allocate a percentage of the anticipated profit to advertising; or you could break it down on a per sale basis, figuring the cost of advertising into every tour ticket sold.

Too often, however, the budget comes out of a consideration of "what we did last year" without much discussion of the wisdom of such a selection process.

4. *Development of media strategy.* This phase could wait until after the campaign theme was conceived, since the theme might have an influence on the media chosen, but media are frequently selected first, based on past experience about their individual effectiveness. You'd program so many newspaper ads; money for production and mailing of direct mail; perhaps some radio, television, or outdoor; and, on occasion, a category of *miscellaneous* for such things as parties or film rental and the like.

The media mix should relate to your established campaign goals. Those media which have performed best for this sort of travel product in the past should get preferential treatment; the remaining media (if you decide to use them) share the remaining budget.

5. *The creative phase.* While these other decisions are taking place, someone should also be working on the creation of the message. The creative people work on the overall theme, the copy platform, and the way this theme will be worked into print and broadcast media.

6. *Integration of all facets of marketing.* You'll want your direct mail to back up the mass media efforts, and you'll want all of the travel consultants to be aware of what is being offered so that they can respond to inquiries intelligently. If the agency has several branches, then each branch should be given sufficient time to develop its own local strategy. Any special events should also be made part of this timetable.

7. *Analysis of results.* Campaigns should be thought out completely before they are launched, checked while they are in operation, and evaluated after they are over. Every attempt should be made to make the analysis as dispassionate and objective as possible. There is no sense in kidding your-

self about results, merely to salve an ego. If you fail, you fail. Profit by the experience and try to discover what went wrong. Don't repeat the mistake.

In evaluating a campaign, remember that there are other reasons for failure besides the advertising itself.

The travel *product* could be at fault, either because it was over-priced, not competitive, advertised at the wrong time, or improperly conceived.

The *strategy* might have been wrong. Perhaps you over-reacted to competition, or pitched an appeal to the wrong audience, or started your ad campaign before your offices were geared up to respond.

You might also have failed in your selection of media, or neglected your follow through, or developed a premise that lacked credibility.

Hypothetical Campaign

Let's assume an agency wanted to concentrate on Hawaiian travel, perhaps as a tie-in with a football game involving the state university. Other agencies, of course, would be competing for the tourist dollars, so this would affect the strategy.

Here's one way the campaign might develop:

1. In marketing strategy sessions, the agency determines that it will focus first on alumni groups throughout the state; then on member's of the university's staff; then on non-alumni football fans; then on students. The decision is also made to move outside the usual geographical limits within which the agency operates, since the volume generated in the larger communities makes it possible to compete favorably with agencies in smaller communities. Servicing out-of-state people means beefing up the usual mail program, so that delivery of tickets can be insured. In this same session, the package is put together. The recommendation is for two options—five days in Honolulu, including round trip travel, game tickets, transportation to and from the game, some sightseeing, hotel, a few meals, and some extras; or a ten-day tour, which would also include two days each at two other islands.

2. Based on previous experience, the agency figures it can sell over six hundred tickets. This means early booking of space and carrier. There might be some easy block sales, so the advertising campaign is aimed at attracting at least five hundred clients.

3. In this instance, the agency decides to invest a certain percentage of the anticipated profits in advertising and comes up with an ad budget of $3,500, which is far above what they would normally spend but worth the risk because of past experience, and because of other factors (like a good team, an early and severe winter, and a solid economy).

4. The media will be varied. In addition to mentioning the trip in the regular Sunday section newspaper ad, the agency decides to run a second ad in the travel pages on Sunday, and one ad a week in the sports pages. These ads will begin two months prior to the reservation deadline.

Prior to this mass media campaign, a direct mail piece will be sent in cooperation with the university, to prime prospects (like alumni and season ticket holders), and ads will be scheduled for several of the game programs. Ads will also be placed in the student newspaper and in certain key papers outstate.

Ten radio stations were selected, based on their geographical reach, and announcements were programmed for the early morning drive time, and adjacent to the evening sportscasts. In addition, spots were scheduled on the broadcasts of three of the team's football games.

Television was used sparingly, with a thirty-second spot scheduled in the 10 P.M. sports news slot, for three nights a week, beginning two weeks before the reservation deadline.

Special flyers were printed up and distributed to the university's fraternities and sororities, and parents of team members were contacted by special letter.

Several football parties were scheduled in key cities in the state, where football films and films on Hawaii shared the spotlight.

5. After considering all the possible differences, the agency decided that the best thing they had going for them was the lower price for their tour package. They settled on that factor as their major selling point.

The creative department of their advertising agency (or the creative person within the travel office) came up with the slogan: ALOHA AND GOOD BUY! The copy platform stressed the many tour features at a low, low price. Readers, listeners, and viewers were urged to send for a descriptive brochure. The newspaper art featured a football decorated with a lei. This also became a concluding slide for the TV spot, with the address and phone number superimposed over it.

For the radio spot, the voice of a familiar sportscaster was used, backed by stadium sounds and Hawaiian music. The television spot centered on the island vacation sites, with football mentioned as a lead in.

6. Footballs and leis were displayed in the agency's three local branch offices, and, for two weeks before the reservation deadline, muumuus and Hawaiian shirts were worn by the travel consultants. Mini-luaus were staged in six outstate communities for community leaders and early registrants.

7. As the campaign progressed, a tally was kept on the number signing up, and the source of their information analyzed. Had the count been running behind expectations, the agency would have committed more money to the media which had been showing the best response.

Once the tour was over and things returned to normal (if that word can be used in the travel business), the original planners sat down to match their expectations with their results, trying to determine which things worked, and which things did not, and why. These conclusions were made part of a written report which was filed for future reference.

* * *

Obviously, while this selling job was going on, someone also stayed on top of hotel and charter space, and other details.

Questions and Exercises

1. Which method of establishing a budget do you feel is the most sensible? Why?

2. Find three examples of a single print campaign—not necessarily for travel, but for any product or service.

Case Problem

Select any tour brochure from the travel agency racks and build a campaign around it, listing these things:

1. Audience.
2. Choice of media to be used, and in what proportions. Give percentages.
3. List the timetable for the advertising.
4. State the theme, and write one hundred words of copy to show how this theme will be carried out.

CHAPTER TWELVE

Publicity and Promotional Techniques

Advertising is often complemented by public relations. This term—public relations—is frequently misunderstood, and even more frequently maligned. In some critics' eyes, it represents an attempt to make something bad look good. Nothing could be further from the truth. While there are inept and dishonest people in the public relations field, there are no more than in any other profession. Perhaps fewer—since the results of public relations are invariably open to public scrutiny.

A short definition of public relations is: "Doing good and getting credit for it." Both parts of that sentence are important. You must first do good, and then you see that this act is publicized.

Public relations (PR) differs from advertising in several ways. You pay to place an ad in the paper or on television, but you don't pay the media to print or broadcast news releases (although you probably pay people to write them). You have more control over advertising, too. Once the ad is accepted, it runs as you submitted it. Not so with publicity. It can be edited, severely cut, even dropped in the wastebasket.

Publicity—which is only *one* tool of public relations—is much more economical than advertising, has more credibility, and has the added advantage of possible placement anywhere in the paper, including page one.

Most practitioners of public relations would view their profession, however, not as a publicity generator, but as a management function, with all the facets this concept entails.

Looked at in its complete form, public relations involves detailed research, elaborate planning, a thorough knowledge of communication, and a precise evaluation. Just as the advertising campaign has its many levels and phases, so does the public relations campaign. The PR person studies the background of every problem, analyzing its causes, and searching out the experience of others; discusses possible alternatives before settling on a course of action; then initiates the action, either through publicity, or special events, or some other form of communication. And then the planners go over the strengths and weaknesses of what ultimately evolved.

Few travel agencies seem to take full advantage of the benefits of public relations, confining their efforts to an occasional party, some club memberships, and a few news releases. In actuality, the opportunities are unlimited.

Human Relations

The basis of good public relations is good human relations. While it is true that public relations is organized and planned—even calculated—the psychology on which PR programs are predicated is a determination of the motives and responses of individuals and groups.

This begins with an attitude. If the travel consultant feels harried and frustrated, this state of mind will be communicated to the clients. Each contact in an agency is a one-to-one contact. The client, consciously or unconsciously, is judging the entire operation on the behavior of the one consultant he meets. Therefore, this relationship should radiate warmth, interest, and efficiency.

In addition to personal contact, the travel agency conducts a lot of business by telephone. This is a trouble spot. One of the problems is volume. There are many incoming calls, plus clients at the counter, and, perhaps, representatives from tour operators and carriers on the premises. It's tough to field all of the incoming calls with dispatch and amiability—but that's what must be done. Curtness, long periods of waiting, cutoffs, confusion, lack of attention, lack of knowledge, failure to follow through—these are all errors that must be avoided. You can't score every time, of course, but it's just as easy to be pleasant as it is to be brusque. Your telephone voice should tell the other party you're glad he or she called and that you'll attend to his or her needs completely and accurately.

If you're going to succeed at human relations, you have to have some idea of what makes people tick. A course in psychology wouldn't be a bad start. Look back at chapter three. The things said there about individual motivation apply as well to human relations and public relations. The more you understand about *why* people do things, the better you'll be able to deal with others.

Community Relations

As with advertising, the goals of public relations involve the identification of certain publics to whom communications must be sent. Present clients form one obvious public; the media form another. Among the remaining publics, the community at large rates a major effort. After all, this is the place where you live and work. You're expected to be a good and a concerned citizen. This means some participation in the activities of the community, including club memberships, attendance at business and social functions, contribution to community causes, purchasing supplies locally, and general support for the aims of the community.

People are bound to have some impression about your agency. Either they like it, dislike it, or know nothing about it. The last two conditions are bad. You want to impart a positive feeling. You do that, not by one big campaign, but by consistent attention to playing the role of good neighbor.

This sort of reputation not only brings the routine customer to your agency, it also paves the way for easier access to commercial accounts.

One final caution. All of the socializing goes for naught, of course, unless the agency is well run, and has earned a name for congenial and effective operation.

Publicity

Public relations has myriad facets, many of which will be untouched in this brief chapter. They are the concern of the practitioner, while all these few pages attempt to do is outline some of the normal PR tasks which could be done beneficially by travel agents. It's unlikely, for example, that any travel agency would do any extensive testing on public attitudes, or on the viability of its communications, or on the community power structure. The basic activities will revolve around media communications, printed materials, and special events.

Publicity refers to news stories which originate outside the normal reportorial channels, and which are *placed* in the media by groups and individuals who have an interest in seeing this news promulgated. There is nothing wrong with this practice. In fact, a majority of news stories on the local scene stem from news releases submitted by persons not employed by the media. There simply aren't enough reporters to go around to cover all the possible events.

This doesn't mean that editors and news directors are sitting around waiting for news to arrive, or that they will be joyously noncritical about every news release that appears. They will try to impose the same professional standards they expect of their own staffs, with some *few* allowances for occasional amateur standing.

First, the person issuing a news release must be able to recognize news. Anyone can appreciate the fact that a big fire is news, or a major crime, but there are thousands of other things that also make news. For example:

- *Important names make news.* The Kennedys and Redfords and Naders of this world generate publicity, even when they do fairly minor things. Fame is relative, of course, and people who would make no national splash may succeed in getting local coverage. A state senator attending the opening of an agency branch office may be worth a few lines in the paper or seconds on the news. So might the departure of some local sports hero from your agency, with a couple of honeymoon tickets in his hand.
- *Unusual things make news.* A couple celebrating their fiftieth anniversary sign up for the "Swinging London" tour. That's news! You'd have to secure the couple's permission, of course, before releasing anything. Whole families touring Europe make news, and so do veterans returning to the site of their combat years, and individuals who opt for an individualized excursion to some off-beat area.
- *Current events make news.* Consider all the possibilities in this area. Readers and viewers are anxious to know about safe travel in world trouble spots; or concerned about the effect of devaluation of the dollar on their travel plans; or want to know about gasoline shortages and prices; or wonder if there are still seats available for the Olympics; or want to find out

when an airline strike will be settled; or would like some estimates on crowded holiday schedules; or are curious about some of the charter bargains. The travel agent has a host of chances to say things that interest the public.

- *Ingenuity makes news.* There are possible news stories all around you; it just takes a little imagination to see them. Suppose you did a survey of client needs and desires for future travel—this would make a news story. Whenever a little-known country makes the news, it's possible you have some staff member who's visited there and can be quoted. There are all sorts of possible ties with national and international stories.
- *Some regular events make news.* Whenever you have an open house, a special film showing, a change in personnel, an annual report that's published, a new service—all of these have news potential. All this takes is a little work and a little know-how, and it's well worth the effort.

The News Release

A news release doesn't have to be a creative work of art; in fact, it shouldn't be. What it *must* be is: *accurate, complete,* and *professional.* This is not an advertisement, so you can't use any puffery. Neither is it a chatty letter, so you can't use cute phrases or homey expressions. Remember that it's supposed to be *news.* You must include all the details and you must have the correct information. Supplying a wrong date or place, or a misspelled name, will make all your future stories suspect. Before any release is sent out it should be checked thoroughly for error, for statements that may be confusing, and for details that may be ambiguous.

The News Release Format

There is a standard way to write a news release, and sticking to this format is a definite plus. At least the news desk will give the story a look, figuring the person that wrote it probably also has news judgment and style.

Here are the elements of a news release:

1. In the upper left hand corner of the sheet, you should type your name, address, and phone number. This *identifies* the person who prepared the release and gives the editor or news director a contact if he or she wishes more information. If the letterhead already gives the address, the name and phone number will be enough. Sometimes PR people also list their home phone numbers. This is a nice gesture, and lets the media people know you will go out of your way to be helpful.

2. Beneath this identification, you supply the details about when the story should be released. This line is usually capitalized and underlined, although there are various ways to handle it. For most stories, you'd use FOR IMMEDIATE RELEASE, meaning that the news director or editor is free to air or print the story right away. If there is a certain time designated for this particular release, you would use that terminology. For example: FOR RELEASE FRIDAY P.M., AUGUST 14. This sort of restriction should be used sparingly.

3. Leave about two inches between the release information and the body of the story. This is so the editor can write his headline when the story is printed.

4. Even though you are writing about something purely local, it's a good idea to get in the habit of using a *dateline*. This means that the story should begin with the place of origin and the date it was written. Like this:

CLAYTON, MO. (August 14, 1980)- -

The place of origin may not always be the same as the place on the letterhead. A New York public relations firm, for example, may represent a Clayton, Missouri, firm, so the story on their letterhead might still bear the Missouri dateline.

The date is important, too. Suppose a story reads FOR IMMEDIATE RELEASE but the person to whom it's directed is out of the city for a few days. Later, that person has no idea how long the story has been around unless it's dated. Sometimes, incidentally, a story may be dated in the upper right hand corner and, occasionally, at the bottom of the story.

5. The news story should be typed, not hand-written. It should be an original or a xerox, never a carbon. A carbon tells the recipient he's second; a xerox or other machine copy indicates he was treated the same as others.

Margins should be wide (1½"), copy double-spaced, and at least 1½ inches left at the bottom of the page. This is so the editor can edit.

The paragraphs should be indented about seven spaces, and the pages should look clean, and be free of strikeovers and messy erasures.

6. News stories themselves are structured in what journalists refer to as the *inverted pyramid,* meaning that the important facts are all up front, in the first paragraph of the story. This is not a short story with a surprise ending.

The first paragraph answers the questions of who, what, where, when, and why (the *five W's*) and, sometimes, how. The remaining paragraphs in the story spell out other details in logical fashion. Sentences should be short and punchy. Ditto for paragraphs. You must avoid flowery language, lines that read like advertising, and copy that works hard to make a dull topic sound like news.

7. If possible, confine the news release to a single page. If you go to extra pages, be certain you don't carry part of a paragraph over to the next page. Splitting paragraphs or sentences is not a good idea. At the bottom of this page, write "-more-" to indicate that additional pages are to come. On the upper left of the next page, identify the story in a word or two, and write the page number like this: 2-2-2-2.

When you reach the final page and come to the end of the copy you indicate this by:

-END-
or
###
or
-30-

The designation *-30-* is the most common form. It's an old typographical and journalistic way to note a conclusion.

8. Before you let the story out of your hands, check it again for accuracy, spelling, grammar, completeness, and tightness.

Robert T. Reilly
HDR Travel Agency
2243 Imperial Mall
Northroads Shopping Center
Altoona, Pa., 16606

PHONE: (814) 551-6797 (OFFICE)
(814) 551-3962 (HOME)

FOR IMMEDIATE RELEASE

    ALTOONA, PA. (August 14, 1980)--An Open House to dedicate the new wing of the HDR Travel Agency has been scheduled for Friday, August 24, starting at 1:00 p.m. and running until 5:00 p.m. Located in the Northroads Shopping Center, the expanded facility will occupy 1200 feet of floor space on the second level.

    Loretta Copper, manager of the HDR Travel Agency, said the new addition will enable the firm, currently the largest in western Pennsylvania, to introduce completely computerized service.

    "We will be able to process tickets in a matter of minutes," said Copper, "when it used to take nearly an hour."

    Visitors to the Open House will be able to view the new computers, see a continuous series of films on European and South American travel, and sample hors d'oeuvres from the recipes of six foreign countries.

    Manager Copper stressed that all Altoona residents are welcome.

    --30--

Figure 12-1

For radio and television, it's a good idea to write a different and shorter release, keeping in mind that these news releases must be written so that they can be delivered, rather than printed. As we saw earlier, writing for the ear is somewhat different. Since time is a more restrictive factor than space, you must keep releases for radio and TV brief. For television, you would also try to come up with some visuals, such as a color slide of the new facility, or an architect's drawing of the addition.

Here are some additional tips for dealing with the news media:

- Treat all media equally. Don't play favorites in giving out information.
- Respect deadlines of the various media. Don't deliver stories to the media when it is too late to get in that day's paper (if that is your intent) or to make that evening's newscast.
- Don't try to get your material used through pressure or pleading. News should sell on its own merits.
- You may be able to get marginal news stories, which would not be used regionally, into a local paper. This is because the local angle makes it news. If a travel agency in Omaha, Nebraska, opened a new wing, that's not news in Altoona, Pennsylvania, but it is in Omaha.
- Be cooperative with the media, offering help when they request it, and passing along news tips you may have, even when they have no connection with your business. Don't try to bury an unpleasant story; just get the complete truth out quickly.
- Don't use colored stock for news release letterheads—at least not shocking pink, or some other flashy color. Also avoid too much ornamentation in the letterhead design.
- If your release includes photos, note this on the release, usually at the bottom, thus:

ENCLOSED: Photo of new HDR wing.

You may also include a caption.

- Keep your mailing lists up to date. Sending a news release to the attention of a person who hasn't been with the TV station for five years marks you as an amateur. Be sure you know the proper name of the travel editor on your local paper.
- Newspaper photos should be 8" x 10" glossy prints, in good focus, and with strong contrast for better reproduction. TV stations prefer slides and film. In both cases, strive for interesting subject matter.

Events for the Press

Don't assume that the news media are anxiously awaiting a chance to attend a news conference; they're not. Only call a news conference when you can't disseminate the information any other way, or when the story will really be enhanced by on-the-spot photo coverage, or when a newsmaker is passing through your city and will be available only for a brief time.

Some firms have periodic press parties for the media. Large travel agencies might want to try this but it makes little sense for small or medium size agencies. These parties are merely good will gestures, without a news reason. They can be expensive and they are not always that well attended. Perhaps an occasional luncheon with those who write travel pieces would be much better.

The Press Kit

If the travel agency does conduct a press conference—let's say for the announcement of a grand opening—consideration must be given to a place (probably the agency itself), a time (a couple of hours before the deadline of the major daily is a good rule), and an invitation list (usually all those who write travel news, plus, in this case, business reporters or general assignment reporters).

You'd also want some kind of *press kit*. These kits may contain such items as a news release, fact sheet, photos, and other information which will help the news person write a good story.

The Travel Article

A majority of travel articles, in all media, are staff written. Travel articles from syndicated sources would make a distant second. The remainder come from free-lance writers and from those people who perform a public relations function.

In an article titled "Gatekeeper Research: How to Reach the Travel Editor," (*Public Relations Journal,* August 1978) Elaine Goldman and Barrie L. Jones list a dozen types of stories preferred by travel editors. In order of preference, from first to twelfth, these were:

1. Budget trips
2. Regional pieces
3. Family travel
4. One-day destinations
5. Price information
6. How-tos
7. Seasonal
8. Convenience/service
9. International
10. Package tours
11. History/nostalgia
12. Luxury vacations

The travel article (and book) has a long and distinguished history. People like Boswell and Dickens wrote travel articles; Ernest Hemingway was a first-rate writer of travel pieces. And there are fine articles on travel being written today, in a much different style than the early chroniclers—more crisp, and more journalistic rather than literary.

When writing travel articles, there are some general and some specific points that need to be made.

1. You should visit the place you write about. This seems like an obvious fact, but a number of authors try to write about areas with which they have no personal familiarity. It usually shows. You should also spend sufficient time in an area to get a decent impression of things. Otherwise, your writing is liable to be shallow.

2. While gathering material for an article, be cautious about the information source that deliberately misleads, or "puts you on." Check every fact.

3. Do your homework in advance, so that you can ask intelligent questions and save both time and unnecessary writing.

4. Develop the requisite writing skills. Good writing is good writing; the only thing different about good *travel* writing is the subject. Good writing means such things as:

- Having something to say.
- Understanding the nuances of the language. This is particularly necessary in travel, where so much depends on the writer's ability to recreate the scene.
- Avoiding cliches—a dangerous temptation in travel writing. Nothing will destroy interest faster.
- Arranging your ideas in some logical sequence, giving the reader a sense of purpose and progression. This may mean an outline before you start writing, and it may also mean considerable re-writing.
- Becoming adept at providing bridges between ideas and between paragraphs. This gives a feeling of easy continuity.
- Learning how to heighten interest. You achieve this through dealing with topics that promise a benefit to the reader; by including meaningful quotes; through a good sense of humor; through the arousal of curiosity; and through the knack of putting yourself in the reader's place.
- Writing clearly, using active verbs, trimming out unnecessary jargon, and by preferring the simple to the complex. Writing should be like conversation, not like instruction.
- Being willing to rewrite—and to cut with judgment and courage.

Like any good article, the travel article starts off with a strong lead, or topic sentence:

> Moving took on a new meaning for American Bob Abrams the day he and his girl friend, Sophie Roberte, negotiated a bank loan here and bought a 60-year-old Dutch barge called Simpatico.
> Stephen McDonnell for *Agence France-Presse*

> How do amusement parks—from Disneyland in California to Disney World in Florida—make customers come back after they've ridden Space Mountain, Pirates of the Caribbean, the Great American Revolution or Rolling Thunder three times?
> Alijean Harmetz, *New York Times Service*

> There was no doubt where I was headed that first day I had ever been in Paris. I consulted the Metro map in its Belle Epoque

frame at a station along the Champs Elysees, determined the route, and surfaced at the Opera. There was the Cafe de la Paix in all its resplendent mystery, greeting guests again.

Horace Sutton in *Saturday Review* (5/12/79)

These are three different ways to start but all share the same quality—you want to read on.

Travel agency personnel don't often write articles, but there is no reason they shouldn't. All of them travel frequently, know the business, have a grasp of what should be of interest to the reader, and should have imbibed considerable local flavor.

It can't hurt to query the local travel editor about doing a piece for his travel section. The article could not, of course, be self-serving, but name identification alone would be worth it. You can always get mileage out of such articles, too, by reprinting them, and including them in mailings to your client list.

The Newsletter

Many travel agencies find that their own newsletters, published quarterly, bimonthly, or even monthly, are one of their best recruitment tools for travel.

As with everything else you do in the travel business, this newsletter should have a professional look. It should be clean, informative, interesting, and attractive. Some of the material used will be purely local—new staff, new branch offices, local travel groups, local package tours, and so on, while other items may have a national flavor.

Laurence Stevens, writing in *The Travel Agent,* suggests keeping a newsletter file into which you drop clips from trade magazines, travel sections of newspapers, and other sources. He further suggests the use of art and photos, avoiding the staged shot of a group around an airplane, and the inclusion of client comments and stories (always, of course, clearing this with them before printing).

Keep in mind that the newsletter is a *selling* tool, but that doesn't mean *hard sell*. The first requirement is that people *read* it. You have to give them something worth reading, and you work your message into that kind of copy. After all, even if you didn't plug upcoming tours but wrote a genuinely appealing newsletter, with plenty of company identification, you'd have a successful mailing piece.

In choosing articles, try to stay current, anticipating reader interest, and, when you can, presenting something truly unique.

If you have the funds, you might have the type set outside your agency and the printing done in a regular printshop. Some travel agencies use electric typewriters or more sophisticated typesetting machines to do their own typography. Others use some quick print method of reproducing the newsletter. If neatly done, these may suffice, even though they will look a cut below the printed newsletter. Above all, however, do not mimeograph these newsletters. This looks cheap, and it's better to have no newsletter than one which presents a poor image.

Figure 12-2

Special Events

Travel agencies frequently put on special events. These can be elaborate office openings or simple film showings. For all such events, however, the watchword is *details*. You must plan in great detail, check every detail, and recheck every detail. Think of all the things that could possibly happen to spoil the event, and try to insure against them.

It makes good sense to jot down a checklist for special events and go over each item until you're certain it has been accomplished. This means that sufficient time must be given to planning. You can't crank up a decent client party in one week. That doesn't even allow time to print invitations. For just about any event, a minimum of six weeks is desirable, with more complicated events demanding longer lead times.

When you contemplate staging a special program, you begin by *clearing the date,* making sure it is one you and your staff can live with, and one that offers a minimum of conflict for the expected guests. Next you *tie down a facility,* such as a meeting room or restaurant, making certain it can handle the anticipated audience. Then you *firm up the program,* arranging for films or speakers, and deciding on the way the function will go.

Now it's time to *issue invitations* and/or *disseminate publicity.* The invitation list must be prepared in advance and you'll want to give the printer a week to ten days to print the invitations, and your staff enough time to address and mail them.

Once these initial tasks have been accomplished, it's time to start looking ahead to the event, and going over all the details. Consider the requirements of the speaker, the need for a film projector, decorations, exhibits, printed programs, food, drinks, heat and air conditioning controls, light switches, sliding panels for noise level control, seating arrangements, microphone and audio controls, lectern, water glasses and so on. There are hundreds of minor items which can spell success or disaster. If everything runs smoothly, nobody notices. But if something goes wrong, everyone notices. That's why you take nothing for granted. Fuses *do* blow; extension cords are forgotten; speakers fail to show; the weather turns nasty; the programs aren't delivered. You have to have alternate plans for things you can anticipate, and you must be able to adjust rapidly to situations you didn't anticipate.

The Film or Slide Program
Film showings aren't original in the promotion of travel, but they are effective. They're also an inexpensive way to attract an audience.

Planning ahead for these shows means considering what films might be topical, seasonal, or otherwise appealing, and then booking them early. If possible, have the films in your office two or three days ahead of the proposed event. Most good films are in demand and, even if the distributor has multiple prints, it could be difficult to get yours when you need it.

How do you locate films?

Air and cruise lines, tourist offices, major resort areas—they generally have films they're happy to loan out. In addition, there are production houses and distributors who publish their own catalogues. Get on their lists and you'll be furnished with an annual roster of available films. Trade publications like *Travel Weekly* publish periodical articles with a rundown of the new and award-winning travel films.

Some films have a rental charge; many are free, except for return postage. You'll be given a date for the return of the film, or for its transfer to another user.

While you're ordering the film, check for an appropriate place to have the showing. Some agencies—very few—have their own facility; others have a hall available in their shopping center or office building. If none of these alternatives is available, check for a local lodge hall, community center, hotel, motel, or even one of the facilities rented or loaned by local business firms. Be certain it's large enough to hold the anticipated crowd but not so large as to brand the evening a failure if fewer people show up.

Decide then what the program will be, and whether you'll serve refreshments, and how you'll get your message across. These events can be as simple as an evening with a welcome, a couple of films, and a dismissal. Or they can be rather elaborate affairs, with films, cocktails, hors d'oeuvres, decorations, even hosts in native costumes. Sometimes the showings combine a film, folk dancing, a talk by a native of the featured country, and other activities.

When the films arrive in your office, preview them. This will give you an idea of the condition they're in and the subject matter. On occasion a film may be too commercial, or too slanted, or inappropriate. Better to catch this before the showing, and either substitute for it, or explain the content in advance. If the film is broken and needs splicing or other repairs, the local film studio or TV news department may be able to help you.

Be sure you publicize the showings—as widely and as imaginatively as possible. This means invitations, news releases, posters, and notices in the newsletter. It also means describing the film to some degree (*Pakistan: Mound of the Dead,* a 27-minute color film about the discovery of Mohenjo Daro, the Mound of the Dead, in the Indus River Valley in the 1920s), rather than just saying, " . . . and a movie about Pakistan."

Arrive early the day of the event and check everything—screen, wall sockets, projector, film, extra projection bulb, extension cord, table for materials, microphone, speakers—everything.

Greet people at the door, and help them meet other people. Name tags might be a good idea, using office personnel to fill them out, or letting them letter their own tags.

Try to keep the program under two hours. This is about the extent of the average attention span. Try to start promptly, avoid idle chatter, and wrap up on time.

Sunday afternoon is a good time for film showings—better certainly than a weekend night.

Be certain that you have enough people to perform the tasks you have in mind. Someone to make out name tags? To serve punch and cookies? To run the projector? To introduce the films?

Slide shows don't have the impact of film, but they also have a role in travel presentations. For one thing, they are more flexible and can be made to fit a program more closely. If the person doing the narration also took the slides, that adds a dimension—providing the slides are good. For example, if the tour leader of a special tour has slides from previous trips, he can whet appetites for an upcoming tour.

Many travel agencies schedule programs relating to upcoming tours, inviting those who have signed up, their friends, other wavering prospects, and clients who should have an interest in this tour. Meeting people who are going has an effect on the recruitment of the uncertain members.

Multi-media slide shows, with half a dozen or more projectors, are not too practical for the average agency. They are too expensive, too complicated. You can, however, improve on the single projector routine at very little extra cost, and with little mechanical risk.

For one thing, you can attach a tape cassette to the projector to drop the slides automatically, at the right places in the script. The advantage of a cassette over a live voice is that you can add music and sound effects, and you can also be assured of more uniform voice quality. The live speaker, of course, also has advantages—like presence, and warmth, and the ability to adjust quickly to unforeseen problems, or to answer on-the-spot questions.

The next step up is to use two projectors, with the cassette, and joined by a *dissolve unit,* which blends one picture into the other, making for a smoother and more artistic flow, rather than the familiar click. To use this combination, you must plan your slides accordingly, using every other one in the alternate projector, or, at least, knowing which one you want on the screen at any given time.

Above all, make the slide show move. There have been so many jokes about folks showing their vacation slides, the audience is already twenty percent desensitized. So keep it brisk, interesting, and short.

It's possible, too, to take both a slide show and a film show to another locale. Many companies use briefcase-size self-contained slide units which project right on the side of the case. These can be carried into an office or board room and set in motion at the push of a button. For commercial accounts in particular, this would be a fine portable tool. The film projector takes more time to set up and you need a board room or something similar. If given the opportunity to show a film, arrive early and check all details before summoning the audience.

Other Visual Aids
Don't neglect the value of such items as flip charts (large or small), descriptive brochures, tape cassettes or records, wall posters, and other items. Some of these don't function well alone, but, in concert with other tools, they perform a real service.

The Speech
Not everyone is gifted as a speaker. It's important that you know your own limitations, and don't try to accomplish things you're not equipped to do. People who can't tell jokes, for example, shouldn't tell jokes. Nothing says every speech must start with a joke. Be natural; be yourself.

The first thing to consider about any speech is the content. Even the best delivery can't atone for a weak message. *Have something to say.*

When you know *what* you're going to talk about, you should determine whether your aim is to entertain, instruct, or persuade. Your approach will differ in each instance.

Then organize your speech, starting with the central idea, then listing the main points under that idea, then developing each point, and then developing the conclusion. After these items are completed, go back and write transitions between the ideas, flesh out the paragraphs, and write your introduction. After these are all done, put them in the proper order, with the introduction first, and write for the style in which you plan to deliver the speech.

It's wise to keep any speech short—under twenty minutes. If illustrated with good slides, you can extend this time, but short is better than long.

Consider your audience makeup. Young or old or a mixture? Experienced travelers or neophytes? Economy minded or deluxe? The toughest audience to address is one that is composed of all types of people, from children to senior citizens.

Decide what system you are going to use for notes. Will you use small cards with topic headings? Or type the entire speech out? Or memorize it and go without any notes? Reading a speech is disastrous. Perhaps the best system—if you can handle it—is an outline on cards which guides you but does not constrain you.

Consider, too, the physical layout of the area where you'll speak. Sometimes a speaker arrives just before he's due to speak and discovers that he's in a large hall, with no loudspeaker system, and half the people screened from his view. Unless you have time to adjust, this can be disconcerting. Test the equipment in advance, too—the mike, lectern light, slide carousel switch.

Above all, don't panic. A relaxed delivery will carry people along. The typical audience doesn't expect William Jennings Bryan each time; they merely want to learn something or be entertained.

Presentations

The presentation is a form of speech, combined with a strong sales pitch. Here are a few tips as outlined in an *Advertising Age* article (January 16, 1978) by Ron Hoff, executive creative director for New York's Foote, Cone and Belding:

- Edit your material. Organize tightly.
- Psych yourself up by convincing yourself you know a great deal about the subject and are well prepared.
- Rehearse—at least ten times.
- Remain cool—even when pressed. Learn how to confess you don't know an answer without appearing dumb.
- Learn how to control your body and hands. Don't look stiff or nervous.
- Slides work better for large groups but charts are more informal and provoke more participation.

- Anticipate questions. If more than one person is involved in the presentation, decide in advance who's going to respond to certain types of queries.
- If there are other presentations preceding and following yours, try to discover what they'll contain.
- Be prepared to fill in if any equipment fails.
- Learn from others.

Other Event Details

Each type of event has its own advantages and challenges. That's why a certain amount of think time is necessary before you stage any event, to make certain you've thought through these separate items.

For example, if you have an open house, have you considered the traffic flow through your establishment; and who will conduct the tours; and what will be said; and when you'll interrupt proceedings for a slide show; and if you'll serve food; and how you'll estimate the crowd; and where you'll stack the literature?

If you sponsor a dinner you'll want to work on the menu, table arrangements, instructions to speaker and toastmaster, guest list, press table, and other facets of the dinner.

Murphy's Law, which says, among other things, that "if anything can go wrong, it will," certainly applies to travel agency events. Think ahead, and you'll save yourself (and your audience) considerable grief.

Other Promotional Ideas

What the intelligent travel agency manager should do is learn to *think* in terms of promotional ideas. After all, when you are dealing in service, there is considerable similarity among agencies in terms of offerings, prices, and other constants. The difference comes down to little things—like employee attitude and ability, and the capacity for merchandising identical items.

Perhaps it's the use of a carousel rack instead of the long wall full of brochures. It might be the use of gift items with the agency name inscribed—items like flight bags, golf bags, garment bags, baby kits, business card files, desk organizers, luggage tags, document holders, correspondence portfolios, and many other giveaway pieces. Perhaps it's merely a distinctive luggage tag for tour members, or an iron-on decal, or a gift pencil.

It might also be a touring travel desk, situated in high traffic areas on set days. Perhaps Monday at a university; Tuesday at a major industrial locale; Wednesday at a shopping center; Thursday at a hospital; and Friday at a military installation.

Some Promotional Campaign Examples
SHAKESPEARE YEAR
In 1967 Great Britain enjoyed an outstanding tourist season by focusing on the 400th anniversary of Shakespeare's birth.

The British Tourist Authority placed more than 700 stories in leading newspapers, managed to get 27 feature stories in top magazines (like *Reader's Digest*), and achieved a total of nearly 140 hours time on radio and television (on nearly 2,000 programs). They also booked hundreds of showings of Shakespeare films, arranged for thousands of posters to be displayed, reached thousands of teachers via direct mail, supplied Shakespeare kits to community and women's clubs, and even flew costumed tavern wenches to New York to dispense mead at the Plaza Hotel.

The planners were also successful in extending the celebration beyond the April birthdate and beyond the confines of Stratford-on-Avon. British tourism rose 16% that year and included a record number of Americans—some 589 thousand persons.

I LOVE NEW YORK

In 1976 New York was talking bankruptcy; tourism was down; a general state of malaise prevailed. William S. Doyle, then a member of the state's department of commerce, convinced authorities to spend nearly their entire budget of $200,000 on tourism research. Armed with responses to an in-depth survey, a comprehensive marketing plan was developed, then funded by the state legislature to the tune of over $4 million. The bulk of this money was spent on television, utilizing an "I Love New York" song delivered by Broadway stars. Major network TV shows (*Today, The Mike Douglas Show, Good Morning America, The Dinah Shore Show*) were used. Cooperative money was secured from five airlines, and co-op funds were supplied by the state to local communities. Collateral material included a 96-page travel guide featuring over 400 New York attractions; a 34-page booklet on nightlife, hotels, restaurants, theatres, shopping, museums, and sports; and a brochure for travel agencies on Broadway shows and package tours. Travel agents also received a strong promotional line on the TV commercials.

Results? The hotel occupancy rate rose to over 85% from a 1970 low of 62%. Broadway theatre attendance rose a third in 2 years. And, in 1977, summer vacation travel income for New York went up $41 million, returning $6 million in additional state tax revenues.

The reasons for this success were a good idea ("I Love New York"), adequately funded, professionally produced, comprehensively backed up with support items and, initially, extremely well researched.

BEAM TRAVEL CENTER ANNIVERSARY

When Beam Travel Center of Ithaca, New York, celebrated its 50th anniversary in 1978, the well-thought-out program attracted about 15% of the town's citizens.

The highlight was a ride in a hot air balloon, which was controlled by a ground tether. Passengers were accorded space by lot. But that was only the beginning. There were bands playing, gift balloons, free cotton candy, popcorn, and lemonade, plus drawings for flight bags, cameras, and tours. Tourist offices and suppliers participated in the promotion, and ads (built around the balloon theme) were carried in football programs, newspapers, and radio. There were cocktail parties, a luncheon, a dinner for selected guests, and a lot of attendant publicity.

The entire celebration was spread over 10 days and cost about seventy-five hundred dollars.

All of these campaigns were backed by some research. A thorough market study is really advisable in any such endeavor. They also featured an awareness of the target audiences, a determination of what materials would work best, a coordination of theme in all that was done, and a tie-in with other firms and organizations that had a mutual interest in the success of the campaign.

The Future?

No one can predict this with certainty, but the wise travel manager reads all he or she can, and tries to anticipate trends and opportunities.

Take the revolutionary idea from American Express, which renamed and redesigned each of its offices, christening them *travel stores,* and organizing them into three divisions—an information gallery, travel-planning conference area, and a service island for transactions. The layout and the minisize computers used by each travel counselor cut time spent by clients by 25%.

This drastic change was dictated, according to American Express officials, because of the complicated nature of today's travel, and the increasing sophistication of the traveler.

Will this change affect the way the average agency conducts business? Of course it will.

Another trend to watch is the increasing number of colleges and universities offering degrees in tourism, including approximately nine masters degree programs in tourism management and one doctoral program. These programs go far beyond the typical travel agent courses or hotel schools, and are producing a new breed of professionals who will eventually make their mark on the industry. As these graduates become available, opportunities will hopefully keep pace in the growing agency structure, as well as in state tourism departments.

The next decade will be an interesting and demanding one for the travel agency. Those best able to cope with the changes will be the managers who combine experience with foresight and daring. They must be solid in their thinking and research, but creative in their advertising and promotional outlook.

For these individuals, next year will always be better, and this year will be darned good.

Questions and Exercises

1. How does public relations differ from advertising?
2. Based on your experience, how would you assess the human relations qualities of travel agencies you've visited? If you've never been to an agency, visit one, and report on this aspect only.
3. Check your local paper, and find examples of five *different* types of events that made news.
4. Do you think you should thank the travel editor for running a feature you sent him or her?
5. Check the travel pages of newspapers and/or magazines, and come up with what you consider to be five good leads in travel articles.
6. Secure three newsletters from local or regional travel agencies and critique them for content and appearance.

Case Problem

Take the following set of facts and turn them into a *complete* news release, remembering to include *all* elements shown in this chapter.

- March 17, 1980, St. Patrick's Day Party
- Globe Travel Agency, 24th and Hickory, Akron, Ohio
- From 4-7 P.M.
- This is an annual event.
- Irish coffee and brown bread will be served.
- Kevin Sheehan, who will lead a trip to Ireland for Globe in May, will show slides of his most recent tour of the Emerald Isle. He is the former mayor of Akron, and was born in County Cork, Ireland.
- Russell Seabrook, manager of Globe Travel Agency, said all are welcome and that dress is informal.
- There will be a drawing for several prizes, including clay pipes, a Donegal tweed coat, and two free tickets to the upcoming Irish Rovers Concert.
- This is the fourteenth straight year Globe has had a St. Patrick's Day Party, and the sixth tour that Sheehan has led for Globe.
- Stewardesses from Aer Lingus, Ireland's national airline, will present all who attend with Irish shamrocks.
- Russell Seabrook said that visitors may also tour Globe's offices. And he said that new brochures from the Irish Tourist Board will be available.

Glossary of Terms

AIDCA—an acronym designating conditions to be achieved by an advertisement; i.e. Attention, Interest, Desire, Credibility, and Action.

accordion fold—a method of folding paper so that it opens like the pleats in an accordion.

account executive—an advertising agency person who works directly with the client on an account.

advertising—controlled, paid promotion of goods and/or services through the use of mass media, with the aim of influencing purchase or attitude.

advertising agency—a firm that specializes in the production and placement of advertising.

advertising mix—a blend of various media in order to conduct an intelligent and effective advertising campaign.

agate line—a unit of measurement in ads which is one column wide and 5½ points (1/14 of an inch) deep.

airbrush—a method of retouching artwork through the use of a fine spray.

asymmetrical balance—see *balance*.

audience—a segment of the public to whom an advertising or promotional message is directed.

audio—the sound portion of a TV script.

audio tape—a tape that records and reproduces sound, used in radio commercials, television, or film.

avails—this term refers to the times and programs which are "available" in the broadcast media.

balance—a condition in layout or design in which the weight of opposing elements seem to equalize each other. When the elements are in near perfect formal balance, this is called *symmetrical balance*; when the elements are not equally divided on both sides in a layout or illustration, but still project balance, this is called *asymmetrical balance*.

Benday—applying shading to a line drawing by the use of adhesive screens.

bleed—if the printed image extends to the trim edge of the page, it is called a bleed.

blow up—a larger version of an illustration, particularly a photo.

body copy—the basic printed information in an ad, making up the "body" of the ad.

boldface—a heavier and darker type.

booklet—a small book, made up of eight or more pages, bound together, usually stapled.

broadside—a large folder, which may unfold to any size from 25" x 19" to 38" x 25". Usually concentrates on a single theme. Sometimes used as a poster.

brochure—another term for a booklet or folder.

brochure shell—a partially printed folder which can be localized by the addition of specific printed material.

CPM—refers to the cost of delivering 1,000 readers, viewers, or listeners to an advertiser. The letters mean Cost Per Thousand.

caption—copy accompanying and explaining illustrations. In newspapers, the caption traditionally went *above* the illustration.

center spread—the right and left hand facing pages in the center of a publication.

chromakey—an optical effect in television.

circular—an inexpensive leaflet used in direct advertising.

circulation—the number of copies of a newspaper or magazine that are distributed; or the number of homes regularly tuned to a radio or television station.

classified advertising—usually small print ads, listed by category, and often without illustrations.

clip art—pre-prepared art delivered by an art service, which can be clipped and used in advertising or other print media.

close up—in television or film, a shot that focuses tightly on a subject. If a close up of a person, this is a head shot.

cold list—a mailing list that is untried by a particular advertiser, so that he has no idea what returns to expect.

cold type—type produced without the use of hot metal, using either photo-composition or a special typewriter.

collateral materials—refers to non-commissionable media used in an advertising campaign, frequently printed materials, like brochures.

color separation—the process of breaking down a full-color illustration into the primary colors. Could also be a black and white negative of one primary color.

column inch—in measuring ads, this would be one inch on whatever column width the publication offers.

commercial—another term for a broadcast advertisement.

commission—a fee paid to advertising agencies by the media, typically 15 percent.

comp—a "comprehensive" layout, one that is in next-to-final form, and good enough to show to a client.

continuity—a radio, TV, or film script.

co-op advertising—a form of cooperative advertising where a supplier and a dealer (or a tour operator and a travel agency) share the cost of running an ad.

copy fitting—the science of determining what space will accommodate a certain amount of copy.

copy platform—the basic idea for the copy which comes out of the thinking and planning stages.

coverage—the percentage of individuals or households in a specific area that are reached by certain media. In broadcast, this term is sometimes used to designate the effective reach of the signal.

crane shot—in film or television, an overhead shot, using a mechanical extension, or crane.

crop—the practice of cutting off portions of an illustration for mechanical or artistic purposes.

cursive—typeface resembling handwriting but with disconnected letters.

cut—in letterpress, a term for an illustration or the engraving made from this illustration. In broadcast, a direction to remove material, or cease filming.
cutline—copy accompanying and explaining an illustration. Traditionally *beneath* the illustration. Cutline and caption are now used interchangeably.
dateline—an indication at the beginning of a news release of the date and place of origin of the story.
design—the arrangement of the various parts to produce an artistic whole.
dingbat—a decorative device in printing, like a dot or a star.
direct mail—a form of advertising which reaches the individual consumer directly, usually via third class mail.
direct sound—the recording of sound at the same time as the filming, producing synchronized sound.
display—a type larger than 14 point, used in headlines and other places requiring emphasis. Also a form of advertising distinguished from classified advertising by the use of illustrations, white space, headlines, and other attention-getting devices.
dissolve—in film and television, a means of moving from one scene to another by momentarily blending both on the screen.
dissolve unit—an attachment to a pair of slide projectors which gives the effect of dissolving one slide image into the other.
dolly—a method of getting closer to a film or TV subject by rolling the entire camera forward (or, if you dolly out, backward).
double fold—a folder folded twice, to produce 6 panel surfaces.
drive time—the morning and evening traffic rush hours, when radio time (particularly AM) is most expensive.
dub—a copy of a video or audio tape.
dummy—the layout for a brochure or booklet or magazine.
duotone—a photograph reproduced in two colors, usually black and one other color.
echo chamber—a sound studio device for adding timbre to a voice.
engraving—a printing plate either hand etched in reverse, or transferred from photographic or other copy through the use of acid.
FTC—Federal Trade Commission
fade—in television, an optical effect where the scene either emerges from black (FADE IN) or goes to black (FADE OUT).
family of type—one design of type in a complete range of sizes.
fees—charges made by service firms (such as advertising agencies) for non-commissionable activities.
film clip—a short bit of film, used for TV news, or to promote some institution or event.
finish—the texture of paper.
flat rate—a standard rate for space or time, without any discounts for volume or frequency.
flop—to print a picture so that it's the mirror image of the original.
flush—to set printed copy even with other copy. *Flush left* means that the

left edge of the copy is aligned, but the right edge (*ragged right*) may not be. A solid even box of copy would be *flush left and right*.

folder—a leaflet that is folded.

font—a complete assortment of type characters in one face and size.

format—the layout and style of an ad, publication, or printed page. (Nine basic formats for ads, for example, are given in the text.) Format also refers to the way elements in a broadcast program follow in sequence.

frequency—in advertising, the number of times an advertising message is delivered within a period of time. Also refers to the character of a broadcast signal.

galley proof—an initial proof, or copy, of an ad, or printed piece.

gatefold—an extended folded page that folds into the booklet like a gate.

gravure—one of the less common methods of printing, where the ink is retained in depressions for transfer to paper, rather than the upright surfaces being inked as in letterpress.

gross rating points—a rating method used in television and out-of-home media.

gutter—the inside margins of facing pages in a newspaper or magazine.

halftone—in order to capture the continuous tones of a photo when reproducing it, the photo (or illustration) is photographed again through a screen, and a printing plate made of the result. This is called a *halftone*.

harmony—refers to all elements of a creative work, including layout, working together to produce an attractive result.

house agency—an advertising agency owned (or controlled) by the person(s) doing the advertising.

ID—short for *identification,* a 10-second spot announcement on radio or television.

in-house agency—see *house agency.*

insert—a page (or pages) printed separately, and then bound into, or inserted into, a publication.

institutional advertising—advertising aimed at building an image rather than the immediate sale of a product or service.

inverted pyramid—a reportorial style in which all essential facts are at the beginning of the story.

italic—a form of type that slants to the right.

jingle—musical treatment of a commercial on radio or television.

junior board—the smallest size of outdoor billboard.

justified margin—spacing out a line to make it full all the way to the right margin.

keying—placing a specific number or letter in an ad in order to check the source of responses.

layout—the arrangement of various elements within an assigned space.

leading—a metal strip (or strips) used to add space between lines. If no leading is used, the copy is "set solid." In cold type, a space.

leaflet—a sheet of direct advertising, usually folded, not stitched or bound.

learning—a relatively permanent behavioral change brought about by some experience.
letterpress—a method of printing using raised surfaces.
letter spacing—opening up spaces between characters, for effect, or to fill a line.
libel—published slander that defames an individual.
lightface—a thin line type, as opposed to the heavy boldface type.
line conversion—a method of producing a special artistic effect by converting a photograph to a line illustration.
list broker—a person who sells or rents direct mail lists.
lithography—a method of printing from a flat surface, using the principle that grease and water don't mix.
live—a performance filmed simultaneously, as against being taped for later showing.
local advertising—advertising paid for and signed by a local advertiser.
logo—stands for logotype, the signature of an advertising, including name and/or design, probably cast in one unit.
lottery—a contest involving chance, consideration, and prize.
lowercase—the small letters as against capital letters. *See also*: uppercase.
mail order advertising—a form of advertising designed to sell goods and services through the mails.
make good—a refund, or re-run, of an ad or commercial, when an advertising medium errs in scheduling or presentation.
make ready—adjustments in a printed form to achieve the desired printing impression.
marketing—a combination of activities designed to efficiently move goods from manufacturer to consumer.
marketing mix—bringing together elements like product, price, distribution, selling, and advertising into a single workable program.
market segment—a limited portion of the total consumer market.
market share—that percentage of the potential market which has been captured by an individual brand.
markup—the difference between cost and selling price.
mat—a papier-mache or composition form made from a plate.
media—the various communication forms—print, broadcast, outdoor and so on.
media mix—a skillful blend of various advertising media in a campaign.
medium closeup—TV shot of head and partial torso.
milline rate—the cost of reaching a million readers with a line of advertising. Arrived at by multiplying the line rate by a million and dividing this result by the publication's circulation.
montage—the combination of several pictures or parts of pictures blended into a single unit. In television or film, the blending of several scenes.
morgue—the name given to the file room at newspapers and other media.
motivation—the root cause of much behavior.
national advertising—advertising by a manufacturer or wholesaler, usually

without any local store information; or advertising in a national publication.

negative—a reversed tonal image of an original photograph.

newsletter—a report issued periodically by a firm or organization to keep employees or the public apprised of current news about the institution.

off camera—an action or sound, including a voice, which occurs without being shown.

offset—lithographic printing where an inked image is transferred from a flat plate to a rubber blanket to the paper.

open rate—the basic rate, subject to discounts for frequency of advertising.

optical effects—film transitions (dissolves, wipes, etc.) which are added after the final cut.

out-of-home advertising—advertising that is seen by people outside their homes, like billboards, exhibits, transit posters and the like.

overlay—transparent sheets used over art or photos to indicate location or shape of special treatment.

package—a complete broadcast program involving script, talent, music, etc.

pan—lateral movement across subject or scene by film or TV camera.

pasteup—in print production, the combination of illustration and type on a single sheet ready for engraving or photographing.

perception—an interpretation placed on sensory experience.

persuasion—a method of bringing about change or conviction.

photocomposition—a method of producing type via photographic impression.

pica—a convenient unit of measurement; approximately 1/6 inch.

point—a unit of measurement for type size. There are approximately 72 points to an inch.

point of purchase—advertising displayed at the location where the purchase of that product or service may be made.

poster—a large sheet of paper containing a message.

preferred position—a specified page or section of a publication, or a specific location on a page. A premium is usually charged for this privilege.

preprint—advertising that is reproduced independently and then inserted in a publication.

press kit—a collection of news-related materials for the communication media.

prime time—in broadcast, the time when there is the heaviest listening or viewing audience.

primary colors—red, yellow, and blue. (Or magenta, yellow, and cyan.)

probability—in surveying, a form of sampling that relies for accuracy on the random method of selecting respondents.

proof—a sample of an ad or other printed material, supplied to the client prior to publishing, so the client may check for errors.

public relations—a planned, organized communication effort designed to build and hold good will.

publicity—a communication about a company or organization released to the media as editorial matter.
quota sample—in survey work, a sampling of respondents with known characteristics.
random sample—in surveying, a form of probability sampling where each unit in the universe has an equal chance of being represented.
rating—a term used in broadcast to define the percentage of homes or individuals tuned to a specific program.
reach—the number of different homes or individuals reached by an advertising message or campaign during a specified time period.
register—the exact alignment of two or more forms in printing.
release—a form used to obtain permission to use a person's likeness or statement; also a media order for placement; also a news release.
remote—a broadcast or telecast originating away from the studio.
reprint—copy of an ad after it has run, or copy of a promotional article.
reproduction proof—a proof of high quality used in making negatives or plates.
retainer—a fee paid in order to retain the services of a professional person or firm for a specified period of time.
retouch—improving an illustration mechanically prior to reproduction.
reverse—a white on black print, like white type on a black background.
ROP—run-of-paper, meaning that the editor may place the ad anywhere in the paper, as opposed to preferred position.
ROS—run-of-station, meaning that the commercial may be inserted anywhere it fits during the broadcast day or week.
rotary board—in outdoor advertising, a single board that is periodically moved from location to location.
rough—a layout stage between a thumbnail and a comprehensive sketch.
sans serif—type without cross strokes above or below the main strokes.
scale of values—the various gradations of gray between white and black.
scratchboard—an illustration technique where ink is scratched off the paper stock rather than inked on.
screen—cross-ruled glass or film used to produce dots and create halftones.
script—a radio, film, or television outline for a program, including the scenes to be shown and the words to be said. Also a specific type face, resembling handwriting.
sequence—in layout or design, a literal or felt progression from one element to another.
series—the full range of sizes in one type face.
serif—short strokes at the top and bottom of Roman type.
shell—see *brochure shell*
showing—in outdoor advertising, the percentage of coverage by a campaign.
signature—the advertiser's name in an ad. Also a number of pages printed on a single sheet.
silk screen—a printing process using a stencil-like method.
single fold—a leaflet folded once.

slander—oral defamation of character.
slide chain—a device used by television studios to project slides on tape, or on a live telecast.
slogan—a more or less permanent advertising phrase.
spec—a term used to describe the "specifying" of type faces and sizes.
spot—a short broadcast commercial, one minute or less in length.
spread—two facing pages, usually in the center of a publication.
stats—short for photostat, a positive or negative photograph.
stock—paper or cardboard.
stock photo—a photo which may be purchased from a commercial vendor.
storyboard—a layout or blueprint for a TV commercial, using sketches or photos to delineate the action, accompanied by the narration or dialogue.
subhead—a smaller, subordinate heading, used to extend the large headline, or to introduce subsequent blocks of copy.
super—a television effect where one image is projected over another on the screen, usually a title or logo or some other print message.
symmetrical balance—see *balance*.
sync—an exact matching of sound and movement, like speech with lip movement.
tabloid—a newspaper about half the size of a standard newspaper.
tag—an addition to a commercial in broadcasting, frequently a specific comment by a station announcer.
tear sheet—a newspaper or magazine sheet containing an ad which is furnished to the advertiser.
testimonial—an advertising message by an identified individual.
thirty sheet—the largest standard outdoor billboard, larger than the twenty four sheet poster because of the extra border.
thumbnail—a small, quick sketch, the beginning stage of a layout.
tilt—vertical movement of the camera in film or TV.
tint block—a colored panel, often screened back to allow type to be overprinted and read.
trademark—a word or symbol that identifies a product or service.
traffic—in an advertising agency, the department that schedules work, and controls the delivery and return of advertising materials.
transfer type—sheets of alphabets or phrases in different type faces and sizes which may be affixed to layouts or illustrations to produce headlines or simulate body copy. Also called *press type*.
tri-vision—an outdoor billboard with three moving panels.
twenty four sheet—see *thirty sheet*.
type—the mechanically produced letter. The four basic forms are: Roman, block, script, and ornamental.
typo—a typographical error.
upper case—capital letters. See also *lower case*.
velox—a particularly sharp photographic print which is suitable for reprinting.
video—the picture portion of a TV program or script.
video tape—a tape containing pictures and sound of a television program.

vignette—a photographic treatment producing soft edges around an illustration.
voice over—written VO. Narration where the narrator is not visible on the screen.
wash drawing—as opposed to a simple line drawing, a drawing that has shades and values, applied with a brush.
weight—a term used to designate the thickness of paper.
white space—that part of a layout which has no copy or illustration.
widow—a short line at the end of a printed paragraph.
wipe—an optical effect where one scene is *wiped* off the TV screen and replaced with another.
zips—short for Zip-a-tone sheets, which may be applied to illustrations to create the effect of shading.
zoom—a change of distance in a TV shot, using a zoom (or "Zoomar") camera lens.

Index

Account executive, 40, 43
Advertising, 5
    appeals of, 28-29
    complaints about, 27, 33-34
    cooperative, 31, 35
    counter, 36
    definition, 24
    donation, 59
    image of, 24, 27, 30
    misrepresentation in, 35
    purposes of, 24-25, 33
    types of, 30-31
Advertising agency, 38-45
    billings, 38, 42
    charges, 40-42
    client relations with, 42-45
    image, 38
    in-house agency, 21, 45
    selecting agency, 42-43
    services, 39, 40, 67
    size, 38-39, 42
    structure, 43
Advertising budget, increasing, 9
Advertising campaigns, 40, 162-165
AIDCA formula, 72
Airline travel concerns, 14-15
American Airlines, 18
Assymetrical balance, 87, 91
Ayer, N. W., & Son, 38

Bait and switch, 35
Balance, 85-86, 90-91
Bates, Ted, 39
Beam Travel Center Anniversary Campaign, 183-184
Behavior, 25, 168
Billboards, 63, 152-153
Billing, 38-39, 42
Block type, 107
Body copy, 72-82
    bridges, 75
    combinations, 81
    featuring an item, 81
    ideas for, 81-81
    styles of, 75-79
    tips for, 79-80
Bridges, in copy, 75
Brochures, 58, 113, 126-129
    assembling, 128
    brochure shells, 129
    copy and layout, 129
    folding and printing, 126-128
    sizes, 113
    value of, 58
Budget, 8, 9, 60, 163

Buying decision, 12

Camera ready copy, 93
Camera, television, 143
Campaigns, advertising, 40, 162-165
Caption, 111
Circus layout, 94, 103
Clichés, 71, 76, 92
Clients, relations with ad agencies, 42, 44
Clip art, 109
Close, in copy, 78
Cold type, 121-122
Collateral materials, 41
Color, 112-113
    color reproduction, 129-132
Column inch, 61
Commercial accounts, 3, 20-21, 58
Commercial advertising, 30
Commissions, 31, 40, 41
Community relations, 168
Comparison shopping, 16
Competition for attention, 2, 4
Comprehensive (comp) layout, 92
Concern about travel, 13
Consumer advertising, 30
Cooperative advertising, 20
Copy fitting, 120-121
Copy heavy ad, 98, 101
Copy platform, 116
Copyright, 36
Copy writing, 68-82, 99
Cost per thousand, 65
Counter advertising, 36
Coupons, 82
Creativity, 67, 163
Cropping (photos), 124

Design of advertising, 84-115
Direct mail, 30, 49-51
    assets, 50-51
    charges for, 62
    copy, 157-158
    liabilities, 51
    lists, 62-63, 155-156
    package, 157
    personalizing, 50
    postage, 159
    production, 50
    prohibitions, 159
    research on, 49-50
    response to, 62-63, 156
Displays, 154
Distribution, 3
Drive time, 53
Dummy, 121, 128

Elements of a print ad, 72
Emotional appeals in advertising, 27
Energy shortage, effect on travel, 16
Enlarging (photo), 123
Envelopes, direct mail, 157
Ethics of advertising, 33
Exhibits, 154

Favorite travel areas, 13
Federal Trade Commission, 34
Fees, advertising agency, 40-41
Feminism, 16
Films, 145, 178-180
Finish, paper, 113
Finnair, 16
First Amendment, 34
Fitting, copy, 120-121
Folding, brochures, 127
Font of type, 121
Foreign visitors, 20, 69
Formats
   print advertising, 93-104
   radio, 53, 135-136
   television, 53, 141-142
Frame layout, 94, 98
Front, Sig S., 11
Full service agency, 39

Gatefold, 126
Gross Rating Points, 53, 57

Halftones, 125-126
Harmony in layout, 85-86
Headlines, 72-74
Hot type, 121-122
House agency, 21, 45
Human relations, 168

Illustrations, 72, 109
I Love New York Campaign, 183
Image advertising, 24, 27, 30
Incomes of travelers, 13
Inflation and effect on travel, 16
In-house agency, 21, 45
Intellectual approach to ads, 27
Inverted pyramid, 171

Labelling, 34
Layout, 84-106, 129
Learning, 26
Legality of advertising, 34-36
Leisure time, 16
Letterpress printing, 122
Liabilities of various media, 49, 51, 52-53, 54, 56-57
Libel, 35
Line, 84-85
Lists, 62-63, 155-156

Local advertising, 30-31, 41
Logo, 72, 82-83, 112
Long range planning, 21-22
Lottery, 36

Magazines, 54-56
   advantages, 56
   charges, 61-62, 65
   color reproduction, 132
   disadvantages, 56
   trade, 30, 54-55
Magazine Network, 54, 62
Mail Order advertising, 30
Management, 3, 9, 11, 21, 44, 59, 67, 182
Marketing, 2
   activities, 2, 162-163
   mix, 6
   segment, 11-12, 16-17
   strategy, 21
Maslow, Abraham, 12
Measuring type, 119-120
Media, 43, 47-66
   charges, 61
   mix, 6, 59
   placement, 61
   position, 62
   schedules, 31
   strategy, 163
   working with, 66, 173-174
Milline rate, 65
Minority prospects for travel, 18-19, 34
Misrepresentation in ads, 35
Mondrian layout, 93, 96, 97
Morley, Robert, 80
Motivation, 26
Multipanel layout, 94, 100

National advertising, 30-31, 41
Necessities, as seen by prospects, 25
Net fare, 4
News in advertising, 24
News conference, 174
Newsletter, 58, 154, 176-177
News media, working with, 173-174
Newspapers, 47-49
   assets, 48-49
   charges, 61
   color reproduction, 132
   liabilities, 49
   number of newspapers, 48
   position, 61
   readership, 48
Newsprint, 113
News release, 170-172
News sources, 169-170
Nielson, A.C., 50
Novelties, 58-59, 182

INDEX

Obscenity, 36
Offset paper, 113
Offset printing, 122
Ogilvy & Mather, 69, 111
Ornamental type, 107
Outdoor advertising, 34
Out-of-Home Media, 56-57, 152-153
    assets, 57
    charges for, 63
    creation of, 152-153
    criticisms of, 56
    disadvantages of, 57
    displays, 154
    exhibits, 154
    Gross Rating Points, 57
    production, 153
    rotary plan, 57
    showing, 57
    sizes, 57, 153
    tips about, 153
    transit posters, 153-154

Package, direct mail, 157
Packaging, legal requirements, 34
Paper, 113-114
    finish, 113
    four color work, 113
    sheet sizes, 113
    weight, 113
Payment, in market segment, 11
Peer identification in ads, 28
Perception, 26
Personalities in advertising tours, 80-81
Personnel, 8
Persuasion, 27-28
Photography, 110-111, 122-126
    cropping, 124
    enlarging, 123
    reducing, 123
    release, 35
    screening, 125-126
    stock photos, 111
Pica, 120
Picture Window layout, 93, 95
Placement of ads, 64
Planning, 21-22
Point of Purchase material, 58
Points, in measuring type, 119
Position, preferred, 61, 62
    magazines, 62
    newspapers, 61
postage, direct mail, 159
Presentations, 181-182
Pricing, 4
Primary colors, 113
Prime time, 53
Printers Ink Model Statute, 36
Printing methods, 122

Product, 6, 12, 164
Production, print, 116, 133
Production, out-of-home media, 153
Production, radio, 138-139
Production, television, 143-148
Profitability, 7, 8
Prohibitions, direct mail, 159
Promotional ideas, 4, 41, 182
Proofs, 31, 119
Prospects for travel, 11-13, 17-20, 59, 69, 158
Psychological appeals in advertising, 28-29
Public relations, 167-184
Publicity, 167, 169

Quantity discounts, 65
Questionnaire, 15

Radio, 53-54, 63, 78, 134-141, 150
    advantages, 54
    charges, 63
    coverage, 53
    disadvantages, 54
    formats, 53, 135-136
    production, 138-139
    ratings, 53
    scripts, 139-141
    travel shows, 148, 150
    writing tips, 136

Sales forecast, 22
Salesmanship, 5, 24, 25, 168
Satisfaction in market segment, 12
Screening, (photos), 125-126
Script, type, 107
    writing, 139-141, 146-147
Secondary motives, 26
Selecting an advertising agency, 47-48
    feature for ad, 81
Senior citizen prospects, 18
Sequence, in layout, 85-88
Series of type, 121
Services, ad agency, 39-40, 67
    travel agency, 6-8, 12
Sex, in advertising, 16
Shakespeare Year Campaign, 182-183
Shells, brochure, 129
Sheets, paper, 113
Short range planning, 22
Shots, television, 143-144
Showings, billboards, 57
Signature, 72, 82-83, 112
Silhouette layout, 94, 102
Simpson, O.J., 80
Size, advertising agency, 38-39
    billboards, 57
    paper sheets, 113

Slander, 35
Slides, 179-180
Small space ads, 105-106
Sound, radio and television, 144-145
Space broker, 38
Special effects, television, 142
Special events, 177-182
Speech, 180-181
Sponsor, 24, 72, 82-83
Standard Rate & Data Service, 54, 65
Stock photos, 111
Symmetrical balance, 87, 90
Television, 52-53, 60, 64, 78-79, 141-150
   advantages of, 52
   charges, 64
   disadvantages of, 52-53
   formats, 53, 141-142
   producing, 143-148
   ratings, 33, 53
   scripts, 146-147
   show, travel, 148, 150
   writing for, 142-143
Testimonials, radio, 135
   television, 141
Thompson, J. Walter, 38
Thumbnail sketch, 92
Time, on radio and television, 63-64
Timing of campaigns, 9
Tours, 3, 39
Trade magazines, 30, 54-55
Transit posters, 153-154
Travel, concerns about, 13
   decisions on, 13
   reasons for, 12, 26
   research on, 12, 14, 15, 47, 67
   time of, 13

Travel agency, marketing, 7-8, 11
   problems, 8
   services, 6-8, 12
Travel article writing, 174-176
Travel desk, 182
Travelers, categories of, 13
   decision making by, 13
   incomes of, 13
   money spent by, 14
Travel shows, radio and television, 148, 150
Trends affecting travel, 15-16, 21, 28, 184
Typeface layout, 94, 99
Typography, 106-109, 119-122
   fitting, 120-121
   font, 121
   hot and cold, 121-122
   measuring, 119-120
   series, 121
   specifying, 118

Understanding travel agency, 4, 14

Vacations, winter, 25
Visual aids, 178-180

Waste coverage, 52, 54, 57
Weight of paper, 113
Wheeler-Lea Act, 34
Women as prospects for travel, 17-18
Working with news media, 173-174

Yellow pages, 58
Young and Rubicam, 38
Youth as prospects, 18

NOTES

NOTES

NOTES

NOTES